GARIBALDI AND THE THOUSAND

The best works of history carry the conviction of great art. They recreate the past with imagination and conviction. They illuminate the tragedies and the triumphs of the human condition. And they help us understand ourselves in time. The aim of Cassell Histories is to reissue some of the most outstanding pieces of twentieth-century historical writing, which were immediately recognized as classics when they first appeared, and have remained so until this day. They address large issues with sympathy and scholarship. They abound with ideas and insights. They are written with vigour and style. They alter our perspective on the past — and on the present as well. They are works of wisdom and humanity, and their appeal to the wise and the humane should be as great today as it was when they were originally published.

G. M. Trevelyan was the great-nephew of Lord Macaulay and was, like his illustrious forebear, the best-known and most widely-read historian of his generation. He was born in 1876 and was educated at Harrow and Trinity College, Cambridge. He was the author of many books, including *The Life of John Bright* (1913); *Lord Grey of the Reform Bill* (1920); *British History in the Nineteenth Century* (1922); *History of England* (1926); *England Under Queen Anne* (3 volumes, 1930-4); and *English Social History* (1944). From 1927 to 1940 he was Regius Professor of Modern History at Cambridge University, and between 1940 and 1951 he was Master of Trinity College. He was, like his father, a member of the Order of Merit, and was Chancellor of Durham University from 1949 to 1957. He died in 1962.

First published in 1909, *Garibaldi and the Thousand* is the second volume of Trevelyan's magnificent Garibaldi trilogy, which was widely acclaimed when it first appeared, and is generally recognised to be his masterpiece. This book begins with Garibaldi's exile and seclusion in the aftermath of his ill-fated defence of the Roman republic in 1848. But it is mainly concerned to describe his triumphant return to Italy as the leader who liberated Sicily from the despotic and degenerate rule of the Bourbons in 1860, and who thus paved the way for Italian unification. Once again, Trevelyan identifies very closely with his hero; he vividly evokes the Sicilian landscape and the sound and smell of battle; and the book reaches a marvellous climax with his account of the taking of Palermo.

CASSELL HISTORY
Series Editor: David Cannadine

Garibaldi and the Thousand
May 1860

May 1860

GEORGE MACAULAY TREVELYAN

CASSELL

TO MY FRIENDS

GEOFFREY AND HILTON YOUNG

Cassell Publishers Ltd
Artillery House, Artillery Row
London SW1P 1RT

Copyright © Longman Group UK Limited
This 1931 edition of *Garibaldi and the Thousand* is published by
arrangement with Longman Group UK Limited, London

Published in Cassell History 1989

ISBN 0-304-31704-7

British Library Cataloguing in Publication Data

Trevelyan, G.M. (George Macaulay), *1876-1962*
    Garibaldi and the Thousand. — (Cassell history)
    1. Italy. Political events. Role of
    Garibaldi, Giuseppe 1807-1882
    I. Title
    945'.08'0924

Printed and bound in Great Britain
by Biddles Ltd, Guildford and King's Lynn

PREFACE

FOURTEEN years ago, when I began to study the life of Garibaldi, and nine years ago, when I published the last of the three volumes of this series, I certainly did not expect that I was going to serve for more than three years with the Italian army, becoming intimate in the field with the sons and grandsons of men recorded in these pages, in the final war of the *Risorgimento*, waged, during its first year, against that very Kaiser Franz Josef whose soldiers hunted Anita and Garibaldi in 1849.

Before the war history seemed to most men a thing outside the main current of life ; the past was like a turbulent but distant ocean, on which we looked out through magic casements from the agreeable bow-window of the present. To-day that flood has broken banks ; we are ourselves tossed on the living stream of history. We have been at war with Metternich and Bismarck. We have fought for the principles of 1688 and 1789. We have settled the undecided issue of 1848. Cavour and Garibaldi gave us Italy for an ally, while Washington and Lincoln gave us America. " The tombs were uncovered ; the dead came to war." Each nation proved to be that which its forefathers had made it. Because of the strange, romantic history recorded in these volumes, Italy in our day fought on the side of freedom. But for that history she would still have been a province of germanised Austria.

The paradox of Italy is this : her civilisation is the oldest in modern Europe, while she herself is the youngest

PREFACE

of the great States. In the thirteenth century of our era
Italians were already supreme in art, in literature, and
commerce, and in the appliances and amenities of civic
and civilised life ; but the Italian State and the Italian
nation sprang into being only sixty years ago. The events
of the Risorgimento, a large portion of which are recorded
in this Garibaldian trilogy, are therefore to the Italian of
to-day more than any single epoch of English history can
be to us. They are to him all that the story of Washington
and Lincoln together are to the American. To be friends
with Italy, we must begin by understanding and sympathising with the movement that gave her birth.

In this edition I have omitted not only the illustrations,
but the elaborate system of references to authorities for
statements made, which in Messrs. Longmans' Library
Edition occupy so many pages of bibliography, appendix,
and footnotes. For several years these books have run the
gauntlet of historical criticism, clad in the armour of those
references—on the whole with a singular immunity. I
would, therefore, venture to refer the student to Messrs.
Longmans' edition. The present reprint has been arranged
in order to place the volumes within the reach of a larger
class of reader.

1920

CONTENTS

GARIBALDI AND THE
THOUSAND

---·---

INTRODUCTION*

WHEN, on New Year's Day 1859, the Emperor Napoleon
III. startled Europe by a few polite but ominous words
spoken to the Austrian Ambassador, Italy of the Italians
was still confined to the small state of Piedmont, nestling
between the Alps and the sea. Strong not in the numbers
but in the character of its citizens, it enjoyed the respect of
Europe, the sympathy of France and England, and the
wistful affection of the inhabitants of the other states of the
peninsula—sentiments inspired by the well-ordered Parliamentary government of King Victor Emmanuel and his
minister Cavour. The rest of Italy, still partitioned among
half a dozen different rulers, was exposed to the absolute
power of priests, of foreigners, or of native despots, bound
together in a close triple alliance against the rights of the
laity, personal freedom, and Italian independence. Two
years went by, and the aspect of affairs had undergone a
change so complete and sudden that many would not believe
that it was indeed destined to be permanent. When, in
November 1860, Garibaldi resigned the Dictatorship of
Sicily and Naples, and sailed back to his farm on Caprera
with a large bag of seed-corn and a small handful of *lira*
notes, he left Victor Emmanuel acknowledged as constitu-

* Written in 1909.

tional monarch in all those territories that we now know as
the Kingdom of Italy—with the exception of two or three
fortresses where the Bourbon flag flew for yet a few months
longer, of the ancient territories of the Venetian Republic,
still guarded by the Austrian Quadrilateral, and of that
narrow ' Patrimony ' of the earlier Popes, where the herdsmen and vine-dressers could descry the cupola of St. Peter's
floating above the evening mist, like the ark of the Church
above the tide of revolution. In the winter of 1860–61 a
patriot could have travelled from Brescia to Reggio and
Palermo by the whole central chain of the Apennines,
without let or hindrance from any anti-national force
except an occasional party of brigands in the Neapolitan
provinces. If it was not till 1866 that the Austrian colours
were lowered from the three great flag-staffs that stand in
front of St. Mark's at Venice, if it was not till after the news
of Sedan that Italy could wisely dare to enter Rome, none
the less the creation of the new State was already an accomplished fact when Garibaldi quitted Naples for Caprera.

We may therefore say that in the years 1859 and 1860
the Italians acquired their national independence, their
civic freedom and their political union. This profound and
permanent change in the European polity was effected contrary to the expectations and wishes of nearly all the rest
of Europe, and under the guns of France and Austria, who,
differing on so many points as regards the fate of Italy,
were at least agreed in objecting to her union under a single
ruler. To neither of these powers could she have offered
a prolonged military resistance, yet she attained her purpose in their despite.

The rapid series of events that led to results so great,
and apparently so improbable, was brought to fruition by
the supreme political genius of one Italian, and by the
crowning achievement of another, whose name is to the
modern world the synonym of simple heroism. The story
of Italy in these two years is rich in all the elements whereby
history becomes inspiring, instructive, and dramatic. In it

we read of all the qualities that make us respect or despise mankind ; here the heroism and there the cowardice of whole populations ; the devotion of individuals and of families, side by side with the basest egoism ; the highest wisdom and the wildest folly ; the purest patriotism and the meanest jealousy, not always found in opposite factions or even in separate breasts. We watch the play of great personalities ; the kaleidoscopic shifting of the diplomatic forces of Europe ; bewildering turns of chance, messengers who would have saved a kingdom stopped by the whim of villagers, decisions of peace or war reached a few days too late or a few days too soon to turn the current of destiny, hair-breadth escapes of men and armies on whom all depended ; heroism, tragedy and burlesque taking the stage of history together. Finally, we witness the success of the most hazardous enterprises ; the fall of kingdoms and principalities ; the dismemberment of the most ancient and terrible Theocracy of the western world ; the realisation of those hopes for which the martyrs of Italy had suffered and perished for two generations, and a full share of the discontent and disillusionment which follows when the dreams of the noblest of men are carried out in actual fact by populations just set free from the corrupting servitude of centuries.

It has sometimes been said that ' Italy was made too fast.' It has been argued that the too rapid introduction of modern political machinery and the too rapid unification of such different populations as those of the north, centre and south, are largely responsible for the shortcomings of the Italy of to-day, though these may with more justice be ascribed to deep-seated sociological causes stretching back through two thousand years of Italian history. But however this may be, it appears highly probable that if Italy had not acquired her independence when she did, and as rapidly as she did, and in the form of complete political union, she might never have acquired it at all. If she had not shaken off Austrian, Pope, and Bourbon, in an age of war and revolution, she would scarcely have done so in a later age of nations perilously armed, but afraid of war and impatient of all questions that might endanger peace. Italy could never have been liberated without one European war at least. Her liberty was not, in fact, fully completed short of three European wars, those of 1859, 1866 and 1870. ⇒ In each of those three years of cataclysm she picked her own advantage out of the clash of combatants stronger than herself. If she had not been freed before 1871, nay, if she had not been three parts freed before the death of Cavour in 1861, her cause would not improbably have declined like that of Poland. Poland's last struggle was in 1863; if Italy had struggled and failed in 1860, the golden moment might never have returned. In the last thirty years of the nineteenth century no country would have gone to war so lightly as did France in 1859 on behalf of oppressed Lombardy, and anything analogous to Garibaldi's attack on the Bourbon would have been prevented by the Concert of Europe, as a wanton outrage on peace and order. But, in July 1860, England broke up such partial Concert of Europe as then existed, and refused to prevent Garibaldi from crossing the Straits of Messina. That decision of Lord John Russell and Lord Palmerston is one of the causes why Italy is a free and united State to-day.

Furthermore, the Risorgimento movement in Italy herself, after two generations of ever increasing heat, was at boiling point in 1859–60. If the cause had failed again in those years as hopelessly as in 1848–49, it may well be doubted whether these ardours would not have cooled and frozen in despair. The 'disillusionment' and 'pessimism,' of which we hear talk in modern Italy, would have been more widespread and of a far more deadly kind if the hopes of achieving the Risorgimento had perished. The Italy of the twentieth century might have relapsed into the Italy of the eighteenth. Again, even if the patriotic movement had continued unabated, the social problem would have arisen to complicate and thwart the political movement for independence, by dividing classes which were united for the national object in the Italy of fifty years ago.

In short, if Cavour, Victor Emmanuel and Garibaldi could not have freed their land in the days of Napoleon III. and Palmerston, and while the impulse given by Mazzini was still fresh, it is doubtful whether anyone would have been able to free her at a later period. She could not afford to await the slow processes of an uncertain evolution in the face of hostile forces really stronger than she, and determined to crush any natural growth by brute force ; she had to seize the opportunity created for her by Cavour before it went by for ever. Like most other great steps that have been made to ameliorate the human lot, the Italian revolution was not inevitable, but was the result of wisdom, of valour, and of chance.

Only outside Italy, and by persons who have not studied Risorgimento history in any detail, do we ever hear it denied that Garibaldi's great expedition of 1860 carried on the main work of Italian unity, at a time when no other means could have availed for its accomplishment. All schools of Italian historians are, I think, agreed that the Sicilian and Neapolitan populations had proved incapable of effecting a revolution in the face of an army of 90,000 men, without external help ; that Cavour was unable, owing to the attitude of Europe, and in particular of France and Austria, to give that help with the regular forces of the North Italian kingdom ; that nothing, therefore, could have liberated Sicily and Naples except an irresponsible ' raid ' by volunteers of the revolutionary party, and that no such ' raid ' could have succeeded except one led by Garibaldi ; finally, that it was only the Garibaldian revolution in Sicily and Naples that put Cavour into the position from which he ventured, in the face of Europe, to attack the Pope's possessions in Umbria and the Marches, and so to unite the whole length of the peninsula in one continuous state. This chain of reasoning, which establishes the supreme historical importance of Garibaldi's expedition, has been fortified by the patient research of Italian scholars during recent years, when so much has been done for the scientific study of the history of the Risorgimento.

The question still in debate among Italian historians is the degree of credit which Cavour can claim for Garibaldi's success. One school, of which Signor Luzio is the able representative, maintains that the great minister aided and abetted the Sicilian expedition from the first, not under compulsion from king and people, but as a part of his own policy ; the opposite school seeks to deny to him even the merit of goodwill. It is possible now to trace many of Cavour's principal actions in the matter, but his motives and intentions from day to day are not always clear and are still in some cases open to different interpretations. But there can be no question that the assistance which he gave was absolutely indispensable to the success of the enterprise.

The technical reputation of Garibaldi as a soldier depends on the history of 1859 and 1860, when he himself was at the late prime of his powers, and in command of an instrument suited to his methods. In 1849, he had not yet fully adapted to the conditions of European warfare the system which he had evolved on the Pampas ; in his later campaigns of 1866, 1867 and 1870, old and lame, he had no longer the ubiquitous personal energy which was the first condition of success in his method of war, he was in command of forces of mixed quality, and, in short, neither he nor his men were any longer

> ' that strength which in old days
> Moved earth and heaven.'

The generation now passing away has judged Garibaldi overmuch by what they recollected of the performances of his decline and decadence, which his partial countrymen have praised too much. But his ultimate place in history, not only as a soldier, but as a patriot and magical leader of men, must depend primarily on those great achievements which I shall here attempt to record.

There is, for the historian, an unique interest in the detailed study of the Garibaldian epic. We can make no such minute inquiry into the lives of Wallace and Tell, and of others who resembled him both in the nature of their work as liberators, patriots and partisan warriors, and in the romantic and old-world circumstances of their achievements. The records of Wallace and the dimmer legends of Tell are so meagre that they leave on us the impression of the heroic figures of Flaxman's outlines, with certain noble stories attached to their names. Even the fuller records of Joan of Arc date from a time so far back in the infancy of historical method, that in our day the learned can still dispute as to the nature of the influences which she underwent herself, and exerted over others. But the records of the Italian national hero and his deeds are detailed to the point of realism. We possess such a mass of evidence, official and unofficial, printed, written and oral, of his friends and his enemies, his followers and his opponents in the field, that we certainly do not lack the material to fill in a living picture of the man and his achievements.

How then, examined in so clear a light, do the legendary exploits of Garibaldi appear? Does the surrounding atmosphere of poetry and high idealism, when considered curiously, evaporate like a mirage? Or does it not rather take shape as a definite historical fact, an important part of the causes of things and a principal part of their value? To my mind the events of 1860 should serve as an encouragement to all high endeavour amongst us of a later age, who, with our eyes fixed on realism and the doctrine of evolution, are in some danger of losing faith in ideals, and of forgetting the power that a few fearless and utterly disinterested men may have in a world where the proportion of cowards and egoists is not small. The story of that auspicious hour when the old-new nation of Italy achieved her deliverance by the wisdom of Cavour and the valour of Garibaldi will remain with mankind to warn the rash that the brave man, whatever he and his friends may think, cannot dispense with the guidance of the wise,—and to teach the prudent that in the uncertain currents of the world's affairs, there come rare moments, hard to distinguish, but fatal to let slip, when caution is dangerous, when all must be set upon a hazard, and out of the simple man is ordained strength.

1909

The above was written eleven years ago, in an era of armed peace unpropitious to revolution and the liberation of races. Since then the most terrible of all wars has liberated the other races subject to Austro-Hungarian and German despotism. But if Italy had not been already, in 1914, a free and united nation, as a result of the events of 1859-60, the Great War of our own day would have had a very different and more tragic ending.

1920

CHAPTER 1

GARIBALDI IN EXILE, 1849–54

' We who have seen Italia in the throes,
  Half risen but to be hurled to the ground, and now.
  Like a ripe field of wheat where once drove plough,
  All bounteous as she is fair, we think of those

' Who blew the breath of life into her frame :
  Cavour, Mazzini, Garibaldi : Three :
  Her Brain, her Soul, her Sword; and set her free
  From ruinous discords, with one lustrous aim. . . .'
        GEORGE MEREDITH. *For the Centenary of Garibaldi.*
                              Times, July 1, 1907.

THE hopes of the revolutionary leaders of 1848–49, after a
brief period of fulfilment, were shattered in Italy as elsewhere by the military force of the powers of reaction.
The idealists, patriots, and demagogues who had for a few
weeks borne rule in half the capitals of Europe, were crowded
into prisons or huddled into nameless graves, while in little
towns overlooking the waters of Swiss lakes, and on board
steamers bound for America or England, groups of emaciated
and ill-clad men, their faces scarred with misery, could be
seen dividing among themselves scanty sums of money with
more than fraternal affection, and imparting in whispers
some new tale of disaster and death.

The most memorable of the closing scenes of the European tragedy had been the defence of the Roman Republic,
which the patriots from the north Italian provinces, led by
Mazzini and Garibaldi, had inspired with heroism and
invested with an imperishable glory. From the moment
when the flag of the degenerate French Republic was victoriously planted on the Janiculum among the corpses of

the Bersaglieri and the Red-shirts, the Catholics of France
enjoyed that coveted occupation of Rome which was destined by a bitter irony to involve them and their cause in
irreparable ruin; and Louis Napoleon commenced to drag
towards the final catastrophe of Sedan the lengthening chain
of servitude and embarrassment, which, as he soon found,
was all that he gained from his protectorate of the Pope.

Meanwhile Garibaldi, not content with having defended
Rome long beyond the last hour of hope, gathered round
him those who would not or could not ask grace of the
restored Papal government, and, carrying the lost cause
into the Apennines, eluded during the month of July 1849
the pursuing armies of Naples, Spain, France and Austria,
until his last forces were captured or disbanded. Then, in
the marshlands near Ravenna, his wife Anita died in his
arms, and he himself, torn away from her death-bed lest
the Austrian searchers should find him there, escaped across
Italy after a series of perilous adventures in company of a
single follower, *Leggiero*. At length, on the 2nd of September 1849, the two fugitives embarked in a fishing boat
provided by the patriots of the Tuscan Maremma.* Some
ten days earlier, the surrender of Venice and its heroic
defender Manin to the Austrians had brought the last
struggle to an end, and ' order ' reigned once more from
Sicily to the Alps.

Before we turn our attention to Italy's convalescence
under the skilful treatment of Cavour, it will be well first
to follow the course of Garibaldi's proscribed and wandering
life, and to note how he preserved himself for his country
through years of banishment and grief, without acquiring
either the faults usual to exiles and fallen chieftains, or
those which marred his own later life after the successes
of 1860. He who is accused of being the most impatient
and headstrong of men, showed a marvellous patience and
a sound political instinct for awaiting opportunity during

---

* The events here alluded to, including the siege of Rome, are told at
length in the author's *Garibaldi's Defence of the Roman Republic*.

the years of his life when he had most to bear, and most temptation to grow weary of delay.

The first occasion for the display of this spirit of patriotic self-restraint arose only a few hours after he and *Leggiero* had landed on September 5, 1849, on the asylum of Piedmontese territory. The presence of the military chief of the late Roman Republic, who, next to Mazzini and Kossuth, was in the eyes of Austria the most obnoxious of all refugees, created a situation of embarrassment and even of danger for the only free State in Italy. Piedmont, not yet recovered from the consequences of the unfortunate Novara campaign of the previous March, dared not too boldly defy the wishes of Austria. It was much that the brave young king, Victor Emmanuel, should venture, in the face of the twice victorious white-coats camped on the Ticino, to preserve the Parliamentary Constitution to which he had sworn, especially as the Parliament was at that time dominated by a somewhat hysterical Democratic party, unwilling frankly to accept the facts of defeat. France, indeed, was the ultimate protection from the insulting demands of Austria, but to France the defender of Rome was as hateful as he was to Austria herself. The external situation, therefore, made it dangerous to harbour Garibaldi. But the internal situation rendered it no less dangerous to expel him, except with his own consent. For in the towns of the long sea-board of Piedmont, especially in Genoa, the hotbed of Republican democracy, in Chiavari, whence Garibaldi's family originated, and in Nice, where it now resided, he was regarded at once as the national hero of Italy, and as the pride of his own Ligurian coast. At Chiavari, where, on the evening of September 6, his arrest was effected in the most polite and friendly manner possible, he would certainly have been released by the populace from the *Carabinieri* who were to accompany him to Genoa, but for his own active collusion with the authorities. And not only was the mob on his side, but the Parliamentary majority, moved by a natural and praiseworthy desire to do honour to the man who had honoured Italy by his heroism, and moved also by a factious desire to render the Moderate government odious, passed on September 10 the following resolution :—

'That the arrest of General Garibaldi and his threatened expulsion from Piedmont are contrary to the rights assured by the Statute, to the sentiments of patriotism, and to the glory of Italy.'

Thus supported by the majority of the Chamber, the claims of Garibaldi to residence in his own country were perilously strong, and if at this point he had yielded to the temptation to exploit his popularity and to accept the flattery of a party at the expense of the welfare of the State, he might have caused grave hurt to Italy. But he had not come to Piedmont with any expectation of being permitted to reside in her territories. He had preferred it to a British ship as his first harbour of refuge, only because he desired to see his now motherless children at Nice. No friendly enthusiasts could persuade him to resist, or even to resent, the determination of the Government to send him again on his travels. To one of his principal champions in the Piedmontese political arena, he wrote with simple gratitude and dignity :—

I sail to-morrow for Tunis with the *Tripoli*. I have been watching all that you and your generous colleagues have done for me. I charge you to convey to them the sense of my gratitude. I have no reason to complain of anyone. The present is a time for resignation, because it is a time of misfortune.'

Before his final departure, the Government allowed him to spend a few hours at Nice. The little port beside whose wharfs he was born and bred is closely penned in by steep hills, which happily still shut out from the old ' Nizza ' of Garibaldi the long modern esplanade which is the ' Nice ' of the visitor,—' the cosmopolitan seat of all that is corrupt,' as its great citizen called it in his anger after it had been ceded to France. But the old town beneath the shadow of the hill was all alive with its simple sailor life on the September evening in 1849 when Garibaldi, having given his *parole* to those who had him in charge, landed from the steamer, and was received into the arms of his own people. A crowd of relatives and friends of his boyhood, at the head of the enthusiastic populace, carried him to the door of his sad home. As he entered it, his old mother fell on his neck, while little Menotti and Ricciotti clung round their father's knees and cried out: ' And is Mama coming too ? ' It was a bitter meeting, and yet all too short. When he was gone, his mother, who was eighty years old, said to a friend that she should never live to set eyes again on her son who was so great and good.

Though driven from Italy, Garibaldi still hoped to remain somewhere on the shores of the Mediterranean. The Piedmontese Government sent him first to Tunis, but the Bey refused to allow him to land. Thus left on the hands of his native state, he was temporarily put ashore on Maddalena, the chief of a group of small islands off the north coast of Sardinia, where he remained for a month as an honoured guest and friend among a patriotic sea-going population. The neighbouring rock ridge of desert Caprera is divided from Maddalena by a channel only a few hundred yards wide, but as yet no thought of settling there appears to have crossed his mind, and no dream that through him Caprera would become a name in history and in song.*

On October 24, 1849, he was taken off Maddalena by a Piedmontese vessel which conveyed him to Gibraltar. There the British governor allowed him to land on November 10, on condition that after fifteen days he should go to England or to some other land of refuge. Garibaldi was

* At Maddalena it was observed that Garibaldi wore a ' mediæval ' costume, ' consisting of a close-fitting blouse of black velvet, trousers of the same, with top-boots, and an Italian hat with brim turned up and feather.' In the following years in America, England and Italy he wore a black frock-coat buttoned up to the neck. Only on the famous evening of May 5, 1860, was the red shirt again unpacked.

hurt at this notice to quit. 'From a representative of
England,' he wrote, 'the land of asylum for all, the blow
cut me to the heart.' *

But he was not entirely abandoned. At this nadir of
his fortunes, he received a welcome invitation from the
Piedmontese consul at Tangier to come and live in his
house. There Garibaldi stayed, from November 1849 to
June 1850, under conditions well suited to heal his deeply
wounded spirit. For he was a man of the old world and
of the open air. He did not require for his distraction
either intellectual stimulants or artificial excitement, but
found the medicine and food for which he craved in long,
solitary gazing on the sea and on wild nature ; in severe
exercise out of doors, varied by some quiet handicraft ;
and in the company of one or more of those numerous
persons, great and small, wise and simple, who could boast
the title of 'Garibaldi's friends.' All these resources he had
at Tangier, as afterwards when he settled for so many years
at Caprera. At Tangier his friends were *Leggiero*, who had
been the comrade of his recent adventurous escape across
Italy, his kind host, and the English consul Murray. He
occupied himself in making sails, fishing-tackle and cigars,
and in using them all when made. Once at least he shot a
wild boar, and he describes himself as the 'scourge of the
rabbits.' Alone with his dog Castor, to whom he became
fondly attached and who died of grief on his departure, he
would spend days together in the wilds, living on the game
he shot, and sleeping out in the southern night under groves
of magnificent olive trees. It was thus that he struggled
with the greatest sorrow of his life.

'Tortured by certain memories,' he wrote in February
1850, 'and by the low condition of our country's affairs, I try
to distract myself by shooting expeditions, and succeed—
materially at least, very well.'

---

* The British islands themselves would of course have been open to
him, as the Governor himself expressly stated. Also he had fifteen days'
notice, not six as he wrongly says in his Memoirs.

His one intellectual employment at Tangier was writing the memoir of his South American life, which still remains as the chief source of our knowledge of his lost Anita, her heroism in obscure skirmishes long forgotten, and her devotion in a love that the world will never forget.

During his seven months' holiday at Tangier, he was constantly but vainly seeking employment as a merchant captain. He had already accepted a pension of twelve pounds a month, offered by Massimo D'Azeglio, Victor Emmanuel's upright premier, which he devoted to the support of his old mother at Nice. His acceptance of the pension proves his friendly attitude to the Piedmontese monarchy. The education of his children, left with the Deideris and other kind friends at Nice, must be defrayed by the labour of his own hands, if he would not depend on the abundant charity of those who loved him. The prospect of regaining, after sixteen years of lawless adventure, his youthful footing in the mercantile marine of the Mediterranean faded away before the opposition of European diplomacy, determined to drive him back across the Atlantic. In April 1850 he had some thoughts of returning to Monte Video, but in June he left Tangier for North America.

Going by way of Liverpool to New York, he was seized on the voyage by the severe rheumatic pains which maimed and tortured him at intervals during the remainder of his life. 'I was lifted on shore like a piece of luggage,' he writes. His hopes of obtaining a ship for himself at New York proved illusory, and he was fain to work as a journeyman candlemaker in a small factory just set up on Staten Island by his good friend and compatriot, Meucci, who treated him, however, not as a mere employee, but as one of his own family. In company with another Italian labourer, and the inevitable Pat, the defender of Rome and the future conqueror of Sicily and Naples might be seen 'bringing up barrels of tallow for the boiling vat' from 'the old Vanderbilt landing.'

New York was at that time full of political refugees,

and the Americans regarded the victims of ' feudal Europe '
with the sympathy due to fellow Republicans. But Garibaldi, unlike Kossuth, politely refused to allow the ' leading
citizens' to fête him or produce him in public, as they
had wished to do on his first arrival in their midst. He
lived among his own people, melancholy and more depressed
than even they were aware, but gentle and generous as
ever. His spare linen and even the red shirt in which he
had defended Rome went to clothe his poorer compatriots.

An American who knew him at this period noted his
' free and athletic movements, notwithstanding ill health
and rheumatism, which disables his right arm,' and his
' easy, natural, frank and unassuming carriage,' ' his freedom of utterance and the propriety and beauty of his
language ' when he spoke in French or Italian. He was
at this time learning English, which he never mastered
so completely as the various Latin tongues. ' Although,'
says the same American, ' I had heard men speak eloquently
and impressively before, . . . Garibaldi raised my mind
and impressed my heart in a manner altogether new, surprising and indescribable.'

But, grateful though he was to the Meuccis and his
other friends, he was secretly unhappy and yearning to be
once more on the ocean. ' One day,' he writes,—

' tired of making candles, and perhaps driven by my natural
and habitual restlessness, I left the house with the intention
of changing my trade. I remembered that I had been a
sailor ; I knew a few words of English, and I went down to the
Staten Island docks, where I saw some coasting vessels loading
and unloading. I approached the nearest, and asked to be
taken on board as a common sailor. The men I saw on the
ship scarcely paid any attention to me, and continued their
work. I went to the second and did the same, with the same
result. Finally, I went to a third, where they were busy unloading, and asked to be allowed to help in the work. I was
told they did not want me. " But I don't want to be paid,"
I insisted. No reply. " I want to work to warm myself."
No use. I was deeply mortified.
' I retired, thinking of the day when I had the honour to
command the fleet of Monte Video, and its warlike and glorious

army. What did all that serve me now ? I was not wanted. I got the better of my mortification, and returned to work at the tallow factory. Fortunately, I had not made known my intention to the excellent Meucci, and so the affront and disappointment, being my own secret, were less bitter.'

At length his merchant friend Carpanetto, of Genoa, came over to New York, and some time in 1851 carried him off on a business tour to Central America. There he fell ill of marsh fever, and was with difficulty nursed back to life by the devoted care of Carpanetto and some Italians of Panama. He then travelled along the Pacific coast to Lima in an English ship, recovering his health on board, and contrasting the scenery of the Andes with the Alpine and Apennine shores of his own Liguria. He was warmly welcomed by the Italians of the South American ports, who, occupying more important industrial positions than those of New York, were better able to help their famous compatriot. At Lima Pietro Denegri gave him command of an old sailing ship called the *Carmen*, bound with a cargo for China. It was a year's voyage there and back, and he wished for nothing better, until Italy again drew her sword in earnest. Meanwhile, he would listen to no rumours of the useless revolts which the Mazzinians constantly attempted to promote. 'Many see Italian risings every day,' he wrote from Lima on his return from the voyage; 'I see nothing and remain a sailor.' In the life of the sea he found the best preparation for the great war, when at last it should come. He wished that all the other exiles would join him. 'A man,' he said,

'must either be a slave or let himself be ruined, or live peaceably in England. Settling in America is even worse : for in that case all is over ; that is a land in which a man forgets his native country. He acquires a new home and different interests. . . . What could be better than my plan ? The whole emigration assembled round a few masts, and traversing the ocean, hardened by a rough sailor's life in a struggle with the elements and danger ; that would be a floating emigration, unapproachable and independent, and ever ready to land on any shore.'

The year's voyage, which began from Callao on January 10, 1852, was prosperous and uneventful. Garibaldi was happier at sea than he would have been anywhere else, but there too he was pursued by memory, and by a fear that was worse than memory itself.

'What shall I say to you of my wandering life, my dear Vecchi?' he wrote next year. 'I thought distance could diminish the bitterness of the soul, but unfortunately it is not true, and I have led a sufficiently unhappy life, agitated and embittered by memory. Yes, I am athirst for the emancipation of our country, and you may be sure that this wretched life of mine, though sadly the worse for wear, would be again honourably dedicated to so holy a cause. But the Italians of to-day think of the belly, not of the soul, and I am terrified at the likely prospect of never again wielding sword or musket for Italy.'

This worst of all terrors came not unnaturally to a man of forty-six, troubled as he now so often was by old wounds and disease, the scars of his conflicts with man and nature in two hemispheres; the fear haunted him in the night watches on the broad Pacific. There, too, he was visited by a strange dream—of the women of Nice bearing his mother to the grave—which, as he declares, came to him on the very day when she died far off on the other side of the world of waters.

Having reached the China ports, and done business for his employers in Hong Kong and Canton, he returned by way of South Australasia. Passing close by Tasmania, he put into one of the Hunter Islands to water. It was a lonely and beautiful spot, and as the Italians landed, a cloud of birds rose from the primeval vegetation, amid the murmur of the clear flowing streams. The scene chanced to make on the mind of this Ulysses, who had seen so many wild and beautiful places all the world over, a profound and permanent impression, such as the daffodils 'along the margin of a bay' once made on Wordsworth. Again and again in after life, in moments of political irritation and despair, he thought of the lonely island with a sudden joy. His atten-

tion and sympathy were also attracted by a comfortably
fitted house and other traces of recent settlement, which
an English family had made and since abandoned, owing
to the death of their comrade, as the carving on a solitary
tomb bore witness. It is not improbable that the memory
of this scene, and the idea of setting up such another home
for himself and his children on such another desert island,
helped soon afterwards to draw Garibaldi to Caprera.

Indeed, he was now, though he did not know it, home-
ward bound for Italy by slow stages. Shortly after his
return to Callao and Lima in January 1853, he was sent off
on another voyage, rounded Cape Horn, and so reached
New York in the autumn. Early in January 1854 he
sailed for Europe as captain of the *Commonwealth*, three
masts, 1,200 tons, with a cargo for Newcastle, whence she
was to carry coals to Genoa. The crew consisted of a dozen
Italian and a smaller number of English-speaking sailors.
By the middle of February they were in London docks, and
Garibaldi and Mazzini met once more.

In all the long life which Mazzini devoted so wholly to
the service of Italy and of mankind, there were only four
months during which he found himself ' drest in a little
brief authority,' and they ended with the fall of the Roman
Republic in July 1849. The ex-triumvir returned to the
dingy lodging houses of London, and resumed, until his
death in 1872, the part which was his as by right,—to suffer,
to meditate, to exhort, and for ever to conspire.

In the summer of 1852, the very year in which Garibaldi
in mid-Pacific had been troubled by the dream of his mother's
death in Nice, Mazzini's mother also died. It was a terrible
blow. He had failed in the ambition of his ' individual
life,' ' to see her in the joy of triumph, when Italy was free.'
' I have now,' he wrote, ' no mother on earth except my
country, and I shall be true to her as my mother has been
true to me.' For the rest, his English friends, men and
women like the Ashursts, the Taylors, the Mallesons, the

Shaens, the Stansfelds, gave him an untiring devotion and all the little that henceforward he had of that *happiness* which he thought it man's duty to despise. The natural fitness of this tender, pure, and withal quietly humorous man, for the endearing trivialities of home life, which he had deliberately foregone at the call of a still higher duty, ensured his welcome at many an English fireside, not only as a teacher who raised life high but as a friend who made it cheerful and kind.

He had need of such an atmosphere to protect him a little from the miseries of his ever-frustrated mission. In 1852-53 the conspiracy of Mantua and the abortive revolt of Milan, followed by the cruel floggings and executions with which the Austrians as usual avenged themselves, were laid at Mazzini's door by the exasperated Liberals of Europe, who cried out that the time for hopeless insurrections on the principle of the ' popular initiative ' had now gone by. The horror inspired by what men regarded as a vain waste of noble lives was successfully exploited by Cavour and the Moderates of Piedmont to draw over the youth of Italy from the banner of Mazzini and the Republic to the banner of Victor Emmanuel and the Monarchy. That this political concentration was necessary as the next step towards national unity cannot be doubted, but it is another question whether the Moderates were wholly in the right when they condemned the Mantuan and Milanese movements as altogether opposed to the interests of the cause. As revolutionary movements they had no chance of success, and ought not to have been undertaken. But as the protest of martyrs they had a great effect in rendering Austria odious in England and in France, and in keeping the hatred of the foreign soldiery hot in the minds of the very men who cried out against the rashness of the victims and the criminality of Mazzini as the supposed instigator. The workmen who were hanged from the red brick walls of the magnificent Castello of Milan, in sight of the spot where Garibaldi's statue rides to-day ; the priest and the band of

gentlemen who, after suffering horrors in the old fortress
of Mantua, stood at last under the gallows outside the town
walls and gazed undismayed over the beautiful and melancholy landscape, across Virgil's marsh and the enslaved
plains, to the heights of Monte Baldo and the towering
Alps of Verona—these men did not die in vain.

Indeed, the Government of Piedmont well knew how to
use the story of these tragedies against Austria no less than
against Mazzini.

' Last night,' wrote Greville in his London diary for March
1, 1853, ' the Marquis Massimo d'Azeglio came here. He was
Prime Minister in Piedmont till replaced by Count Cavour,
and is come to join his nephew, who is minister here. He is a
tall, thin, dignified looking man, with very pleasing manners.
He gave us a shocking account of the conduct of the Austrians
at Milan in consequence of the recent outbreak. Their tyranny
and cruelty have been more like the deeds in the Middle Ages
than those in our own time. . . . They have thrown away a
good opportunity of improving their own moral status in Italy,
and completely played the game of their enemies by increasing
the national hatred against them tenfold. If ever France
finds it her interest to go to war, Italy will be her mark, for
she will now find the whole population in her favour, and would
be joined by Sardinia . . . nor would it be possible for this
country to support Austria in a way to secure that Italian
dominion which she has so monstrously abused.'

In this strangely correct prophecy, made by a man who
was as far removed from a Mazzinian as a typical Englishman can possibly be, we see the connection between the
tragic events of Mantua and Milan in 1852–53, and the
battles of Magenta and Solferino in 1859. And yet, perhaps,
the most important effect of those events was to diminish
the prestige of Mazzini, and to hasten the process by which
the youth of Italy withdrew from him their allegiance
and transferred it to Victor Emmanuel, to Cavour and to
Garibaldi.

And so when, in February 1854, the captain of the
Commonwealth landed in London docks and went to find
his old friend and teacher, Mazzini was in fact face to face

with one of his supplanters.   But his only thought was at once to use him and all that his name was worth to initiate another revolt.

'Garibaldi,' he wrote on February 16, ' is here ; ready to act.   Garibaldi's name is all powerful among the Neapolitans, since the Roman affair of Velletri.*   I want to send him to Sicily, where they are ripe for insurrection and wishing for him as a leader.'

It appears, however, that Garibaldi's ' readiness ' to go to Sicily was entirely conditional on the Sicilians first rising themselves and calling on him to come over and help an insurrection already afoot.   These were the conditions on which he absolutely insisted, both now and on every later occasion when the scheme was proposed, until its successful execution in 1860.   Indeed, in August 1854, only six months after this interview with Mazzini, he wrote to the Italian papers to warn the youth of his country against ' rash enterprises ' initiated ' by men deceiving and deceived, which only serve to ruin or at least discredit our cause.'

But whatever really passed between the two men with regard to Sicily, the most significant word spoken by Garibaldi to Mazzini at this time in London was that related for us by an ear-witness, Alexander Herzen.   It would not, said Garibaldi, be well to offend the Piedmontese Government, for the main object now was to shake off the Austrian yoke, and he doubted greatly whether Italy was as ripe for an United Republic as Mazzini supposed.

Garibaldi spent more than a month in London, making some close friendships, and forming those strong ties of mutual attachment which ever afterwards bound him to our country.

The disinterested affection for Italy and her champions that grew up in our island during the fifties and sixties, left a mark on the literary, political, and social life of Great Britain.   Apart from the unrivalled appeal to the

* For battle of Velletri, 1849, see *Trevelyan's Gar. Rome*, chap. viii.

imagination which Italy of all lands can make ; apart from the knowledge, then so prevalent among educated Britons, of her history, her literature ancient and modern, her art, her music, her cities and her landscape ; apart from the attractive personal qualities of her champions, who captivated the English as no other body of refugees ever did before or since, there were other special causes for that Italian enthusiasm of our grandfathers, which now began to be an important factor in Garibaldi's career.

In the first place, the bulk of the propertied classes, having secured their position against a narrow oligarchy by the Reform Bill of 1832, and being no longer alarmed, after the failure of Chartism, by any serious pressure from below, could afford to indulge in a good deal of speculative Liberalism. Social reform had not yet become a leading question, and Liberal sentiment ran largely into anti-clerical and anti-despotic feeling, for which it found more vent upon the Continent than at home. Domestic politics were in an unusually stagnant condition, and many public spirited men had therefore ample leisure to found the society of ' Friends of Italy ' in 1851, and to carry on the work of its propaganda for many years with ever increasing success. The most exciting alleviation of the dullness of English politics was the ' no-Popery ' cry, which, however futile and misdirected as an influence on our home affairs, led a large section of the religious world, not usually very prone to revolutionary sympathies, to take a generous interest in the cause of freedom in Italy. Lord Shaftesbury himself lived to be one of Garibaldi's ardent admirers. The fact that the Irish were on the side of the Pope, and occasionally disturbed the pro-Italian meetings, dispelled the last doubts of the average Englishman as to the propriety of the movement.

Furthermore, when the revolutionary governments of 1848 were replaced in one country after another by absolutism and military rule, it was very natural that we should begin to pride ourselves on the unique position occupied by

2

Britain as the only free country among the great powers of Europe. We were to the whole Continent what Piedmont was to Italy. Because we harboured the exiles, and held up in that night of time the beacon light of an ordered freedom, we were hated whole-heartedly at St. Petersburg, Vienna, Berlin, Naples and Rome, and half-heartedly and with secret envy by the would-be Liberal who sat discontented in the Tuileries under the protection of priests and bayonets. We were soon made aware of this ill feeling and its cause. Our national pride thereupon took fire for freedom, and under Palmerston's spirited lead those forces and passions which in a later generation were termed ' Jingo,' were enlisted on behalf of Continental Liberalism. When the Austrian General Haynau unwisely came over to England in 1850, a personal assault was made upon him in Barclay's brewery on the ground of his barbarity to women and to better men than himself, and it is noticeable that not only *Punch*, but the Foreign Secretary, Lord Palmerston, applauded the draymen's undiplomatic zeal. The Crimean war was regarded by many as an attack upon the arch-despot who had aided Austria in 1849. Not only the *Daily News* and the Liberal press proper, but Palmerston's organ, the *Morning Post*, were strongly pro-Italian. The *Times* indeed remained Austrian until well on in the year 1859, when it became evident that the Italian cause might not improbably succeed.

While many of the propertied classes were thus growing hostile to the Italian tyrannies, the only part of the working class which then had any political consciousness was deeply sympathetic with Mazzini and Garibaldi as the champions of European democracy. This feeling was specially strong on Tyneside, whence Joe Cowen sent out Mazzini's proscribed literature to Italy concealed in the famous bricks which he manufactured at Blaydon. He brought down distinguished exiles to instruct industrial Northumberland. Here Father Gavazzi lectured to audiences wholly unfamiliar with the Italian tongue, who sat enchanted by his

Demosthenic gestures and delivery in a style unknown in
Northern Europe, and applauded loudly when he was understood to be saying something against the Pope, or when they
caught the words ' Mazzini ' or ' Garibaldi.' When, therefore, the men of Newcastle learnt that Garibaldi was coming
in his ship to fetch away a cargo of their coals, they bought
him a sword of honour, and since, according to his custom at
this period, he declined to attend a public reception in the
town, they sent a deputation on board the *Commonwealth*
to present it to him as he stood among his little crew. The
miners tramping about the deck in heavy hob-nailed boots
amused the Italian sailors.

' The sword,' said Cowen in presenting it, ' is purchased
by the pennies of some hundreds of working men, contributed
not only voluntarily but with enthusiasm, and each penny
represents a heart which beats true to European freedom.'

Garibaldi replied in a carefully prepared English speech :—

' One of the people—a workman like yourselves—I value
very highly these expressions of your esteem, the more so
because you testify thereby your sympathy with my poor,
oppressed and down-trodden country. . . . Italy will one day
be a nation, and its free citizens will know how to acknowledge
all the kindness shown her exiled sons in the days of her darkest
troubles.'

It is doubtful whether this brotherly reception of the proscribed champion of a ruined cause and an enslaved country
by the working men of Tyneside and their middle-class
leaders is not as much to the credit of England as the por-
tentous uprising of the whole nation to welcome the same
man in 1864, as the world-renowned liberator of Sicily and
Naples.

CHAPTER II

CAVOUR AND THE CONVALESCENCE OF ITALY—GARIBALDI AT CAPRERA

> ‘Italy, what of the night ?—
>   Ah, child, child, it is long !
>   Moonbeam and starbeam and song
> Leave it dumb now and dark.
> Yet I perceive on the height
>   Eastward, not now very far,
> A song too loud for the lark,
>   A light too strong for a star.’
>   SWINBURNE. *Songs before Sunrise :*
>   *A watch in the night.*

IN the spring of 1854 Garibaldi returned to Italy and
settled down to live at Nice, apparently without any communication with the Government of Piedmont.   The fear
of Austria lay less heavy on the land than five years before,
when it had been judged dangerous to harbour the revolutionary chief.   In those evil days, after an obscurantist
régime lasting for a whole generation (1815–48), followed
by a brief period of sudden change at home and ill-con-
ducted and disastrous war on the frontiers, the ship of
State had almost foundered.   Destitute of many of the
accessories of modern life, with ruined finances and an
ill-organised and defeated army, threatened by a reactionary
priesthood on the one side, and an excitable and not too
loyal democratic party on the other, the Liberal monarchy
had just escaped destruction, thanks to the character of
the young King Victor Emmanuel and the services first of
the honest D’Azeglio, and then of the great Cavour.   This
marvellous man, hated alike by Democrats and Reactionaries, and disliked personally by the king, had imposed

himself on king and country, by astute Parliamentary manœuvres and alliances, and by the display of a genius for government which both king and country had the sense to value at its incalculable worth. Like our own William III. in his superiority to the men and parties who disliked him, but could not do without him, he too was not invariably scrupulous in the means by which he baffled the yet more unscrupulous champions of clerical and despotic predominance in Europe.

Cavour had trained himself—for no one was his teacher—in what was then the British school of politics. Passionate Italian as he was, his political and economic ideas were based on acute observations made in England, and on a close study of the work of Grey and Peel. Believing in civil and religious freedom to a degree unusual among Continental statesmen of any party, he regarded freely elected Parliaments as the essential organ of government, and force as no remedy, except to expel the stranger and the despot. Any fool, he said, could govern by martial law. According to him, it was the business of a statesman to govern by Parliament, not indeed obeying every behest of ignorant partisans and corrupt interests, but persuading the country and the Chamber to take the right course, by weight of the authority due to wisdom, knowledge and experience. This ideal, seldom realised in any country, was the actual method by which Cavour governed Piedmont in the fifties. If he had lived to govern all Italy in the same manner during the sixties and seventies, the country which he created would have avoided many misfortunes besides those of Custoza, Lissa, and Mentana. And if then the example of Cavour had been preferred to that of Bismarck as the model for the patriots and statesmen of modern Europe, the whole world would now be a better place than it is.

Garibaldi, having settled down to live under the government of this man, soon became aware of the stir of new hopes and energies in the changed country to which he had returned. The life of Piedmont was, during this decade, enriched by many thousands of exiles from the other States of Italy, the very pick of the land which they were all sworn to make into a nation.   As soldiers, statesmen, journalists, business men, they served Piedmont as the microcosm of the Italy to be.   One section of these exiles, still clinging to the Republican faith, and only half pleased with the Government that sheltered them, was for ever striving to stir up Mazzinian revolts in different parts of the peninsula. But the other section, enthusiastic supporters of Cavour, ready to wait for his initiative, and unwilling to compromise his deep-laid plans by any rashness on their part, had accepted the monarchy as the only way to national unity and independence.   This party was increasing its numbers by conversion from the Republicans, and to this party Garibaldi attached himself.

When he first returned to Italy the two questions of the day in Piedmont were the suppression of the monasteries, and the participation of the country in the Crimean war, both of which he strongly approved.   The first was naturally popular with the Liberal * parties of almost every shade, though fiercely contested by the influence of the priests and reactionaries, still very strong among the peasantry especially of the Savoyard mountains.   The Crimean expedition, on the other hand, had few hearty supporters.   It was generally regarded as a folly of Cavour's, a waste of those slender resources of Piedmont which ought to be carefully husbanded for the coming struggle with Austria.   But Garibaldi was from the first almost as much delighted by the expedition to the Crimea as by the suppression of the monasteries.   The suppression was the first thing that gave him confidence in Cavour.   Of the expedition he said, that

Italy should lose no opportunity to unfurl the Italian flag

---

* I take this opportunity of explaining my use of the word ' Liberal ' in this book.   I use it in the sense in which it was used in the Italy of that day, to cover all the parties, Republican or Monarchist, Federalist or Unitarian, who desired to see changes in the various Italian States in the direction of liberty from autocratic government.

on any battle-field that should recall to the remembrance of European nations the fact of her political existence.'

Probably he did not understand the further and more definite object of Cavour, which was to prepare the way for an alliance with Napoleon III., or with England, or with both, against the Austrian power in Italy.

But however much Garibaldi approved of the war, he could take no part in it, for the French would have considered his presence at the front in any capacity as an insult to themselves. The 17,000 Italians whom General La Marmora led to the Crimea had to wait long for an opportunity of proving to Europe anything to the advantage of their country, except that their commissariat was better organised than that of their British allies. At length, in August 1855, they were taken into battle on the banks of the Tchernaya, and behaved well. At the news of the battle, public opinion in Italy caught fire, and Cavour's Crimean policy was at length endorsed by the nation.

Garibaldi, meanwhile, used the immense weight of his influence with the Democratic party to discourage premature movements of insurrection, by a strongly worded letter to the papers. This was the more creditable on his part because he himself had the best of all reasons to be impatient :—

'I do not enjoy good health,' he wrote to his old friend Cuneo, in January 1855, 'and I wish I might use what is left of me on behalf of my country before I am quite broken up.'

Meanwhile he did his best to keep himself in training. Rising at dawn, he roamed the mountains behind Nice for four hours every morning, with his now inseparable friend and secretary Basso, in pursuit of partridges. The middle of the day he spent in teaching his younger boy to write, tracing out the large letters in pencil with his own hand for Ricciotti to cover them over in ink, and in visiting his daughter Teresita, who had been adopted by his friends the Deideris. The evenings he spent at a house rented by an

English widow lady to whom he was for a time engaged.
He appeared to Jessie White, one of our countrywomen
who was of the party, as 'a quiet, thoughtful, unpretending
gentleman,' very ready to make friends, but subject to
childish gusts of anger that passed away often with laughter,
and always without bitterness, as when the ladies mimicked
the peculiarities of his speech, or failed to learn to shoot
against the coming of the holy war, or praised Mazzini as
the first man of the age. This was when he was ashore ;
but he often went on short cruises in command of the screw
steamer *Salvatore* to Marseilles, Civitavecchia, and elsewhere, taking his elder son Menotti as cabin boy.

In the autumn of 1855 his brother Felice died, leaving
him an inheritance of 1,400*l.* (35,000 *lire*), which, together
with a smaller sum saved out of his own earnings as a sea-
captain, placed him in a position to alter his mode of life.
Short of another war of liberation, the thing he most desired
was, as he told his friends, to end his days far from the
world, in communion with the grand solitudes of nature.
He remembered the rocky coast and islands of northern
Sardinia, and in December 1855 he sailed for that region,
intending, as he wrote,

' to traverse the Gallura, where I think it will be possible
to choose a place on which to make a settlement, to pass some
of the spring months there or perhaps to stay there permanently if I find a suitable place.'

The point in the Gallura which he had in view was the
Capo Testa (Santa Teresa di Gallura), a headland on the
coast of Sardinia running out into the Straits of Bonifacio.
But when he touched at the Island of Maddalena, where
he had spent a month in 1849, some old naval friends of
his in that port, particularly the Susini family, anxious to
have him yet nearer to themselves, warned him that if
he settled on the solitary *Capo Testa* he might easily be
carried off or murdered by an expedition fitted out in
French Corsica. It was not easy to frighten Garibaldi,

but he believed Napoleon, ' the man of December,' capable
of any crime, and perhaps also he saw greater convenience
as well as safety in a closer neighbourhood to Maddalena.
Before the end of the month he had agreed to buy the
northern half of the island of Caprera for about £360. —

His new home was indeed admirably suited to all his
purposes, and to the purposes of Italy in him. Stationed
within an hour's row of the little port of Maddalena, where
the ships of the Piedmontese navy often touched, ' the
hermit of Caprera ' was never in the way and never out of
the way from the point of view of Victor Emmanuel's
Government. He could be fetched off the island at two
days' notice if his sword was wanted. If peace was made
and he was angry, he could retire there and work off his
feelings in piling up the granite rocks into rough walls,
or taking what he called his ' spade bath.' Safely back
on Caprera, he was less in the mood to listen to politicians
and makebates, nor did they find it easy to follow him to
his lair, since the ordinary steamers crossed from Genoa
to Maddalena only once in a month. Thus he preserved
his dignity by a picturesque seclusion, and his vigour by a
healthy and hardy existence. In the great years 1859 and
1860 Caprera proved, as we shall see in the course of this
book, an institution of no small value to Italy. And even
after 1860, when during the last twenty years of his life he
regarded himself overmuch as a privileged being, endowed
with the right of levying war on his own account, Caprera
saved him from making more numerous and worse mistakes.

The island, which is roughly five miles in length and
fifteen in circumference, appears to-day almost * exactly
as Garibaldi left it—that is to say, very much what it has
been from the beginning of time. And so long as the State,
whose property it now is, preserves it free from the profanation alike of modern improvements and of national
monuments, it will, in the rugged grandeur of its scenery,

---

* There is now a long bridge joining Caprera to the nearest point of the
island of Maddalena. A road has also been made on Caprera.

and in its untouched record of what has been, remain in itself the noblest of all monuments of the Italian Risorgimento. From on board ships working southward along the coast of Corsica from Genoa and Leghorn, or eastward through the Straits of Bonifacio, Caprera and its white house are seen from a considerable distance out to sea. From the base of the rock precipice that crests the top of the island, the ground on the western side inclines somewhat less steeply to the shore, and there, shining white on the moorside, a quarter of a mile from the water's edge, appears the long flat-roofed house of one storey, built by the labour of Garibaldi and his friends. It is the only object that catches the eye, amid the grey rocks and dark green plants that share the island between them. Caprera is still, and may it for ever remain, a desert moorland, only to be traversed on foot by pushing through the odoriferous brushwood and leaping or climbing from one granite crag to another. Every cranny in the rock where earth has lodged, every space between the tumbled boulders, is the cradle of wild vegetation—orchid, lavender, red saxifrage, the stately asphodel, the spurge with its yellow flower, the tamarisk and the evergreen lentisk with its smooth leaves. But more than all else the cistus, raising its white rock-rose to the traveller's knee, delightfully impedes his progress over the greater part of the island. Only here and there are miniature lawns of grass, breaking the thickness of the jungle. The trees are few, stunted and hidden among the rocks. Indeed, swept as it is by a peculiarly fierce and persistent wind, Caprera has in it more than a touch of the feeling of our northern landscape. Even on a fine day, when the wind has dropped a little, when the sun brings out the odours of all the aromatic plants together, and the fraction of Mediterranean waters enclosed by the little archipelago swells gently in its granite basin—even then, if cistus and lentisk could be changed into purple heath, the scene would pass for one of those inlets on the western coast of Scotland, where, amid shelving moorland and jagged heaps of rock,

The great sea-water finds its way.'

Such an island is not altogether characteristic of Italy, but it is altogether characteristic of Garibaldi.

When, in the spring of 1856, Garibaldi came to occupy his newly-purchased property, he was not quite the only inhabitant of Caprera. During the period of the Marlborough wars, a bandit named Ferraciolo, pursued by justice, took refuge with his wife and child on the island, which they found completely deserted, though there were traces of habitation in Roman or pre-Roman times. For a hundred and fifty years, generation after generation of this wild man's descendants perpetuated their race on this lonely spot, living as goat-herds and smugglers in the hut which their ancestor had built of stones and mud. In Garibaldi's time the Ferraciolo of the day still continued to dwell there with his family, on excellent terms with the new-comer. Half a dozen other herdsmen kept their goats on Caprera, one or two housing there themselves in huts or in natural grottoes, others on Maddalena. Not many years before Garibaldi's arrival, an eccentric and ill-conditioned Englishman named Collins, together with his rich wife, whose attachment to him was considered at once romantic, touching and inexplicable, had bought a large part of Caprera from the Piedmontese Government, and built a house upon it, though they lived chiefly in Maddalena. After Garibaldi had bought from them and from the Ferracioli the northern and more mountainous half of Caprera, his relations with Mr. Collins became strained. The Englishman's goats and pigs, wandering loose as of old through the brushwood, soon found out the general's potato and cabbage patch ; the cows of the new settler retaliated, and international complications ensued. But Garibaldi solved the problem by turning out with his friends, and building a rough stone wall right across the island from west to east, along the border of his property. About 1859 Mr. Collins died, and his faithful but more sociable widow made friends

with the Italian colony.   In 1864 a number of Garibaldi's
wealthy admirers in England purchased the southern half
of the island from Mrs. Collins, and presented it to the hero
of their choice.   But the visitor struggling through the
brushwood of Caprera still comes unexpectedly upon the
now useless wall half hidden by the tall vegetation.

Wall-building and house-building were indeed the chief
occupations of Garibaldi's early years on the island.   His
first habitation, in 1856, was a tent, which the winds often
carried away at night.   He and his stalwart son Menotti
lived under canvas until they had run up the still existing
wooden pent-house in which to receive his daughter Teresita.
From that new base of operations they then proceeded,
with the help of Basso and some other friends, to build the
pretty, flat-roofed mansion in the style of the architecture
of Montevideo.   The first part of it was habitable, after a
fashion, by the end of 1857, but a second part was afterwards added.   This second portion, finished in 1861, had
an ill-fated upper story, which was taken down again five
years later because it was not sufficiently solid to resist the
winds of Caprera.

Garibaldi was the first to attempt the cultivation of the
island soil on any extensive scale.   But even his cornfield,
olive yard, and potato patch, picked out from among the
stones, was the land of a crofter rather than of a farmer.
He was first and foremost a shepherd and goat-herd, rearing
a particularly fine breed of goats, which he imported from
Malta to run loose among the rocks.   The cows were each
known by name, and they were most tenderly treated.

' He is as kind,' wrote Vecchi, ' to the brute creation as to
man, and is so pained to see an animal struck that he never
permits it in his presence.   He takes a special delight in planting
and cultivating useful vegetables, and is highly displeased if
a plant be trodden on, or pulled up by mistake.'

Garibaldi himself, in a curiously emotional description
of his own gardening operations in Caprera, exclaims :

' The soul of the poor plants was in communion with mine, as I know when, thrown back into this sea of misery, far away from them, I turn my thoughts back to them, and feel myself cheered and exalted.'

He himself, the plants, and the butterfly that flits around them, are alike ' part of the soul of the universe, part of the infinite, part of God.' This thought, he tells us, ' raises him above miserable materialism.'

The frugally furnished little house was often overflowing with guests, who gladly took part in the gardening, building, and herding occupations of the day.

' Here is liberty in all things,' writes Vecchi in 1861, ' even to the cellar, although the General drinks nothing but water ; . . . for supper he has new milk. For the rest there are salted viands, with coffee, tea and milk at discretion. He helps his neighbours, beginning with the women, and invites his distant guests to take care of themselves. When he speaks to his daughter, he says " Teresa " in such a soft voice that it is impossible to imitate it. If he is in good spirits, he lights his cigar, and—excited by some name or deed which I allude to on purpose—he narrates, modestly of himself, but with full meed of praise for others, the great feats of arms in America, or particulars of the more recent events in Lombardy, Sicily, and Naples. . . . If he is oppressed by gloomy thoughts, he rises immediately from table, and walks out ; for he constantly suffers from the feeling of desolation, repeopling in thought the battlefield with fallen friends, and those who died for the noble cause for which he has ever drawn his sword.'

One evening, as Vecchi narrates, the party in the house heard that a new-born lamb had been lost among the rocks. Long searches by lantern-light, guided by Garibaldi over the crags and through the brushwood, failed of success, both before and after supper.

' It was nine o'clock and raining, and we were very tired, so we once more returned to the house, and went to bed. An hour afterwards we heard the sound of footsteps in the next room, and the house-door opened. . . . About midnight we were roused by a voice : it was the hero returning, joyfully carrying the lost lamb in his arms. He took the little creature to his bed, and lay down with it, giving it a bit of sponge dipped

in milk to suck to keep it quiet, . . . and he spent the whole
night caressing and feeding the foolish creature. . . . At five
in the morning we found him planting potatoes in the garden.
We took our spades and began to work also.'

The qualities which endeared him to the simple souls
who lived in his house on Caprera similarly won the hearts
of the most critical and experienced judges of men in Italy
and England.   The fond simplicity of a child, the sensitive,
tender humanity of a woman, the steady valour of a soldier,
the good-heartedness and hardihood of a sailor, the imposing majesty of a king like Charlemagne, the brotherliness
and universal sympathy of a democrat like Walt Whitman,
the spiritual depth and fire of a poet, and an Olympian calm
that was personal to himself—all plainly marked in his port
and presence, his voice and his eyes—made him, not the
greatest, but the unique figure of the age.   That this rare
creature had no head for administration or politics need
cause no surprise.   That he had an instinctive genius for
guerilla war was a singular piece of good fortune.   Such
another nature will never be bred in cities or by the typical
life of modern times.   It had been nurtured in the solitudes
of the sea and of the Pampas, and was preserved intact by
the life of Caprera.   'He loves solitude,' wrote Vecchi,
'and the sea, itself a solitude, conducive to dreams and
deep emotions.'   He used often to climb alone on to the
rocky crest that crowns Caprera, and thence cast his eye
on all sides over sea and mountain and moor : to the north,
across the strait, he beheld the magnificent peaks of Corsica ;
to the south, some of the lower Sardinian hills ; to the
west, close below him, the group of uncultivated and rocky
islands, and the lodge that he had built for himself in that
wilderness.   But to the east, where the granite crags
sloped down from under his feet so ruggedly and steeply to
the sea, that its murmur round their base was, even on calm
days, audible on the summit, no attempt at human habitation had been made ; only the wild plants clung and trailed
round the rocks, the eagle cried above his head, and the

deep primeval quiet, undisturbed by man since the beginning of time, filled him here with the breath of liberty, the utter release from crowds and courts and officials and the whole scheme of modern life, to which he was always in mind and heart a stranger ; and this liberty would have sufficed him to the end of his days as he gazed over the unbroken surface of the sea, had he not in his mind's eye seen beyond the eastern horizon those still enslaved Italian shores.

CHAPTER III

THE NEAPOLITAN PRISONERS

'O miseri, o codardi
Figliuoli avrai, miseri eleggi.'
LEOPARDI.
' Thou shalt have children either cowards or unhappy ; choose then the
unhappy.'—LEOPARDI. *To his sister, on her marriage,* 1821.

IT was the work of the French Revolution, and of the
many national movements to which it gave rise in other
countries, to destroy three distinct systems :—the feudal
rights of the noble, the secular privileges of the church,
and the absolute political power of the monarch. In no
country of Europe was this triple revolution more lamen-
tably overdue than in Naples,* where the tyranny, uncontrolled through long centuries, of priest, of noble, and
latterly of king, had left marks of devastation not only on
the welfare of a few passing generations, but deep in the
national character itself. In the Middle Ages, Campania
and Apulia knew no burgher life such as that which rendered
Lombardy and Tuscany the hearth of European civilisation. Indeed, the feudal rights exercised by the nobles of
Germany and France were inferior both in number and in
kind to those acquired by the Norman adventurers of
the eleventh century and their degenerate descendants over
the hill towns of Southern Italy. In those miserable abodes
of fear, poverty and superstition, the Dark Ages were prolonged down to the end of the eighteenth century, and it
was there that the character of the Neapolitan people was

* I have left over to Chapter viii. what I wish to say about Sicily, the
other half of that Bourbon State officially called the ' Kingdom of the
Two Sicilies,' which was overthrown by Garibaldi in 1860.

moulded. It is then scarcely matter for surprise that the mountain shepherds who might claim to be the descendants of the Samnites and the Bruttii displayed a half-animal savagery ; the tillers of the plain a dull helplessness ; and that the cities of the coast, once the seat of Hellenic civilisation, had developed the vices of the *Graeculus esuriens* into the proverbial qualities of the ' Lazzaroni.'

Then suddenly came the armed inrush of the French Revolution, sworn to ' shake the dead from living man.' The Napoleonic kings, Joseph Bonaparte and Joachim Murat, abolished the feudal system with a completeness characteristic of that epoch of reform, but with an equitable consideration for all parties that secured the permanence of the change after the Restoration of the Bourbon Monarchs.

Feudalism, which had in fact long been yielding to the principle of Monarchy, thus disappeared. But the rule of priest and king was not so easily disposed of, and when Murat had been shot, and Waterloo had decided for awhile the fate of Europe, it was not difficult to subject once more to the obscurantist despotism of the Spanish Bourbons a people prepared for slavery by so many centuries of abject oppression at the hands of feudal lords, by ignorance and poverty still almost universal, and by peculiarly gross superstition.

Yet there were other elements in the Neapolitan kingdom. At the first coming of the French armies, in 1799, the small educated class which alone had any real public spirit had hailed the opportunity of progress, and though the *lazzaroni*, under a protection which Englishmen would like to forget, had aided their royal master in making a hideous massacre of the most respectable inhabitants of Naples, the subsequent rule of the Napoleonic kings had raised and encouraged that section of the community. After five years of restored Bourbon rule (1815–20) this class succeeded, through the agency of the secret society of the Carbonari, in winning over the military forces of the

kingdom and extorting from Ferdinand I. the famous
constitution of 1820. The unexpected news thrilled all
Italy, and for awhile many observers, besides the impatient
Byron at Ravenna, believed that all Italy would rise in arms.
But another generation was to pass before the time was
ripe for such a national movement, and meanwhile the
Neapolitan Liberals did not know how to use the power they
had so easily seized. They quarrelled with the Sicilians,
who had also revolted against Ferdinand I., perorated
ceaselessly in their Parliament, made no effective preparations for resistance, and fell an ignominious prey to the
armies of Austria, sent down by Metternich and the Holy
Alliance to eradicate from the European body this plague-
spot of constitutional government. Ferdinand I., who had,
according to the family custom on these occasions, sworn
to the constitution and then brought in foreign troops to
put an end to it, took a horrible vengeance. Henceforth
cruelty and espionage became the leading features of
Bourbon rule, which, from 1815 to 1820, had been corrupt
and obscurantist indeed, but not wantonly tyrannical.

> From 1821 to 1860 the history of the government of
Naples is little more than the annals of the police, who
were assisted by all the other civil functionaries, by the
remodelled army, by the priesthood, and by innumerable
spies. The local authorities, chosen by the central government from among the fiercest reactionaries of each district,
were primarily delators and police-agents—little or nothing
was done in the way of road-making, public works or local
improvements of any kind. The whole energies of government, local and central, were devoted to repression. Every
private person had to bribe and fawn upon the *Capi Urbani*
(mayors and headmen of villages), the police, the priests
and their innumerable dependants, or he would incur the
greatest risk of being ruined, however innocent he might
really be. There was, in practice, no law but the will of
these harpies of government. Sometimes the soldiery put
in their oar ; one poor wretch in the province of Salerno

was given a hundred lashes by the order of a colonel ' for despising the authority of the king.' The comic element is never long absent in Italy ; to wear a beard was considered a sign of Liberalism, and the police marched men off to the barber as readily as to prison. In such a state of society the ridiculous scrupulosity of the censorship, which practically barred all serious modern literature, was one of the lesser evils. It caused no surprise that a barber of Reggio was fined 1000 ducats for having a volume of Leopardi's poems in his shop. ' The police,' wrote the British Minister in July 1856, and he might have written the same words with equal truth any time during the previous thirty years,

' the police, composed as it is of the most brutal and reckless set of individuals, who have the power to imprison and maltreat any person without affording him the means of defence or redress, of course intimidate individuals, and prevent any concerted plan or action, as the fear and corruption introduced by the system is so great that nobody can trust his neighbour.'

This system was so humiliating, so ubiquitous, and so corrupting that men of any public spirit or even of any self-respect became actively hostile to the authorities. The mild and tender Luigi Settembrini, one of the most ' sympathetic ' characters ever produced by Italy, thus records the reasons why in 1839 he deliberately abandoned his happy and idyllic family life and the easy career of a provincial Professor of Greek and Rhetoric to spend the best twenty years of his manhood, either in filthy prisons or in obscure poverty :

' In Lombardy and Venice,' he writes, ' there was the foreigner, worse than native tyranny ; but there the Austrian was strong, not stupid. He punished ferociously every political crime, but favoured good administration, and was just to all within certain limits. In the North there were two camps ; in one the foreigner, in the other the whole people. . . . But we in Naples, on the contrary, had fraternal tyranny, the cruellest of all ; and it was not Ferdinand who was the tyrant, no, it was the priest, the gendarme, the royal judge, the tax-gatherer, every employee of government : these men left us no hour of peace, but continually, daily, in the public square and in the private chamber, stood by us, crying like robbers, " Give, or I strike." Such oppression corrupts a nation to the bones.'

The embodiment of this rule was King Ferdinand II. (1830–59), the *Bomba* of Italian and English history. Like other exceedingly bad kings he had a fair share of domestic virtues, and he was not devoid of a queer personal attractiveness. It is true that his first wife, the refined and lovable Maria Christina of Savoy, the representative of a higher type of civilisation, was miserable at Naples. Whether or not the traditional story be true, that he pulled away the chair from under her as she sat, and that she leapt up in anger and called him the ' King of Lazzaroni,'—he certainly was bored by what he regarded as her airs of superiority, and treated her with scant attention. She died in 1836, revered as a saint by the Neapolitans, and leaving a son Francis, feeble alike in body and mind, destined to forfeit the throne and end the dynasty.

Ferdinand's second wife, the Austrian Maria Theresa, suited him better. He was invariably faithful to her. They lived a simple, secluded and frugal life, somewhat after the manner of George III. and his queen, except for the coarse practical jokes which were Ferdinand's delight. It would have been well for him if he had been of a more widely sociable disposition. A few jovial words spoken, as he knew so well how to speak them when he wished, to the leading men of the kingdom, a few more court ceremonies, a few more public appearances, a few largesses and smiles to the mob would, in the opinion of those who knew Naples, have done much to establish his dynasty. But he could not endure either court functions or general society. He would not even have the clergy as his companions, though he was superstitious to a degree that was remarked and ridiculed even in Naples, and though it was his fixed policy to increase the already extravagant privileges of the Church. When he chose, he could fascinate an enemy in a few minutes' conversation : but there was often a malicious humour under his cordiality. ' Keep beside him,' wrote one shrewd observer, ' and he was all you could desire; lose sight of him for a moment, and you might find yourself in the next five minutes under arrest.' He was clever with the cunning of a Neapolitan street lounger, but ignorant, and proud of his ignorance. Men of education he always spoke of as ' scribblers ' (*pennaruli*). He was politically a complete cynic, disbelieving in all public virtue, and disliking those who had a reputation for it, as tedious fellows who would not play the game. Deceit and tyranny were the two main principles of the art of government which had been taught him in youth and to which he adhered all his life.

But, though unscrupulous as to means, he was faithful to what he regarded as the ends of politics. He was a true Neapolitan patriot : he disliked the idea of Italy a nation, but he kept Austria at arm's length more than his predecessors had done, refusing a strict alliance that would have made his throne secure. He knew how to resent with spirit the hostile interference of England and France. He was abler than his father. He reformed and strengthened the army, within the limits set by the universal system of corruption, which he made no effort to change in any department of government. He worked with industry as the head of an over-centralised system. He was his own prime minister and his own favourite.

The Bourbon rule was odious to all good men, even to the few who, like Generals Filangieri and Pianell, loyally served it in the vain hope that it would some day be reformed. But it remained unaltered from 1821 till its destruction in 1860, except during four months at the beginning of the year 1848, when, owing to the outbreak of revolution in Sicily, the Neapolitans secured from Ferdinand II. another of those constitutions which this royal house was ever ready to swear to at need. The story of 1820 repeated itself with a difference. This time, indeed, as all Italy rose, and the national war against Austria was waged in the North, there was no Austrian invasion of Naples, and the reaction there was effected without foreign intervention. In May 1848, while the fortunes of free Italy were still at their zenith in the valley of the Po, while Radetzky was still at bay behind the Quadrilateral, the Neapolitans succeeded in forfeiting their newly-won freedom. There was a general want of experience, and, with honourable exceptions, a general want of public spirit. Violent counsels and cowardly conduct, the impolitic erection of barricades, and the refusal to fight behind them when erected, destroyed the Liberals, and enabled Ferdinand II., by the help of his Swiss regiments, to re-establish his despotic power on May 15, 1848. One of the most powerful arguments for the necessity of that union of Southern to Northern Italy which took place in 1860 was the utter failure of the Neapolitans to maintain their own freedom when left to themselves in 1848.

An ill-supported rising of the more spirited Calabrian peasants was speedily crushed, and Sicily was more gradually reconquered (September 1848–May 1849), with those horrors of bombardment and sack which won for Ferdinand II. the cognomen of *Bomba*.* The Neapolitan troops, who had been foolishly insulted by their Liberal compatriots during the excitement of the days of freedom, had rallied to the throne, and henceforth hated the Liberals of the mainland hardly less than they hated the Sicilians. With this force Ferdinand was strong enough in the spring of 1849 to conduct a crusade against the Roman Republic on behalf of his guest, the exiled Pope Pio Nono. But the only result was the defeat at Palestrina at the hands of Garibaldi, and the disgraceful retreat from Velletri, fatal to the confidence which the army had begun to feel in itself after the Sicilian victories. Such was the terror inspired by the 'red devil' in this campaign, that eleven years later the mere rumour of Garibaldi's approach could unnerve the Neapolitan regiments.

* Short for *Bombardatore*, ' the bombarder.'

So King Ferdinand returned from the vain pursuit of military glory to a task for which he had greater qualifications—the persecution of his subjects. In the summer and autumn of 1849, the prisons of Naples and the provinces were rapidly filled with men, of every shade and variety of political opinion, who had taken part in the movement of the previous year. Some, especially in Calabria, had risen in arms against the reaction, but others had been opposed alike to the Calabrian and Sicilian rebels, and were guilty of no more than trying to work the constitution which the king had granted. It is impossible to estimate the number of Ferdinand's subjects who were languishing in prison for political offences by the year 1851, because the Government never published, and probably never compiled, lists of any except two very restricted classes of prisoners ; but the number, 20,000, which Mr. Gladstone quoted as 'no unreasonable estimate,' is considered as probably below the truth by Signor de Cesare, the impartial and well-informed modern historian of Naples. This high figure would include the large numbers who were being detained year after year before trial, or after acquittal, or 'correctionally'—that is, by administrative order. But, besides the prisoners, there was an equally indefinite number of *attendibili*, or suspects under police supervision—estimated by Signor de Cesare at 50,000 ; these men, generally the most intelligent and often the wealthiest citizens of the districts where they severally resided, were cut off from all civil and academic functions, were forbidden to leave their houses without special licence from the police, and had every action supervised by the authorities, who found pleasure in annoying them, and profit in extorting money for the least concession.

These proceedings of *Bomba*, as our grandfathers almost invariably called him,* became known to the whole world,

---

* 'The captain of an English merchantman once horrified a party of very loyal Neapolitans by saying, on seeing the portrait of Ferdinand, in what he meant to be a very respectful tone : "So that is King Bomba !"

and particularly to England, in their true colours, without
the decorous coating of phrases and reticences in which the
official world usually drapes such matters.   Englishmen,
for reasons which I have discussed in a previous chapter,
were not at that period in the habit of finding excuses for
this sort of tyranny.   So the drama was unveiled to England
and to Italy not only in its horror, but in its strange beauty
for the leading victims—Poerio, Settembrini, and Castromediano—were men of such lofty idealism and gentle
but resolute character as must qualify the sweeping condemnation so often pronounced on the inhabitants of the
land of Vesuvius.   If, in the terrible words wherein Filangieri unloaded the bitter experience of a lifetime, ' it is
often a great calamity to a man of honour and spirit to be
born a Neapolitan,' the worst consequences of that calamity
have been endured without such complaint by some of the
choicest spirits who ever adorned the history of a people.

Carlo Poerio, a man who held what would in England
be called Conservative views, had opposed every sort of
armed insurrection in Sicily or elsewhere.   This man,
whom Mr. Gladstone justly compared to the most high-
minded of his own English colleagues and rivals, was by
reason of his character and abilities regarded as the natural
head of the Constitutional party.   He had been one of
Ferdinand's ministers under the constitution of 1848, and
as such had been treated by his master with even more than
usual *bonhomie*.   Ferdinand introduced him with effusion
to the Queen, called him *Carlino*, and pressed on him his
best cigars.   For the ' King of Lazzaroni ' had a very real,
though peculiar, sense of humour, and he had determined
that his *Carlino* should rot in a noisome dungeon.   Poerio,
Settembrini and forty others were brought to trial in June
1850 ; the case lasted till February 1851, although it was
shortened by the fact that the prisoners were not allowed

The terror of his audience, who thought that the invisible and ever-present
police would at once swoop down on the auditors of such a treasonable
remark, it is not easy to describe.'

to bring their witnesses into court. After a patently forged document had come to grief and been ' reserved for further investigation,' a false witness named Jervolino was set up to swear one ridiculous absurdity after another against Poerio, floundering through with the help of the judges. There was this difference between Jervolino and Titus Oates, that no one in court believed a word he said. This formality sufficed to secure for the most respected subject of the Crown a sentence of twenty-four years in irons. While the tragic farce proceeded, Poerio's forty fellow-prisoners, including several of the noblest men in Italy, looked on in despair, pre-doomed, as they knew, to ruin and long years of horror. One of their number, named Leipnecher, had already died of gaol fever, having been dragged from his couch and carried into court as a malingerer. ' God, the avenger of the oppressed, will exact retribution for this man's death,' his friend Pironti cried out to the presiding judge. Little did they dream that the man who should be sent to avenge them was earning his daily wage in carrying up barrels from the wharves of Staten Island. Still less did they suppose that his forerunner was in court among the spectators. But there on the public benches sat an English visitor, come to Naples for his daughter's health, a man of middle age, but with more than the fire of youth in his eyes, as he glowered with ill-restrained indignation at the wicked judges and false witnesses, and shook to think that this was perpetrated in the name of order and of religion.

Mr. Gladstone, who found himself at Naples for reasons entirely unconnected with politics, had no belief in the idea of Italian unity and nationality, which for many years to come he regarded as an idle dream. So far from sympathising with revolution, he was still, as he declared on his return to England, ' a member of the Conservative party in one of the great family of nations,' ' compelled to remember that that party stands in virtual and real though perhaps unconscious alliance with all the established Gov-

·ernments of Europe as such.' Any man so situated, and
made of ordinary clay, would have been well content to
spend his time at Naples in ' diving into volcanoes and
exploring buried cities.' But in this man's heart, deeper
than party associations and personal predilections as to
European politics, deeper even than the curiosity of the
classical scholar, and far deeper than the desire for ease on
a well-earned holiday, flamed the disinterested hatred of
injustice and cruelty, often found as the handmaid of other
passions, but seldom thus the lord and dictator of the soul.

At the British Embassy he had come across its legal
adviser, a worthy Neapolitan gentleman, shortly afterwards
exiled and naturalised in England, where he rose by public
service to high estimation as Sir James Lacaita. He told
Mr. Gladstone much, and showed him more. Naturally
the Liberal clergy were sought out with eager sympathy,
but the friend of Newman acknowledged with a sigh the
connection of another section of the clergy with the Government, and the services rendered by the confessional to the
police. Then came Poerio's trial. After that the glories
of the most beautiful bay in Europe lost hold upon his
imagination, and when he looked out at ' the picturesque
and romantic forms ' of ' those lovely islands scattered
along the coast,' knowing now that they were the prisons,
he could think of nothing but ' what huge and festering
masses of human suffering they conceal.' His spirit,
shaking itself free of every impediment of interest and old
association, rose in its native majesty, and, heedless alike
of the scandal to official Europe, of the discomfiture of his
own colleagues, of the triumph of Palmerston, to whom
he would be forced to apologise, he determined on a line
of action which, as his friend and biographer tells us, was
the turning point of his own life, and may well be counted
as the turning point in the shrunken tide of Italy's fortune.*

It must be remembered that Mr. Gladstone was recanting. Gladstone and Molesworth, wrote Lord Palmerston in 1851, ' say that they
were wrong last year in their attacks on my foreign policy, but they did
not know the truth.'

Poerio and his forty companions, except a fortunate half-dozen, were condemned. They were consigned to various terms of imprisonment—in the case of the principal leaders, for life, or for terms of years which it was thought probable they would not survive. Mr. Gladstone thereon determined to visit the Vicaria prison in Naples. The Government was so confident of its strength, and so ignorant of the visitor's intentions and power, that he obtained entry. The horrors of the Vicaria, probably the best prison in the kingdom, as being in the capital and therefore more exposed to inquiry and criticism, Mr. Gladstone was accused of exaggerating. But when an English friend of the Neapolitan Government had seen it, he was obliged to confess that ' the atmosphere was as thick as in a London fog from the horrible exhalations,' that the prisoners were ' evidently always addressed and treated as brutes,' and that ' human life was in a living tomb, assisting at the spectacle of its own decay.' It was here, then, that Mr. Gladstone saw

the official doctors not going to the sick prisoners, but the sick prisoners, men with almost death on their faces, toiling upstairs to them, because the lower regions of such a place of darkness are too foul and loathsome to allow it to be expected that professional men should consent to earn bread by entering them.'

On the island prison of Nisida, whither he next proceeded, he found Poerio and other distinguished men, in the coarse red garb of convicts, each of them chained either to a fellow-sufferer in the cause, or else to a common criminal.

The prisoners had a heavy, limping movement, much as if one leg had been shorter than the other. But the refinement of suffering in this case arises from the circumstance that here we have men of education and high feeling chained incessantly together.'

The couplings were never removed on any occasion either by day or by night.

' I myself,' wrote Mr. Gladstone, ' saw a political prisoner, Romeo, chained in the manner I have described to an ordinary offender, a young man with one of the most ferocious and sullen countenances I have seen among hundreds of the Neapolitan criminals.'

Another unfortunate, by a refinement of cruelty, was chained to the false witness named Margherita, who had been suborned against him at his trial.

I must say,' wrote Mr. Gladstone, ' I was astonished at the mildness with which they spoke of those at whose hands they were enduring these abominable persecutions, and at their Christian resignation as well as their forgiving temper, for they seemed ready to undergo with cheerfulness whatever might yet be in store for them. Their health was evidently suffering. . . . I had seen Poerio in December during his trial, but I should not have known him in Nisida. He did not expect his own health to stand, although God, he said, had given him strength to endure. It was suggested to him from an authoritative quarter, that his mother, of whom he was the only prop, might be sent to the king to implore his pardon, or he might himself apply for it. He steadily refused. That mother, when I was at Naples, was losing her mental powers under the pressure of her afflictions.'

This lady died, in fact, in September of the following year. Her other son, Alessandro, of more fiery temperament and advanced politics, had fallen fighting for Italy in Venice. She had brought them up for such service, preferring unhappy sons to cowardly, but when the inevitable end came, it broke her heart.

It was here in Nisida that the chained prisoners implored their visitor not to consider the further penalties which any public action on his part might bring down on themselves, but to consider only how he might accelerate the liberation of their country. Before he left the island prison he had agreed with Poerio that public exposure was what was needed. ' As to us,' said that generous man, and his companions re-echoed him, ' as to us, never mind ; we can hardly be worse than we are.'

Having made this agreement with Poerio, it was perhaps

a mistake on Mr. Gladstone's part that on his return to England he persuaded himself, or allowed Lord Aberdeen to persuade him, to delay publication until the elder statesman, ' as an old friend of the Austrian Government ' in pre-Waterloo times, had applied privately to Vienna. Lord Aberdeen, convinced and shocked by what he heard, hoped that Austria, as the patron of Ferdinand, would use her influence to obtain ' some improvement.' Two months elapsed before Schwarzenberg's answer came to hand, and during the interval Mr. Gladstone not unnaturally became impatient. Early in July 1851, two days before the arrival of the Austrian's reply, he published his famous ' Letters to Lord Aberdeen.' He should have done so two months before : publishing them when and how he did, he slightly offended his benevolent and honourable colleague. The Austrian negotiation with Naples, unsympathetically but honestly * undertaken by Schwarzenberg, was from the first predestined to futility if it was in any way intended to fulfil the agreement with Poerio and his companions at Nisida. It is not conceivable that Austria, with her own black record as it then stood, and her entire policy based upon repression in Italy, would or could have obtained from Ferdinand—who was moreover no such complete slave of Austria as his predecessors had been— more than the release of a certain number of prisoners. The question was not of a few dozen men but of many thousands, not of a single state trial but of a political system.

* Lord Stanmore tells me that the reason why his father, Lord Aberdeen, was left so long without an answer by Schwarzenberg, was that the latter had written to Naples to get private assurance that Ferdinand would accede to the Austrian request when it was officially made. Lord Stanmore says that Schwarzenberg had got this assurance, though the exact nature of the promised concessions is not ascertainable. On the other hand, *De Cesare*, i. 65, 66, says that the Neapolitan Ministry absolutely disregarded the warning sent them by Castelcicala, their representative in London, of the forthcoming publication of Mr. Gladstone's letters (of which Aberdeen had notified him), and concealed these warnings from King Ferdinand.

' It is not,' wrote Mr. Gladstone in his first letter, ' it is not
mere imperfection, not corruption in low quarters, not occasional
severity that I am about to describe ; it is incessant, systematic
violation of the law by the power appointed to watch over
and maintain it. . . . It is the wholesale persecution of virtue
when united with intelligence, operating upon such a scale
that entire classes may with truth be said to be its object, so
that the Government is in bitter and cruel, as well as utterly
illegal,* hostility to whatever in the nation really lives and
moves and forms the mainspring of practical progress and improvement ; it is the awful profanation of public religion, by
its notorious alliance, in the governing powers, with the violation
of every moral law. . . . It is the perfect prostitution of the
judicial office. . . . I have seen and heard strong and too true
expressions used, " This is the negation of God erected into a
system of government." ' †

This terrible invective, and the yet more terrible array
of facts supporting it, produced a profound and permanent
effect on the sympathies of our country.   It moulded
English opinion on the subject of Naples, as Burke's more
abstract ' Reflections ' moulded it on the subject of the
French Revolution, and in both cases the pamphlet was the
more persuasive because the author was a noted adherent
of the English party least inclined to the views advocated.
The press, almost without exception, joined in the outcry,
and the *Times* gave up King Ferdinand, whom it had
supported in 1848.

In political circles abroad the letters aroused more con-
troversy, but scarcely less interest.   The reply of the
Neapolitan Government convicted Mr. Gladstone of a few
small mistakes which he readily acknowledged, but only
served to demonstrate by its silences the truth of the bulk
of his accusations, and was pounded to pieces in his ' Exam-
ination of the Reply,' and in an anonymous ' Detailed
Exposure.'   The hatred felt for England in the Papal and

---

* The constitution granted in January 1848 was never repealed, but
was treated as a dead letter. This insolent indifference to the law was
what chiefly offended Mr. Gladstone's Conservative instincts.

† '*La negazione di Dio eretta a sistema di governo.*' It is to be noted
that this famous epigram was not originally Mr. Gladstone's, but of Italian
origin.

reactionary world rose to extravagant heights. One of the principal historians of that party, De Sivo, in his elaborate ' History of the Two Sicilies,' more than ten years later, answered ' Lord Gladston ' by saying that the English sold their wives with ropes round their necks for a few ' pences,' and then had the impertinence to complain of ' little trials in Naples.' Although an important section of the French press, especially the Catholic papers, loudly defended the King of Naples, although high Parisian society made a dead set against England and Mr. Gladstone, yet the ultimate effect was very considerable on Napoleon III. and his subjects, who had moreover their own ' Murattist ' designs on Southern Italy. In 1856, France joined England in withdrawing her minister from Naples as a protest against the royal misgovernment, and in the supreme crisis of Garibaldi's fate in 1860, the sense that the Neapolitan Bourbons were pariahs prevented Napoleon from interfering on their behalf. For that strange man, though he had himself committed a great political crime, was not, like the despots of Eastern Europe, insensible to the moral responsibilities of diplomacy. Mr. Gladstone, in fact, created in France and England the feeling which kept the international ring clear for Garibaldi's final attack on the kingdom of the two Sicilies. When, in 1864, the Liberator of Naples came to our island, at a great reception held in his honour at Chiswick, Mr. Gladstone stood among other distinguished men to receive him on the staircase. As he came up in his red shirt and *puncio*, he saw the friend of the prisoners, seized his hand, and said with deep feeling the single word : ' *Précurseur.*'

But the most terrible sufferings of all—those which were endured in the mountain fortress of Montefusco and the island of San Stefano—were never witnessed or described by Mr. Gladstone. Posterity, however, possesses a yet more lifelike and intimate record than any which he could have given, for these experiences were narrated by the chief victims themselves, in the *Memorie* of Castromediano and the *Ricordanze* of Settembrini—memoirs such as can be written only by men of remarkable character and intellect under circumstances of transcendent interest.*

The Neapolitan nobility as a whole, while often disapproving of the action of the Government, left the constitutional movement in the hands of the class just below them in the social scale.   But there were exceptions to this rule :—

' Sigismondo Castromediano, Duke of Morciano, Marquis of Caballino, lord of seven baronies, died on the 26th of August, 1895, in the smallest room of his vast, ruined castle, a few miles from Lecce. He left no heir to his poverty. With him disappeared a house which was already illustrious and ancient when one of its members fought for fair-haired Manfred of Benevento. On his coffin were placed the chain of a galley-slave and the red jacket worn by Neapolitan convicts. These, he used to say, were his decorations.'

The man whose life history is thus epitomised was more an antique Roman than a Neapolitan Liberal.   He had the qualities of that aristocratic and stoic ideal adumbrated in the characters of Plutarch.   His pride differed from the pride of other Neapolitan nobles, being inward not outward, moral not social; he wished for no approval save from his own conscience.   But he knew what the ancients did not always know, that the true pride is generous to enemies, and when, in the hour of triumph, Garibaldi asked him for the names of his unjust judges, he replied : ' I have forgotten them.'   He was no politician, and he held in scorn the secret societies of Southern Italy with their ' ridiculous mystical rites.'   He had no ambition save to live and to die in his old castle, vastly remote from

* Those who cannot read these works in the original, will find the two stories told in an admirable form in the *Italian Characters* of Countess Martinengo Cesaresco. Only the later edition (1901) contains the essay on Castromediano. I take this opportunity of thanking the authoress of Italy's book of heroes for the many services which she has rendered to me in the study of Garibaldian history.

the world in the scorched Apulian wilderness. There, in fact, after 1860, he passed the remaining thirty-five years of his long life. But in the early months of 1848 he felt bound to take his proper part as local magnate in the welcome given by the neighbourhood to the brief reign of liberty. For this he was seized, tried and condemned by the provincial court of Otranto to thirty years in irons.

In the prison on the island of Procida, where he was first confined after his sentence, the *camorra* ruled among the prisoners with little interference from the gaolers. The criminals had knives, and murdered each other with relative impunity, while vice of every kind was rampant and uncontrolled. The more respectable inmates some· times begged to be confined in the worst penal dungeons of the place in order to avoid this terrible and dangerous society. But Castromediano was treated by the most abandoned wretches with the awe due to a superior being. At last, one day, the gaolers burst in with cries of ' *Viva il Re! Libertà, libertà,*' and informed the ' politicals ' that they were released by the clemency of the king. They were sorted out from the common criminals and put on board ship for the mainland. For some hours the pitiless jest deceived many, but it soon appeared that they were only being moved to a place of yet more cruel torment. On the way thither, they were joined by another group of prisoners from Nisida, including Poerio and the men whom Mr. Gladstone had visited. Poerio was hailed by them all as their father and chief. Soon it was whispered in their ranks, but for long it was not believed, that they were bound for the up-country fortress of Montefusco, which had been closed seven years back as no longer fit for human habitation. In the damp walls of this mediæval ruin, Ferdinand had determined to confine fifty of the principal political prisoners under harsh rules specially approved by himself, and under a gaoler who was the incarnation of cruelty. As the files of chained prisoners, already fainting with hunger and misery, wound up the mountain road to this dreadful place,

3

a gaunt, half-naked beggar suddenly rose up on the wall of a town beneath which they were passing, and waving his great stick cried out in devilish glee : ' *Viva 'o Re !* Carbonari ! Jacobins ! Montefusco is waiting for you.' And then, breaking into song, he croaked out :

> Whoe'er comes back to life
> From Montefusco's towers
> May boast himself twice born
> Into this world of ours.'

They passed on with sinking hearts.

On their first arrival in the damp and vermin haunted dungeons, they were almost starved to death, and only obtained food as the result of long expostulations. The chief gaoler exhausted every device to aggravate their misery. Though they were all men of refinement, orderly and long suffering, they were daily threatened with flogging, which was actually carried out upon one of them. Their letters were not only read by the gaolers, but were often kept back with cruel insult, except on those frequent occasions when the death of some broken-hearted wife, father, mother, or sister was announced ; then, indeed, the letters were handed on with alacrity, but without a sign of compassion. Many of them were permanently ruined in health, eight died of disease, and none were ' born again ' without carrying away lasting traces of their entombment. Castromediano's hair turned white, but he and Poerio, though both shaken by illness, supported the spirits of their comrades, which were indeed of metal kindred to their own. The song of a nightingale pouring out from bushes below the castle gave them comfort and hope ; it was therefore killed by the gaoler.

At last half a dozen out of the fifty were corrupted and became spies on the rest. They were perpetually worried to sue for pardon. Indeed, it is probable that the worst severities were applied in order to break the spirit of the men whose names now stood for so much in Italy and in

Europe, and induce them to recant and humble themselves
before the throne so gravely imperilled by their now famous
sufferings and their continued defiance. But they knew they
were in the forefront of Italy's battle, and were ready to die
at their posts.

Meanwhile on the desert island of San Stefano, ten
leagues out to sea off Gaeta, Luigi Settembrini, under a
sentence of death commuted to that of perpetual imprisonment, was shut up with thirty other ' politicals ' in the
famous *ergastolo*, among eight hundred wretches condemned
for murder and other more abominable crimes to hopeless
and unending punishment. Over a doorway opposite the
prison-house ran a Latin inscription :

*' Donec Sancta Themis scelerum tot monstra catenis
Vincta tenet, stat res, stat tibi tuta domus.' ***

These words,' wrote Settembrini, ' were not read or not
understood by most who entered, but they froze the hearts of
the political prisoners, warning them that they were entering a
place of everlasting woe, among a lost people, of whom they
themselves were to become part. One must have great faith in
God and in virtue not to despair.'

Here no one was chained. There was in fact much licence.
Drink went the round among the worst of the inmates,
perhaps alleviating their misery and certainly shortening
its term, but greatly adding to the discomfort of the respectable prisoners. Knives were common, and murder was an
ordinary incident. Ten men were shut up together in each
cell, the political prisoners being carefully scattered about
so that they should in all cases be physically and morally
at the mercy of their dreadful companions. ' Men become
beasts, descended to the utmost depth of moral degrada-
tion,' wrote Settembrini, although he succeeded in forming
close human and spiritual relations with one or two of these
children of unutterable woe.

* While sacred Justice holds in chains so many monsters of crime, your
wealth and house stand safe.

The diary of this man's agony, written in the gaoi of criminals condemned for life, has become an Italian classic.

' The three years,' he wrote, after that time had elapsed, ' are for me as one sole day—both short and long. I turn to contemplate this lapse of time, unmarked by events, and it seems brief ; one day does not differ from another ; one always sees and suffers the same things. Here time is like a shoreless sea, without sun or moon or stars—immense and monotonous. Many of the prisoners who have been here for thirty years say, when they speak of what they did or saw thirty years ago, " Not long since I saw this, I did that." I also say, " Not long since I was condemned to death." But when I look upon myself and my soul and this poor, torn heart, when I reckon up my woes and uncover the wounds which reach even to the depths of my soul, oh, then these three years seem to be infinite ! I cannot recall the few pleasures and the many griefs I had before: the griefs of these three endless years seem all my life. Three years, and if I have to say ten, and twenty, and thirty ? I shall never say it, for I shall not live so long.

' My body and my clothes are soiled ; it is of no use to try and keep clean ; the smoke and dirt make me sickening to myself. My spirit is tainted ; I feel all the hideousness, the horror, the terror of crime ; had I remorse, I should think I too were a criminal. My spirit is being undone. It seems to me as if my hands also were foul with blood and theft. I forget virtue and beauty.

' Oh, my God, Father of the unfortunate, consoler of those who suffer, oh save my soul from this filth, and if Thou hast written that I must here end my sorrowful life, oh let that end come soon. Thou knowest grief does not frighten or subdue me ; I bear my cross ; even on my knees I drag it after me ; but I fear to become vile, I fear my soul growing perverted ; even now, I recognise it no more.'

In April 1854 he wrote to his wife :—

I kissed your portrait, my beloved one, but I kissed it in secret. The men among whom I live, if they had seen me would have laughed at me, because they have no knowledge of virtue or of love. . . . Were anyone to read the words I write to you he would laugh at me and at my love. But you will not laugh, my beloved. Those who have not suffered as we have suffered cannot understand how misfortune strengthens and purifies love.'

Settembrini preserved his life and his reason in this hell

by applying his mind to his famous translation of Lucian, and by enjoying the friendship of his fellow-prisoner Silvio Spaventa.

In the winter of 1854–55 the political prisoners were at length separated from the criminals and confined together in two rooms overlooking the sea. Here they began seriously to devise means of escape, concerted by secret correspondence with their Italian friends through the medium of Temple, the British Minister at Naples. Anthony Panizzi, an exile from Modena ever since 1821, famous in the land of his adoption as the Librarian of the British Museum, formed a plot for the release of Settembrini and Spaventa. Money was collected for this purpose from Lord and Lady Holland, Mr. Gladstone and others. Sir James Hudson, the British Minister at Turin, who had already earned the confidence of all parties of Italian patriots, from Cavour downwards, introduced the English conspirators to the Democrats of Genoa, well knowing that they were better suited than Moderates and Cavourians for an enterprise of this character.* The Italian end of the plot was therefore placed in the hands of three men : Medici, who had so gallantly defended the Vascello, the key to the Janiculum, in the siege of 1849 ; Bertani, the head doctor of the Roman hospitals on that occasion, now the chief agent and friend of Mazzini in Italy ; and Garibaldi himself— three old friends who were destined ere long to organise and execute a more important but no less hairbrained adventure than the release of Settembrini from San Stefano. Garibaldi, all agog for action on however small a scale, undertook to command the expedition, and a detailed plan of escape was arranged with the prisoners. But the ship, purchased by the English sympathisers, was lost off Yarmouth in October 1855, before ever Garibaldi had set foot on her deck. The plot never fairly recovered from this blow, though Garibaldi paid a flying visit to Panizzi in the British

* Cavour, indeed, knew of the plot, and believed that Palmerston knew also.

Museum in February 1856. But Temple had long thought it imprudent, and Panizzi was won over to that opinion. By the end of the year even Bertani gave up hope. So Garibaldi remained on Caprera, and Settembrini on San Stefano for another three years.

While the emissaries of this abortive plot were passing between Caprera, Genoa and England, the stir of movement began again in the Neapolitan dominions. After 1848 all hope had been dead, and even indignation had been muffled by fear, until Cavour's Crimean policy encouraged the Italian cause in general, and England and France raised the Neapolitan question in particular. Finally, in October 1856, the two Western powers withdrew their representatives from Naples for no reason in the world except that the king sturdily refused to listen to our advice as to his methods of governing his own subjects. This action of Palmerston and Clarendon, though it was shrewdly criticised by men of the world as being at once interfering and impotent, had real effect in encouraging King Ferdinand's rebellious subjects, who saw in it a promise of help, and an official endorsement of Mr. Gladstone's accusations. The victories of the Italians in the Crimea, and the importance of the English and French action at Naples, were both greatly exaggerated as rumour passed secretly from mouth to mouth among the Sicilians and South Italians, whose ill-informed and easily excited minds were rendered doubly credulous by the artificial ignorance imposed by the censor. The era of hope and conspiracy began again.

But in order to understand the three rival policies directed against the King of Naples—the Murattist, the Mazzinian and the Cavourian—and Garibaldi's relation to each, it will be necessary to take a wider survey of Italian affairs.

CHAPTER IV

CAVOUR BRINGS THE DEMOCRATS AND NAPOLEON III. INTO HIS CAMP—PISACANE'S EXPEDITION—PLOMBIÈRES AND THE DECLARATION OF WAR AGAINST AUSTRIA— 1856–59

The adhesion of Garibaldi to our principles is an event of immense importance. We must make the utmost of this event, which secures for us the sympathies, and, when required, the active assistance of all the youth of Italy.'—Letter of PALLAVICINO to MANIN, 1857.

THE Democratic party, in which resided most of the faith, vigour and initiative of the Italian *Risorgimento*, as well as most of its unwisdom and rashness, had in the summer of 1849 come into deadly conflict on the walls of Rome with France and Napoleon III. Nothing short of the supreme genius of Cavour could in ten years' time have brought these irreconcilable enemies side by side into the field against Austria. Indeed, Cavour was one of the very few men who so much as realised the necessity for this strange combination, but he saw from the first that the Piedmontese statesmen and soldiers could not overcome Austria and the princes dependent on her in Italy, without the assistance both of France and of the Italian Democrats. In September 1856 he made his pact with the Democratic leaders. In July 1858, at Plombières, he made his pact with the French Emperor. In the spring of 1859 he forced on the war and the revolution.

On the side of the Italian Democrats, the originators of the alliance with Cavour were Manin, the creator and defender of the Venetian Republic of 1848, and his intimate friend Pallavicino. The immense value which they attached to the adhesion of Garibaldi to their new policy is shown by the words which stand at the head of this chapter. That adhesion was readily given. On August 13, 1856, Garibaldi, introduced by Pallavicino, had his first interview with Cavour. The guerilla chief was received with courteous familiarity, and went away rejoicing and speaking of the great minister as ' his friend.' The interview was secret, but Garibaldi next year publicly proclaimed his acceptance of Victor Emmanuel's kingship as the basis of Italian unity. When the world knew that the defender of the Roman Republic had, at the instigation of the defender of the Venetian Republic, accepted the principle of Monarchy, all chance of further disruption in the Liberal ranks was removed, and the Italian patriots, with a few important exceptions, were united under one flag. Mazzini's policy of the ' neutral banner '—that is, the policy of temporary alliance with Piedmont against Austria, leaving the question of Monarchy or Republic to be settled after the war—was now repudiated. Garibaldi never ceased to think that a Republic was ideally the best form of government, but he remained for the rest of his life actively loyal to the Italian monarchy, and never, though often under severe temptation, consented to raise the ' neutral banner.'

To this great decision, the most important and the best political action of his long career, he was urged by many motives. Above all else he saw that the Monarchy would unite a country which the Republic would divide. ' I was and still am a Republican,' he wrote, ' but I have no belief in a system of popular government so uncompromising as to impose itself by force on the majority of a nation. Another motive perhaps was irritation with Mazzini, the legacy of their quarrels during the defence of Rome, and the result of the natural incompatibility of their characters.*

* When Garibaldi came to London in 1864, Mr. John Morley, who had seen his triumphal entry, was describing it in the evening to Mazzini. Mazzini asked, ' Well, Mr. Morley, have you ever seen a lion ? ' ' Yes, I have, at the Zoo.' ' Have you noticed the face of a lion ? Do you not think it is a very foolish face ? Well, that is Garibaldi's.' I have this story at first hand.

Another, closely connected with this feeling, was his soldierly dislike of the Mazzinian method of undertaking wars with undisciplined and insufficient forces, and his perception that the regular army of Piedmont was essential to the expulsion of the Austrians. We must also take into account at this period his confidence in Cavour, and his belief that Italy was on the eve of war and revolution, stirred up this time 'from above.' He had, besides, at all times, a vague belief in the uses of a popular Dictator to supplement or replace Parliamentary government, and this theory, which ran strangely athwart his democratic and republican principles in his illogical mind, predisposed him to accept the headship of Victor Emmanuel. Last, but not least, we must count his personal devotion to the chivalrous warrior king. Garibaldi's belief in Victor Emmanuel survived by many years his belief in Cavour, and was ended only by death.

In the summer of 1857 the leaders of the new 'National party' formed the 'Italian National Society,' modelling its organisation on that of the English Anti-Corn-Law League. Italians of all the provinces, free or enslaved, were invited to join, and did so in thousands. The officers of the society were converted Republicans; Pallavicino was president, Garibaldi vice-president, the Sicilian La Farina secretary. Manin, in his exile in Paris, signed the articles of the society on his death-bed in August 1857, and did not live to see the ripening of his well-laid scheme for the liberation of Italy.

Hitherto the policy of the House of Savoy, even when patriotic and Liberal, had been 'provincial'—or 'municipal' as the Mazzinians tauntingly called it—aiming at the extension of the boundaries of Piedmont, not at the creation of an Italian State in which Piedmont should merge its own existence. Hitherto the 'men of the revolution,' the Democratic party inspired by Mazzini, had been the leaders of the movement for national unity, which had seemed a chimera to Piedmontese statesmen. Cavour's

3 *a*

predecessors and many of his colleagues ' wished to annex
Lombardy and the Duchies but not to make the nation.'
But now things had changed. The Prime Minister of
Piedmont was in secret alliance with a society, headed by
ex-Republican chiefs, whose avowed aim was to place the
crown of all Italy and Sicily on the head of Victor Emmanuel.
Each side had accepted something of the programme and
spirit of the other.

But the degree to which Cavour was conspiring with
Pallavicino and Garibaldi against the Pope and the King
of Naples had to be concealed, lest Napoleon should take
alarm and so the other conspiracy against Austria in the
North be utterly frustrated. For Napoleon would not
allow North Italy to annex either Rome or the South.
On the one hand he was protector of the Pope, and on the
other he had designs of placing on the throne of Naples
his own kinsman Lucien Murat, who, through his father
Joachim, had some rights of memory in that kingdom. All
that Cavour dared do, to thwart these Murattist designs
so dangerous to the prospects of Italian unity, was to
put the English diplomats on their guard. In September,
1857, he explained his position frankly to La Farina, the
Sicilian secretary of the National Society :—

I have faith,' said Cavour, ' that Italy will become one
State, and will have Rome for its capital. But I do not know
whether it is ready for this great change, for I do not know the
other provinces of Italy. I am minister of the King of Piedmont, and I cannot, I ought not, to say or do anything prematurely to compromise his dynasty. Make your National
Society, and we shall not have long to wait for our opportunity.
But remember that among my political friends no one believes
the enterprise (viz., the union of Italy) possible, and that
haste would compromise me and the cause. Come to see me
whenever you like, but come at daybreak, and let no one else
see or know. If,' he added smiling, ' I am questioned in
Parliament or by diplomats, I shall deny you, like Peter, and
say, " I know him not." '

From that time forward La Farina regularly visited Cavour,

coming up to his bedroom every day before sunrise, by a secret stair.

For the present, therefore, the Piedmontese propaganda in Naples and Sicily had little open support from the Piedmontese Government. But it was vigorously pushed by Cavour's Neapolitan friends living in exile at Turin, like Antonio Scialoja, as also by La Farina and the National Society. It was also favourably regarded by the men who from the Neapolitan prisons exercised a profound influence over Neapolitan opinion. Poerio managed to smuggle out from the dungeon of Montefusco a pencilled note with the words : ' Let our pole-star be always and only Piedmont.' Both he and Settembrini condemned the French Murattist movement as anti-national, and the action of the Mazzinians as factious, premature, and sometimes criminal. For the Mazzinian party, though it did useful work in combating the Murattists, attacked the Bourbon rule by some very questionable methods. The attempt to assassinate King Ferdinand, in December 1856, made by the soldier Agesilao Milano, who wounded him with the bayonet during a review, was the act of a solitary individual, a Mazzinian fanatic ready to sacrifice his own life, and endowed with moral qualities which explain, though they can hardly justify, the high esteem in which his memory was held by Italian and English sympathisers. But to Mazzini himself and a large section of his followers must be assigned the praise and blame for Pisacane's expedition of the following summer.

The Mazzinians, alarmed at the progress of Murattism, determined on immediate action in the south. A plan was formed to invade the Neapolitan coast from Genoa, the sea-cradle of Italian democracy. Mazzini himself left England, and came disguised to the base of operations. But the resources of his party, after the recent secessions to the National Society, were so small, the reports from the Neapolitan capital so discouraging, that half even of the faithful remnant tried to persuade their chief to abandon

the rash project.   His old friend Saffi, who, having shared
his triumvirate in Rome, now shared his exile in England,
and Bertani, his agent in Genoa, were alike opposed to
the design.   The best Neapolitan soldier among the exiles,
Cosenz, afterwards Garibaldi's able lieutenant in Sicily and
Naples, refused to lead men to destruction.   Garibaldi
himself, when Jessie White Mario upbraided him for de-
clining to join the expedition, replied to her with kindness
and good humour, but declared that he disapproved of
sending men to the slaughter ' to make the *canaille*
laugh.'

But Mazzini found men of the right temper for his
purpose in the Neapolitan Carlo Pisacane, the Calabrian
Nicotera, and the Sicilian Rosolino Pilo.   On June 25, 1857,
Pisacane and Nicotera sailed from Genoa in a small steamer
named the *Cagliari*, taking with them two dozen young
men of a spirit no less determined than their own.   They
missed Pilo, who was on the look out for them with a similar
force in another small ship, and sailed on alone to meet
their fate.

The original design had been to land first on the island
of San Stefano, and release Settembrini, Spaventa, and their
fellow prisoners.   But Spaventa, whom they round means
to consult, would have nothing to do with the plan, for
fear that the forcible capture of the island would involve
the release of the malefactors as well as of the political
prisoners.*   Pisacane therefore landed instead at the
neighbouring convict island of Ponza, which the little force
captured by a brilliant stroke.   There followed the disgraceful scene averted from San Stefano by Spaventa's
unselfish caution.   Pisacane released and took away with
him on the *Cagliari* some 200 common convicts, besides a
dozen ' politicals ' and a hundred old soldiers of the War
of Liberation.   With this undesirable force they landed at

---

* The Panizzi-Garibaldi plot for their release (see p. 69 above) had
involved no risk of freeing the common convicts, as stealth, not force, was
the principle of that plan.

Sapri. Some of the Liberals of the neighbourhood tried to raise the cry of *Viva Murat*, but the cries raised by the invaders were *Viva l' Italia* and *Viva la Repubblica*. As they marched up country into the mountains of the Basilicata, they found the peasantry in some villages neutral, while others turned out to defend their homes against a force which they justly believed to be principally composed of criminals, although Pisacane was able to repress any tendency to misconduct during the short time the expedition lasted. Reactionary feeling, stirred up by the village priests, was not wanting, and the Liberators found themselves opposed not only by Neapolitan troops, but by armed peasants, and even by women and children. After two severe conflicts with the troops and peasantry at Padula and Sanza, in which the convicts bore themselves well, the Republican force was overpowered. A pitiless massacre ensued, for the peasants were mad with rage. Pisacane died fighting; Nicotera and others were captured, desperately wounded.

Meanwhile at Genoa, Mazzini plotted to surprise and capture the royal arsenals, in order to fit out further expeditions in aid of Pisacane. The Piedmontese government had warning, and forestalled the attempt. Thereupon, by Mazzini's advice, it was decided to abandon the project, but one small party of the conspirators proceeded to carry out its original orders, and a scuffle took place in which a Piedmontese soldier was killed. Throughout the peninsula the indignation of patriots was aroused against the men who had fired on the national uniform and wantonly risked a civil war in the State which was now regarded as Italy in embryo. Public opinion enabled Cavour to indulge to the full his lifelong hatred of Mazzini, which contrasted so strongly with his admiration for Garibaldi. Mazzini escaped to England, but was condemned to death in his absence, and many of his followers were sentenced to long terms of imprisonment. His prestige had received an even more severe blow than that which it had suffered from the affairs of Mantua and Milan five years before. His party was in ruins.

Pisacane's expedition against the Bourbons is related to Garibaldi's successful expedition three years later, exactly as John Brown's raid on Harper's Ferry is related to the American Civil War. Pisacane was at the time condemned by almost all the friends of freedom, as having brought discredit on the cause, but a few years later his name was the watchword of that cause in the hour of its triumph, when the ghosts of the forerunners seemed to be marching in front of the triumphant columns of liberation. Like John Brown, he had exacerbated the feud, made compromise impossible, and so helped to bring on the final struggle. Like Brown, he had committed some acts that were criminal, and some that were sublime, and above all else he had known how to die. The Genoese part of the plot, the attack on the Piedmontese arsenals, had scarcely the shadow of an excuse, but its failure served at least to show that without the secret connivance of the Piedmontese authorities no effective expedition could sail from Genoa against the Bourbons. In 1860 this lesson was not forgotten by Garibaldi—nor by Cavour.

Although Cavour's severe reprisals on the Mazzinians for the Genoese insurrection incurred some censure from contemporaries, and more from posterity, those measures were thought too lenient by the nervous usurper in the Tuileries, who denounced Genoa as the most dangerous city in Europe, and, like a true Bonaparte, ceaselessly complained that political exiles were permitted to live in Piedmont, and that the press there enjoyed a relative freedom. His querulous outcries about exiles and newspapers were treated with scorn when addressed to Great Britain, but caused grave anxiety to Victor Emmanuel and Cavour, who on the one hand could not abandon the system of liberty in Piedmont without sacrificing the newly-won attachment of the Democrats throughout the Peninsula, nor, on the

other, offend Napoleon without losing their last chance of
driving the Austrians out of Milan. From this dilemma
they escaped in strange fashion through an event which
seemed certain by its very nature to precipitate them into
the abyss.

On the night of January 14, 1858, as the Emperor
Napoleon and the Empress Eugénie were driving together
to the opera, three bombs were hurled at them near the
entrance of the theatre. The horses were killed, but the
Emperor, like his uncle under the curiously similar circumstances of the royalist plot of 1800, stepped out unhurt
from the ruins of the carriage. Around lay 156 wounded,
of whom eight expired. When Cavour heard of this wanton
slaughter, equally provocative to the sovereign who had
been the intended victim and to his people who had been
the actual sufferers, he exclaimed in an agony of apprehen-
sion—' if only this is not the work of Italians ! ' Soon his
worst fears were realised. The criminal turned out to be
Felice Orsini, ex-official of the Roman Republic of 1849,
in the service of which he had distinguished himself by
suppressing terrorism and political crime at Ancona. Since
then he had lived much in England, seeing Mazzini's English
friends, and still sharing his political views. Of these
views, perhaps the most erroneous was a fixed belief that
only Napoleon prevented France from going to war on
behalf of Italy, whereas the exact opposite was the case.
Under this delusion as to politics, and a yet worse delusion
of his own as to ethics, Orsini, who had at this time quarrelled with Mazzini over some private affairs, devised his
plot without the knowledge of his old associates, but with
the help of some mean tools of his own finding.

Austria herself could not have wished for an event more
compromising to the hopes of Italy, except for the one
circumstance that the bombs and bomb-throwers had
come to France not from Piedmont but from England.
The anger of France was expended against ' perfidious
Albion,' with whom a long and complicated quarrel arose

out of the affair. At first, indeed, Napoleon was scarcely
less angry with Piedmont, and demanded of her in set terms
the expulsion of the emigrants and the silencing of the
Democratic press. The moment was one of extreme peril.
But now, as on several later occasions, the King came to the
rescue of his great minister. In a spirited but friendly
letter Victor Emmanuel stated the position with a wise
frankness.

'If the Emperor wishes me to use violence in my kingdom,
let him know that I should lose all my influence, and he all the
sympathies of a generous and noble nation. . . . that he has
no right to treat a faithful ally in this fashion ; that I have
never endured violence from anyone ; that I follow the path
of honour without reproach, and am responsible for that
honour only to God and my people ; that our house has carried
its head high for 850 years, and that no one will make me
bow it ; and that with all this I desire to be nothing but his
friend.'

In accordance with instructions received, General Della
Rocca ' committed the imprudence ' of reading to the
Emperor these words which would have goaded the first
Napoleon to some outburst of vulgar fury. ' That is what
I call courage,' was the generous reply ; ' your king is a
fine fellow ; I like his letter.' The doubtful and weak-
willed guide of Europe's destiny was touched by the undiplomatic sound of truth, purpose, and courage ; the
adventurer was held in envious admiration of ' that ancient
royalty which was the one thing he could not purchase.'

And, indeed, the fiery little warrior, with the immense
moustache, who strutted about, head in air, as though he
were vainly trying to overtop his courtiers, was ' every
inch a king.' Victor Emmanuel came of a royal stock so
ancient and so honourable that it could afford to have democratic sympathies without losing caste. Like the warrior
of Navarre, who, two centuries earlier, had done for France
a work somewhat similar to that which he himself was
doing for Italy, he had been nursed to hardihood as a moun-
taineer and hunter, and had early learnt, by the discipline

of evil times, to estimate men and things as they were, and not as they seemed when viewed from palace windows. Though of rougher speech and blunter manners than the 'gentle Henry,' he too was loved by the common people whose welfare he had at heart and whose company he was always glad to share in war and in the chase. He, too, hunted women with as little rest or scruple as he hunted game. But, in other respects, Victor Emmanuel had great virtues. His personal and family pride, perhaps the strongest motive in all his actions, took a noble form, for it was his first rule of life to be the 'man of honour,' the *galantuomo* in all his dealings—with his subjects, to whom he had sworn constitutional oaths, with Napoleon, with expectant Italy. He too often deceived, or allowed Cavour to deceive, perfidious enemies, but those to whom he owed an obligation, or who put their trust in him, never had reason to repent it. His courage was boundless, his good sense remarkable, and his Italian patriotism stronger than his religious devotion, with which it so often came into conflict.

It soon appeared, to Cavour's astonishment and joy, that not only was the master of France not alienated from Italy, but that he had now at last decided actively to befriend her. His conduct towards the man who had tried to murder him is one of the strangest chapters of the fascinating and mysterious book of the psychology of Napoleon III. He permitted the trial to be so conducted as to become rather the apotheosis of a martyred patriot than the condemnation of a criminal. Though Orsini perished on the scaffold, it was in the odour of a sanctity cast about him by his executioners. The letter in which he appealed to Napoleon to win the gratitude of twenty-five millions of Italians by freeing their country from Austria, was not only allowed to be read in the most impressive manner at the trial, but was printed in the French papers, and even, at Napoleon's special request, in the Piedmontese Official Gazette. Cavour, who had no sympathy with murderers anywhere, nor with conspirators outside diplomacy, was almost shocked at Napoleon's prostration before his would-be assassin ; but since the publication of Orsini's letter was a direct challenge from France to Austria, he gladly printed it, and it remains perhaps the strangest document that ever enlivened an official newspaper.*

The reasons why Napoleon relented to Orsini and to Italy will always be open to conjecture. His enemies attributed all to fear of assassination, remarking that by a campaign in Lombardy he could make reparation for Rome, and so sleep at nights without dreaming of that single-minded Italian ferocity of purpose which otherwise would dog him to the grave. But those know little of Napoleon who think that fear or any other single passion or single object can explain his conduct in anything. If he had been summoned before the throne of Omnipotence to give an account of his intentions, he could hardly at any moment of his reign have given a clear and consistent answer. He was at once a selfish and scheming adventurer who murdered liberty in his own country and protested against its natural manifestations in neighbouring lands, and a romantic idealist who wished to extend the principles of the French Revolution over Europe. The liberticide heard the cry of Poland and of Italy, which rose in vain to the ears of many who disapproved his tyranny in France. He was touched by the spectacle of Orsini's self-sacrifice, and remembered the day when, twenty-seven years before, he had himself conspired and revolted on behalf of Italian freedom. The Buonapartes were of ancient Italian origin. The founder of their modern fortunes had first leapt to European great-

* ' Que Votre Majesté se rappelle que les Italiens, au milieu desquels était mon père, versèrent avec joie leur sang pour Napoléon le Grand, partout où il lui plut de les conduire ; qu' Elle se rappelle qu' ils lui furent fidèles jusqu' à sa chute ; qu' Elle se rappelle que tant que l'Italie ne sera pas indépendante, la tranquillité de l'Europe et celle de Votre Majesté ne seront qu'une chimère ; que Votre Majesté ne repousse pas le vœu suprême d'un patriote sur les marches de l'échafaud ; qu' Elle délivre ma patrie, et les bénédictions de 25 millions de citoyens la suivront dans la postérité.'

ness by his Italian campaign of 1796, and perhaps the purest and best result of all his mighty activities had been the resurrection of Italian life after two centuries of death-like trance. Was that resurrection now to be completed or to be suppressed ? And if military glory was to be one of the bases of the restored Napoleonic dynasty (' peace, of course, was to be another), where could it be better won than in the plains of Lodi and Marengo, and in sight of the hills of Rivoli ? *

Such were Napoleon's personal aspirations, encouraged by his intimate friend, the Italian Count Arese, and by his cousin Prince Jerome Napoleon, who, with all his faults, felt a strong and disinterested enthusiasm even for the extreme idea of complete Italian unity.† But, for the most part, Napoleon III. was served, surrounded, and maintained by reactionaries and Clericals. His wife, whom he had married for love, was a Clerical. His throne depended on the French Catholics, and the fixed price of their support was the defence of the Pope's temporal power by the armies of France. The story runs that Cardinal Antonelli was asked one day—' When will the French garrison be withdrawn from Rome ? ' ' When I withdraw my garrison from Paris,' was the reply. The flagrant contradiction between the terms on which Napoleon held his throne in France and his desire to liberate Italy involved him, during the remainder of his reign, in weak and crooked courses which led him to ultimate disaster. If he had been more far-seeing or less generous he would certainly have shrunk from stirring up the Italian question.

It was characteristic of his mind and method that when he entered into negotiation with Cavour for an offensive

---

* Material for the fascinating study of Napoleon III. is most easily available in La Gorce's fine work, and in Ollivier's *Empire Libéral*.

The best works on the subject in English are Mr. H. A. L. Fisher's *Bonapartism* (1908) and Mr. F. A. Simpson's *Rise of Louis Napoleon* (1910).

† I call Prince Napoleon (*Plon-Plon*) ' Prince Jerome,' as he was usually called, though his real name was Joseph ; Jerome was also the name of his father (ob. 1860) and of his elder brother (ob. 1847).

alliance against Austria, he did not dismiss the reactionary Walewski, but was content to deceive him, carrying on the most important diplomatic transaction of his reign as a profound secret behind the back of his foreign minister. Through the agency, first of Prince Jerome and then of the Emperor's physician, Dr Conneau, a meeting was arranged between Cavour and Napoleon at the quiet health-resort of Plombières during the holiday season of 1858. On July 21, a single conversation, protracted for nearly eight hours, partly indoors and partly in the Emperor's phaeton among the wooded valleys of the Vosges, sufficed for the two men to adjust the fate of Italy. When the diplomatic world heard that Cavour had been at Plombières *incognito*, there was some uneasiness, but the secret of what he had done there was well kept.

The result of that long day's conversation was at once epitomised by Cavour in letters to General La Marmora and to the King. A suitable cause of quarrel was to be found with Austria, to give colour before Europe to a pre-meditated attack. Then 200,000 French and 100,000 Italian troops were to drive the Austrians from Milanese Lombardy and from the Venetian Quadrilateral, and finally to dictate peace at Vienna. The Cisalpine domination of the *Tedeschi* was to come to an end. Liberated Italy was not, however, to be united in one state ; Napoleon, as a good Frenchman, could no more tolerate a united Italy than a united Germany—though by the irony of fate he was destined to be instrumental in the creation of both. By the pact of Plombières Italy was to consist of a federation of weak states, nominally under the Presidency of the Pope, really under the protection of France. Of these the strongest would be that of North Italy, under Victor Emmanuel, which would include Piedmont, Lombardy, Venice, and the Pope's Adriatic dominions. His Umbrian dominions would be added to Tuscany to form a Central Italian State, while he himself would retain Rome and the province in which it stood. Naples must be reformed, or, as Napoleon did not attempt to conceal, given to Lucien Murat. In return for these benefits Italy would cede to France Savoy and possibly also Nice, and Victor Emmanuel would be asked to give his daughter Clotilde in marriage to Prince Jerome.

There were two miscalculations in this great plan. One was that the French and Italian forces were not strong enough to reach Vienna or even Venice. The other was that the French Catholic world would never allow the Emperor to despoil the Pope of three-quarters of his Italian dominions. Not only Napoleon but Cavour was still under some delusion as to the attitude of the Papacy. A month after Plombières, Cavour sounded Count Pasolini, the old friend of Pio Nono in his more Liberal days, and learnt that there was no chance at all that the Church would consent to surrender any part of her temporal power. And if she would not consent, Napoleon dared not be a party to her coercion.*

But if Cavour did not at first realise all the difficulties of executing the pact of Plombières, at least he understood all the dangers that would arise if it were executed. It would substitute French for Austrian supremacy in the peninsula. Cavour desired this no more than Garibaldi or Mazzini, but he had the nerve to risk the new danger as the only possible way of getting rid of the old incubus. He hoped, not without reason, that he would somehow be too clever for Napoleon in the end, and that Italian patriotism would rise to the level of the occasion. In the interval between Plombières and the outbreak of war he set himself to cultivate that patriotism in its most uncompromising form, partly in order to strengthen his position against his too formidable ally, and partly as a means of provoking Austria to war. For this dual purpose he summoned the

* The Pope, in January 1859, told Odo Russell, the British Resident, plainly that he would not even consent that any part of the Papal States should be administered by laymen : the ' States of the Church ' must be governed by priests.

patriots of all the other Italian States to flock to Piedmont
and enlist in the National forces. A secret organisation
for smuggling young men over the frontiers was established
by the National Society in almost every town of Northern
Italy. Many thousands from Austrian Lombardy and
Venetia, from the Papal States and the Duchies were enrolled in the Piedmontese regular forces, and in March and
April 1859, 3,000 more were formed into a small volunteer
corps called the *Cacciatori delle Alpi*, to be commanded by
Garibaldi.

By this policy of the enlistment of volunteers from all
Italy, including Austria's own subjects escaped from her
odious conscription, Cavour succeeded in provoking the
war. In December 1858, he had told Odo Russell, who
happened to be passing through Turin, that he would
' force Austria to declare war about the first week in May ' ;
he kept this extraordinary promise with a week to the good.
He kept it in spite of the most adverse circumstances. The
first four months of 1859 were perhaps the greatest, as
they certainly were the most agonising, of Cavour's life.
On January 1, Napoleon opened the ball by saying to the
Austrian ambassador that he regretted to find his relations
with Francis Joseph not as good as he could wish. Nine
days later Victor Emmanuel introduced into his speech to
the Parliament at Turin the famous words suggested by
Napoleon himself—*il grido di dolore*—' the cry of suffering
that rises to our ears from so many parts of Italy.' The
alarm thus fairly given, all France and all diplomatic
Europe rose up in protest to prevent the war. Napoleon
found himself deserted by the elements in French society
on which his dynasty depended—the Catholics and the
propertied classes—while the Liberals and Republicans
could not be expected at once to put confidence in their foe,
or to hail the prospect of his triumphant return as the Cæsar
of a victorious army. In England the Conservative ministers
of the day, who pleased themselves with the belief that
Italian grievances could be remedied without the expulsion

of Austria, placed themselves vigorously at the head of the peace movement, but with a strong Austrian bias. They took their stand, wrote Lord Malmesbury, on ' the terri-torial arrangements of 1815, which have ensured the longest peace on record.' Most Englishmen, though more sym-pathetic with Italy and less well disposed to Austria, shared the ministers' terror lest this war should be the prelude to another age of Napoleonic conquest. Hostility to France at this moment damped our enthusiasm for Italy, just as six months later it served greatly to enhance it.*

France and England together were too much for Napo-leon's infirm purpose. He shrank before the storm which he had raised, threw over Prince Jerome and Cavour, and in the middle of April joined England in recommending that Piedmont should reduce her armies to a peace footing while France and Austria similarly and simultaneously dis-armed. Cavour knew that in the state to which patriotic feeling had then been worked, an order to disarm issued in Turin would mean mutiny, revolution, anarchy, and the disappearance of the House of Savoy. To fall fighting Austria single-handed would be a better way to perish. For some hours Cavour contemplated suicide. He was found by his friends burning his papers, and he did not deny that he had had ill thoughts.

But meanwhile he had left no stone unturned. There

---

* This terror of France, with whom we had just been quarrelling, explains the inconsistency of the common British attitude to Italy in the spring and autumn of 1859, so amusingly exposed by Matthew Arnold in *Friendship's Garland*. Ruskin, though he despised the Italian Risorgi-mento, despised still more the English attitude towards the war of 1859. He writes on June 15 : ' The Italian nation is unhappy and unprosperous ; its trade annihilated, its arts and sciences retrograde, its nerve and moral sense prostrated together; it is capable only of calling to you for help, and you will not help it. The man you have been calling names, with his unruly colonels, undertakes to help it, and Christian England, with a secret hope that, in order to satisfy her spite against the unruly colonels, the French Army may be beaten, and the Papacy fully established over the whole of Italy—Christian England, I say, with this spiteful jealousy for one of her motives, and a dim, stupid, short-sighted, sluggish horror of interruption of business for the other, takes this highly Christian position,' &c., &c. *Arrows of the Chace*, 13.

was still a desperate chance that Austria would refuse the
simultaneous disarmament, and in this hope he had himself
accepted it—though he could scarcely have intended really
to fulfil the agreement.   But meanwhile his provocations
to Austria, consistently prolonged for so many months,
had at last broken down the counsels of wisdom at Vienna.
Austria refused the English proposals for simultaneous disarmament, and on April 23 her couriers arrived at Turin
bearing an ultimatum with three days of grace.   Never
were messengers of victory or of peace received with greater
transports of delight.   That night Cavour dined in triumph
among the small circle of his intimate friends.   On April
27 Austria ordered her troops to invade Piedmont, and
Napoleon, with the sullen acquiescence of England and
amid the rising enthusiasm of France, came to the rescue
of the peaceful little State against the wanton aggressor.
Bismarck, in 1870, may have equalled but did not surpass
this masterpiece of Cavour.   England, angry with Austria,
angry with Napoleon, retired for a season, soon to reappear under a new government and in a very different
temper.*

But Italy, rejoicing in her opportunity thus snatched
from the claws of fate, confident in such a group of leaders
as few nations have ever had at the crisis of their history,
remembering her past failures only as lessons, and thinking
of her dead as arising from their graves to watch, entered
upon the two years of war and revolution which secured
for her the right to be.

* 'Though it is *originally* the wicked folly of Russia and France that have
brought on this fearful crisis, it is the madness and blindness of Austria
which have brought on the war *now*.'—Queen Victoria to the King of the
Belgians, April 26, 1859.

CHAPTER V

GARIBALDI'S ALPINE CAMPAIGN, 1859

'Sì scopron le tombe, si levano i morti,
  I martiri nostri son tutti risorti !
  Le spade nel pugno, gli allori alle chiome,
  La fiamma ed il nome d' Italia sul cor !
Veniamo ! Veniamo, su, o giovani schiere,
  Su al vento per tutto le nostre bandiere !
  Su tutti col ferro, su tutti col foco.
  Su tutti col foco d' Italia nel cor.
     Va fuora d' Italia, va fuora ch' è l' ora,
     Va fuora d' Italia, va fuora, o stranier.'
                      Garibaldi's Hymn.

'The tombs are uncovered, the dead come from far,
The ghosts of our martyrs are rising to war,
With swords in their hands, and with laurels of fame,
And dead hearts still glowing with Italy's name.
Come join them ! Come follow, O youth of our land !
Come fling out our banner, and marshal our band !
Come all with cold steel, and come all with hot fire,
Come all with the flame of Italia's desire !
    Begone from Italia, begone from our home !
    Begone from Italia, O stranger, begone !'

TOWARDS the middle of December 1858, Cavour summoned Garibaldi, who, leaving Caprera, landed at Genoa on the 19th, and spent the evening there with his friends of the Democratic party. Neither he nor they knew of the pact of Plombières, but they already scented powder in the air. ' Write me a hymn for my volunteers,' he said to Mercantini. The result of this commission appeared in ten days' time, in the shape of ' Garibaldi's hymn,' destined in the coming years to resound on the battlefields of Italy from the Alps to the Sicilian mountains.

On December 20, Garibaldi proceeded to Turin, and was taken by La Farina, the secretary of the National

Society, on one of his secret visits to Cavour. It was probably at this interview that Garibaldi was told of the important part assigned to him in a plot of Cavour's, soon afterwards abandoned, for beginning a revolution in the Carrara district in order to provoke Austria to war. It was certainly at this interview that Cavour told him that he was to be put in command of a volunteer force to be raised among his own friends. Returning to Genoa, he at once commissioned Bixio to begin privately enrolling names. He sailed back to spend Christmas at Caprera, telling La Farina that a steamer must be sent to fetch him when he was wanted. A few days later, at the New Year, came Napoleon's public warning to the Austrian ambassador.

At the end of February Cavour sent once more for the hermit of Caprera. The design of the Carrara revolution was being gradually abandoned in favour of an easier method of provoking Austria, the enlistment of her run-away subjects under the banner of Piedmont. Thousands were being drafted into the regular army, but Cavour's favourite scheme was the formation of Garibaldi's corps of volunteers. On March 2, 1859, the decisive interview on this subject took place. Garibaldi had reached Turin the night before, and in the morning Cavour's confidential valet came into his study to announce that there was a man demanding to see Monsieur le Comte. " What is his name ? " " He will not give it ; he has a big stick and a big hat, but he says that he has an appointment with Monsieur le Comte." " Ah ! " said Cavour rising, " bring him in ! " The man entered, whose appearance had so much astonished the valet. His skin was tanned by wind and weather, his hands were hardened with daily toil. His eyes

'were surrounded by a network of fine lines. This had no trace of cunning, as is so often the case with wrinkles round the setting of the eyes, but was obviously the result of habitual contraction of the muscles in gazing at very distant objects. In short, Garibaldi's eyes, both in this respect and in respect

of a certain steadfast, far-away look in them, were the eyes of
a sailor.'

All was soon arranged between Cavour and his visitor with
regard to the volunteers, and on the same day Garibaldi
was taken to see Victor Emmanuel. The occasions, of
which this was the first, when these two met face to face
were nearly always pregnant with fate for Italy. And
whenever they met, Garibaldi left the king's presence with
an increased sense of loyalty and a more docile spirit.

On this occasion indeed he required no royal persuasion.
He returned that night, in the highest spirits, to Genoa,
and there summoned about him the chiefs of the old Democratic armies, the Republican and Garibaldian veterans of
'48 and '49. It was in vain that Mazzini denounced the
war, on the ground that

  if successful, it will give Louis Napoleon a greater hold than
he has ever had on the French mind through military glory and
territorial increase. The Lombardo-Sardinian kingdom will
be, morally, a French dependency. Through other, more
southern schemed acquisitions, the Mediterranean will be a
French lake.'

This attitude, though it had much influence in London
among the Italian exiles, had little in Italy, where the war
fever was at its height. The Garibaldini did not deny the
danger pointed out by Mazzini, but strove to provide
against it by giving to the ultra-patriotic forces an independent military organisation so formidable that Cavour
would not feel the need to depend on France, nor the power
to betray Italy even if he wished. Hardly one of the old
fighting men but came to Garibaldi's call. Even Dr.
Bertani, who had so long been Mazzini's agent in Genoa,
undertook to organise the medical service for the *Cacciatori
delle Alpi*, as he had organised it for the defenders of Rome
ten years before. Medici, who had fought in the red shirt
on the Pampas and had held the ruins of the Vascello for
three weeks against the French army, and Nino Bixio,

who had been carried back from his wild charge up the steps of the Corsini and laid in the hospital beside his dying friend Mameli, were both again ready to Garibaldi's hand. Cosenz, Neapolitan by birth but Northerner by temperament, a quiet, modest and benign gentleman in spectacles, as cool in battle as Bixio was hot, already famous as one of the defenders of Venice, now entered Garibaldi's service, and was henceforth his good angel in politics and in war. The *Cacciatori* were organised in three regiments, each consisting of a full thousand men and each divided into two battalions. The first regiment was entrusted to Cosenz, the second to Medici, the third to a less able officer, Ardoino. But one of Ardoino's battalions was led to battle, and would, if necessary, have been driven into the mouth of hell, by Nino Bixio— strangely popular with his men, although he was always falling upon them with the flat of his sword in gusts of blind anger which would soon have earned for any other officer a bullet in the back.* The list of captains and lieutenants of the *Cacciatori delle Alpi* is filled with such names as Bronzetti, Sacchi, Carrano, Piva, Cadolini, familiar in the history of the sieges of Rome and Venice and of the last stages of Garibaldi's retreat.

In allowing Garibaldi to choose his own officers, Cavour showed that he was not afraid of ex-Republicans, or even of Republicans who were ready to fight for the king. It had been his own device, suggested to him by no one and opposed by many, thus to create a force which should represent the idea of the national uprising as distinct from Piedmontese officialdom and the French alliance. If Garibaldi, the known enemy of Napoleon and the champion of Italian nationality, could achieve some romantic feats of war in the Alps, both the English public and the Italian

---

* Nino Bixio's constant apologies for his conduct in these matters, found in his letters to his wife during the campaigns of 1859–60, show that that lady was always doing her duty by taking him to task on the subject. Nino was adored by his family, among whom he was always as gentle as he sometimes was with his soldiers.

Democrats would feel greater sympathy with the war and confidence in its author, Cavour.* The plan succeeded to perfection, owing to the valour of the *Cacciatori* and the genius of their leader, which made up for the lack of numbers, artillery, cavalry, commissariat, and good fire-arms. For of these advantages the volunteers were deprived by the jealousy of the War Office, of which General La Marmora was now the head. Cavour in those days was too busy to see to everything, and 2000 good carbines which he had ordered for the *Cacciatori* were sent after them too late, and distributed by a foolish official among the civic guard of Lago Maggiore. No horses or waggons were provided for the ambulance, so that Bertani and his staff of able doctors had to rely on the liberality of the inhabitants in the seat of war. There was no commissariat. There was no artillery, except a mountain battery that arrived too late to share in the principal achievements of the campaign. There was no cavalry except fifty *guide*, or scouts, who came on their own horses. Another similar, though probably inferior, corps, raised from the exiles of Central Italy and called the *Cacciatori degli Apennini*, was deliberately sent off under another command, contrary to the express orders of the king that all the volunteer regiments should be placed under Garibaldi. One good thing, indeed, the War Office provided—the services of General Cialdini, most enthusiastically rendered, to organise the three regiments in the depots ; for Garibaldi himself was a bad organiser.

Fortunately these raw volunteers and their veteran officers had three weeks of active service with the regular army before they were called upon for any great effort on their own behalf. When war was declared on April 27, Turin was in the greatest danger. General Gyulai, with over 100,000 Austrians ready to his hand, was on the banks

* It is remarkable how the *Times*, hostile to Italian hopes in the early part of the year, on account of its fear of Napoleon, at once took up Garibaldi and his volunteers at the very beginning of the war, *e.g.*, leading article on May 28. It saw in Garibaldi a way to combine friendship for Italy with hostility to France.

of the Ticino, while the French were far away across the
Alps. But Gyulai's not very acute mind was distracted
by the precedent of former wars, when Austria's safety had
lain in the defensive and in a judicious retreat to the
Quadrilateral. He crossed the Ticino on April 29, and
wasted three weeks, each worth an army corps to Austria,
in futile and hesitating movements, while regiment after
regiment of French infantry, Zouaves, and cuirassiers
marched down the winding valley from the frozen summit
of Mont Cenis pass, or came steaming up by sea to Genoa
and thence by train into the valley of the Po. During this
anxious period of waiting for the French, the entire forces
of Piedmont, 60,000 all told, were concentrated near the
great river to defend the heart of the State. The *Cacciatori
delle Alpi* served side by side with the regular troops,
occasionally skirmishing with marked success on their own
account, and enduring the frightful discomfort of the rain
and floods, which were perhaps one of the minor reasons
of Gyulai's inactivity. Garibaldi, as a subordinate, proved
on this occasion the most ready and obedient of men, and
won the hearty goodwill of his superior officers.

When at last the French had arrived, and the allies were
in a position to take the offensive, the *Cacciatori* were sent
up north to invade Alpine Lombardy as a detached and
advanced left wing of the army. Garibaldi was far too
well pleased with this independent command and the chance
of being the first liberator on Lombard soil, and he was
moreover far too good a soldier, to utter in his men's
hearing any discouraging complaint of the unprovided
condition in which they were being sent on an errand so
hazardous.

The force which he led into the enemy's territory consisted of just over 3000 young men, each with an abomin-
ably bad old pattern musket of shorter range than the
weapon of the regular army. But at the end of each
musket was fastened a serviceable bayonet, the weapon
destined to win the little campaign. The fifty rifles were

the private property of as many crack shots from Genoa, ' gentlemen-merchants, artists and professional men,' who under the title of the ' Genoese carabineers,' formed a fine body of skirmishers, always in the forefront of battle. There was, besides, an excellent rifle in the skilled hands of the gigantic Peard—once the terror of the Oxford ' town ' —destined now to obtain, without seeking it, a European celebrity as ' Garibaldi's Englishman.' But the other units of the division, not only miserably armed but untrained to shoot, and unaccustomed, as townsmen, to the mountains or, indeed, to great physical exertion of any kind, were required to take Alpine passes from the splendid Tyrolese sharp-shooters and well-drilled Croats and Hungarians with rifles and artillery. The task would have been impossible if the *Cacciatori* had been of the ordinary stuff that armies are made of, stirred only by the usual passions of war. But their ranks contained the very pick of the first families of Milan,* and were for the most part filled by Lombard students, artisans, landlords, professional men, and runaway school boys. They had been selected from among their fellows by the devotion with which they had risked, and the energy by which they had saved, their lives among the Austrian watchers on the frontier, for each one had stolen into Piedmont ' crossing the mountains and wading the rivers on St. Francis' horse ' (viz. on foot). They were mostly men of education and of ideals. Their solid English comrade was astonished and touched to hear them round the camp fires entertain each other with long recitations of Tasso, Ariosto, and Alfieri. No youths ever

---

* Mrs. Gurney Buxton tells me that in 1881 the following patois verse was still being sung by the peasants along the shores of Lago Maggiore, celebrating the liberation effected by the *Cacciatori* of 1859 :—

> ' Evviva Garibaldi !
> Tutti i sciuri (signori) di Milano
> Li ong fa' scappa i Tedeschi
> Coll' la bandier' in mang ' (mano).

' All the gentlemen of Milan have driven out the Austrians with the banner in hand.'

went to battle with a stronger motive to conquer. They were fighting their way back as liberators to the homes from which they had lately fled like hunted criminals. They did not find the words of Garibaldi's hymn too high-flown for the occasion. They were to make their country and to avenge at last the long catalogue of her martyrs. Privately, too, each one was consumed with the remembrance of some story of injury and shame wrought on his family or his dearest friends by the rough and stupid soldiery of Eastern Europe. They had confidence in their veteran officers, and far more than confidence in their general, who was the god of their idolatry. The fear of his reprimand, of which he was never sparing either to individuals or to companies, was an ever present terror, while the hope of his measured and lovingly spoken words of praise, the certainty of seeing his calm face and hearing his low pene-trating voice in the midst of the decisive charge of the day were moral forces which would alone have made them superior to any ordinary regiment.

The red shirt did not appear in this campaign ; it would have been a gratuitous insult both to Napoleon and to the Piedmontese official party. Garibaldi himself was properly dressed as a Piedmontese general, though on the march he was seen to change his ' tiresome hat ' for a broad-brimmed felt, and to wrap himself up during the rain in the folds of his American *puncio*. But in the king's battles he always displayed the king's uniform. His men, dressed after the ugly, conventional pattern of the line regiments, had none of the theatrical picturesqueness of Rome ten years before, or of Sicily in the following summer. But on the eve of entering Lombardy, Garibaldi made them leave their knap-sacks behind and be content with as much linen and pro-visions as could be forced into their bread bags and into the large pockets which he caused to be sewn on to their coats. He thus gained that mobility which was the first principle of his method of war, but increased the difficulties of the commissariat and of food supply. Fortunately, in the country which they were about to invade, every household was passionately on their side.

The Ticino, which divided Austrian Lombardy from Piedmont, issues from the Lago Maggiore in a broad, swirling flood that no regiment could hope to ford. It thus offered, in continuation of the lake commanded by Austrian steamers, an easy line of defence against Garibaldi's unsupported infantry advancing from Biella. But he had at least an imitation of one other arm of the service in the fifty mounted scouts, and by great good fortune, their able leader, Simonetta, was a popular landowner in this very district. On May 21 and 22 Simonetta made a rapid tour in disguise along both the free and unfree shores of the lake, and although the Austrians laid an embargo on every stick that could float, and had their steamers on the look-out, he skilfully and secretly collected a number of barges at an appointed place. This *rendezvous* was Castelletto, on the Piedmontese shore of the Ticino, three miles below its debouchment from the lake, and one mile below Sesto Calende on the opposite shore, where lay a slender detachment of Austrians. At Gallarate lay a single battalion, enough if properly used to have delayed the passage until immense numbers had been brought up from Milan. But the Austrians did not suspect Garibaldi of intending to pass the river. Their delusion was maintained by one of his most customary devices, for he ostentatiously ordered provisions for his troops at Arona and Meina, as if he intended to march northward along the Piedmontese shore of Maggiore. As usual, his own men were equally deceived, and it was with surprise that they heard the order given on the night of the 22nd, just outside Arona, not to enter the town but to turn sharply to the right. They proceeded south by a forced march under cover of unusually thick darkness. The clock of Castelletto was striking midnight when the column, still ignorant of its destination, reached the top of the high bank above Simonetta's barges, and saw

4

the faint gleam of water through the trees below. Only
then did they realise that they were to invade Lombardy
before dawn. While the rear companies were still struggling
through the brushwood of the steep incline down to the
river's edge, a flood of moonlight suddenly burst over the
long reaches and swirling eddies of the Ticino and lit up
the busy and memorable scene. By that time the first
companies, already on the opposite bank, were marching
up in perfect silence and order to Sesto Calende, where they
captured the fifty Austrians in their beds. In the grey of
the morning the remainder of the division crossed, all in
the highest spirits at being the first liberators on the soil
of their own Lombardy. The inhabitants, ' who had gone
to rest slaves and awoke free,' were prodigal of thanks and
of such hospitality as they could provide, and would on no
account accept payment.

Next morning, by five o'clock, the troops were already
on the road for Varese. The weather was the loveliest of
the early Italian summer; the atmosphere had been washed
bright by the recent rains; the landscape and the people,
both among the finest in Italy, were in gala to greet their
deliverers. All day Garibaldi guided his men by intricate
country roads winding in and out of hills green with chestnut, oak and fir, across rivulets rushing between banks of
flowers, along the soft and richly cultivated southern shores
of Comabbio and Varese lakes, to the north of which rose
the great mountain ridges. And everywhere as they passed
from hay-fields and wayside factories and entrances of
village streets, there poured out, with shouts of *Viva
Garibaldi, Viva l' Italia*, handsome and prosperous looking
peasants, a cross between the Italians of the plain and the
men of the higher Alpine valleys. As they neared the foot
of the great hill on which Varese stands, the summer night
descended, and the fire-flies danced among the moving
columns, making the young soldiers laugh as one tiny spark
after another settled in the bushy beard of their immense
English comrade. Then, as they mounted the wearisome

ascent to the ever-receding city, an Alpine thunderstorm broke in splendour upon them.   Just before midnight they entered Varese under a deluge of rain, but it fell unheeded on the frantic joy of the people, who embraced the Garibaldini in the open before they suffered them to take refuge under the fine mediæval colonnades that flank the street. The city had revolted some hours before their arrival. Many a banner of '48, with the three colours long faded, like the dead who had borne them, had been pulled out that afternoon from holes among the roof tiles.   In the autumn of that year of disaster, when Garibaldi had for a few weeks continued the lost war against the Austrians in this very district, he had passed through Varese on his way to the skirmish of Morazzone.   That now, after eleven years, it was Garibaldi who had come back to deliver them made deliverance itself more enchanting.   This welcome in the midnight storm at Varese was the first of a thousand such scenes to be enacted in the next two years round Piedmontese or Garibaldian liberators in more than half the cities of Italy.

The revolution was spreading on all sides, and far in front of the line of march.   As fast as the news arrived that Garibaldi was across the Ticino, townsmen and peasants alike along the shores of Como, and up the Valtelline to the very foot of the snows of Stelvio, drove out the Austrian police, formed revolutionary committees, and put themselves in touch with the King's commissioner, Emilio Visconti Venosta, whom Cavour sent after Garibaldi to take over the administration of the liberated districts.   These patriotic and manly populations were the same as those which, in the spring of 1848, had left their mountain homes and marched to Milan in time to take their share in the ' five days.' * Now again, by their premature uprising, they risked and in some cases experienced the severe reprisals of

* Readers of Meredith's *Vittoria* will remember the patriotic mountaineers of the Valtelline; his description of their action is quite in accordance with fact.

the Austrians, of whom they were not fairly quit till after the battle of Magenta. These popular movements, though in Cavour's eyes of high political importance, were of little military service, owing to the lack of weapons. The search for arms had been the main part of Austrian policy for ten years past in these districts, where many a brave fellow had been shot for possessing a long knife or an old gun. Neither had the *Cacciatori*, themselves so badly equipped, brought with them the means of arming the revolution.

Garibaldi had yet to make good his challenge to fortune in thrusting himself far across the Ticino so many days in front of the allied army. He saw that Varese offered an admirable defensive position, and spent May 24 and 25 in fortifying its approaches and resting his men. General Urban, who was coming to dispose of him, enjoyed not only a deserved reputation among the Italians for brutality, but a name among his own countrymen as a dashing commander specially fitted to cope with the famous guerilla at his own game. He was called ' the Austrian Garibaldi,' but the events of the next few days showed that he was a very Austrian Garibaldi indeed. As soon as Gyulai heard that the *Cacciatori* had crossed the Ticino, he had sent this officer against them at the head of the brigade Rupprecht, consisting of rather more than 3,000 infantry, and a full complement of artillery and cavalry. Urban advanced from Como by the Camerlata road, and attacked Varese from that side only, after detaching a column over the hills to his right in the vague hope that they would reappear at the critical moment on the north of the town. But they were not seen again, so that Garibaldi's force present in Varese was actually larger than the 2000 and odd infantry who attacked it, although the latter had the advantage of bringing artillery into the field.

The scene of Urban's attack in the early morning of May 26 was Lower Biumo, a suburb lying at the north-eastern foot of the group of wooded hills on which Varese is so pleasantly situated amid its gardens and villas. In this suburb on the plain Garibaldi had stationed Medici, while he himself occupied the wooded hill of Upper Biumo not far to the north, the direction from which both he and Urban expected the approach of the lost Austrian column. Medici's men down below held a large villa and its little walled garden along the south of the Camerlata road, just outside Lower Biumo (the house is easily to be distinguished to-day by a bust of Garibaldi on its outer wall); on the other side of the road were some smaller houses, and a few trenches which had been constructed the day before. The Austrians drove in the Italian outposts from Belforte farm, and thence advanced through a plain a mile long, covered with mulberry trees standing out in rows above the high corn. Their artillery unlimbered and shelled the volunteers in Lower Biumo at close quarters but without impairing their *morale*. Indeed, when the white-coats advanced to the charge, the young Italians, inferior in firearms, but superior in spirit to the enemy, leaped from the trench and from over the garden wall, and fell on them with the bayonet. The guns limbered up and were not seen again that day. As the sun sucked up the last of the early morning mist, Garibaldi, having satisfied himself by careful scouting that no column was approaching Varese from any other direction, galloped down from Upper Biumo and headed the advance ; Cosenz led down other bodies of *Cacciatori* from the hills on the south, and turned the left flank of the Austrians. They retired slowly, halting to fire behind every line of mulberry trees, and making a last attempt to rally at the fine old group of farm buildings on the knoll of Belforte. But soon the last of the white-coats had been cleared off the ground.

The battle of Varese had cost the mother of the Cairoli the first of those four sons whose lives she gave for Italy. It was Ernesto, a young doctor of law, fighting as a common soldier ; he was deeply mourned by Garibaldi, who already knew and loved the Cairoli family, the leaders of patriotic

Pavia. The eldest of the five brothers, Benedetto, who alone survived the heroic era, though not for lack of exposing himself in the forefront of Garibaldi's wars, became prime minister of the country ransomed by his brothers' blood.

The Austrian rout was complete, but there was no cavalry to follow it up. Part of the *Cacciatori*, unbreakfasted but eager to go on when Garibaldi asked them to ' see our friends a little further along the road,' pressed on with him over two more miles, down through wooded ravines and water-courses, up again through Malnate village, and across the cultivated table land beyond it. They were brought to a stop by the Austrian rearguard, rallied on S. Salvatore heights to cover the further retreat of the main body through Binago. A deep gorge, with sides so steep that it was not possible to climb them except by clinging to the bushes, divided the Austrians from their pursuers. A first attack was repulsed, but the position was finally turned from the north, where the gorge was shallower. While the enemy's rearguard was evacuating S. Salvatore, Garibaldi gradually withdrew his men to Malnate and thence to Varese, as rumours that the lost Austrian column had been seen in the hills to the north gave him momentary fears for the safety of Varese. At midday he led his men back to the city, all in the highest spirits. Seeing Peard, who had used his rifle well in the thick of the battle, and had now walked the skin off his feet, dragging his heavy weight along the road, he spoke kindly to the Englishman and made one of his staff lend him his horse.

The well-planned defence and spirited counter-attack had given the new generation of Garibaldi the needful self-confidence. But the battle of Varese, though a faultless piece of minor tactics, was no very wonderful feat of war. Next day, however, Garibaldi was to display his peculiar strategical genius at its best, in effecting the capture of Como from a force more than double his own.

On the evening of his defeat at Varese, Urban telegraphed

to headquarters that his victorious enemy had employed 7000 troops that morning—more than twice the real number. Gyulai was thoroughly alarmed as to the effect which these northern operations might have on his own position at Milan. The allies might at any moment attack him in front on the Ticino with their main force, and meanwhile the Alpine districts on his flank and rear were rising, the steamers on Lake Como had been seized by the local rebels, and Garibaldi would soon join them at the head of his victorious troops. Might he not then march on Milan at the critical moment of the struggle of the main armies on the Ticino ? And would not Milan then rise as in '48 ? It was necessary to dispose of Garibaldi. That very night (May 26) Urban was put in command of three brigades— that of Rupprecht which had just been defeated at Varese, and those of Augustin and Schaffgotsche, amounting in all to over 11,000 men. In the course of the morning and early afternoon of the 27th, all four battalions of the brigade Augustin had come up by train from Milan and joined the brigade Rupprecht for the defence of Como city. Thus, although the third brigade Schaffgotsche was still on its way, Urban had eight battalions of infantry, that is about 6400 men, besides artillery and cavalry, with which to hold Como against the 3000 Garibaldini, still unprovided with cannon.

Como, lying low by the lakeside, is guarded from approach on the west by a line of forest-clad mountains, so steep that no troops can cross them except at two points, the pass of San Fermo on the north, and the town of Camerlata where the mountains end on the south. All that Urban had to do was to hold these two points with a force more than double that of Garibaldi. But he preferred to leave part of the brigade Augustin down in Como city on a level with the lake, where it was absolutely useless. He very properly massed another strong force to defend the approach to Camerlata, but he occupied the pass of San Fermo with only one or two companies of Hungarians, apparently not knowing that a city in a hollow must be defended on the hill tops.

Garibaldi, advancing on the morning of May 27 over the battlefield of the previous day, marched at first along the main road towards Camerlata, as if he were about to attack the defenders of Como on that side. And there they continued to expect him, deceived by masking operations of Cosenz at Olgiate, long after the main body of *Cacciatori* had turned off northwards to the left. Guided by small country roads through a maze of wooded and vine-clad hills, the Italians arrived about four in the afternoon opposite the ill-guarded San Fermo pass flanked on each side by high mountains. As the *Cacciatori* passed through the village of Cavallasca they obtained a full view of the position which they were about to attack : a little valley and stream lay below them, and beyond rose the smooth slope of a hill, on the top of which towered the apse and campanile of the old church of San Fermo. This building on one side of the road and a little wayside inn upon the other were both crowded with Hungarians, whose rifles, projecting from long rows of loopholes, commanded the ascent from the stream. Flanking parties went out to right and left to capture the two hills commanding the church and village, and another company had Garibaldi's orders to charge up the road in front as soon as the firing began on the flanks. The leader of this company was the gallant De Cristoforis, a student and patriot of the very best type of that golden age of Italian publicists. Although he had already distinguished himself in the little campaign, unfortunately he now neglected to deploy his men. As they rushed in column up the road, they were checked by a terrible volley from the church and inn. De Cristoforis fell mortally wounded, and two of his officers were laid low at the same moment. But the flank attacks were meanwhile being developed, the frontal attack was renewed, and the two weak companies of Hungarians were soon bayoneted, made prisoners, or sent flying through the rear of the village.

The Garibaldini had thus effected a lodgment on the broad neck of the pass. When, now too late, large bodies of Austrians came hurrying up from Como and from other directions, a series of confused and petty actions raged among the vineyards and brushwood on the pass-top, and on the slopes of the wooded mountains at either side. The Italians fought chiefly with the bayonet, and Garibaldi was everywhere in the thick of the fight. The officers, according to the Garibaldian formula for successful leadership of raw volunteers, exposed themselves in the front of every danger. Cosenz led on his men, and Medici drove another division of the enemy southwards towards Camerlata. Bixio wrote to his wife next day, ' Garibaldi gave his orders only by gestures, and our men cast themselves down like a torrent. I am living in a world of poetry (*sono nella poesia*).'

At last the Austrians gave way and fled down the ravine by the steep zig-zag road that falls for many hundred feet from San Fermo to Como. Halting on the edge of the pass the victorious Garibaldini could see the reserve of Augustin's brigade, like little white specks far below, crawling about in the *Piazza d' Armi* outside the city, and their unused artillery standing in limber. Now came the moment for one of Garibaldi's great decisions. Was he to bid his men descend the mountain side and enter Como, into the midst of a more numerous but demoralised enemy ?

' For some time,' writes Peard, ' a steady fire was poured down on the ravine from the height above, and just as the sun had gone down, and it was beginning to get dusk, the whole of the troops on our left were collected and formed in the high road.

' After a short time Garibaldi rode to the front with his staff, with the peak of his cap pulled down close to his eyes, the only indication he ever gave of his thoughts being more intensely occupied than usual. It was as usual a barometer of his feelings, as the working of the stump of Nelson's arm. Slowly our whole body began to move. As we descended the wide road, darkness began to close in. Every one expected some hot work before we should be in Como, for they had seen the formidable column that occupied the *Piazza d' Armi*. As we got nearer what was naturally supposed would be the scene of a hand to hand struggle, the halts, though of only a few minutes' duration, became frequent. The men were careful in arranging the position of their canteens and anything that might make a noise. They seemed to step lighter than usual, for not a footfall was to be heard. The silence became almost painful. In this way the first of the houses of the suburb was reached. The inhabitants instantly, as the column advanced, showed lights at their windows. They began to cry " *Viva Garibaldi*," but some one would run over immediately and beg them to remain silent. We were rapidly passing the suburb. Where were the Austrians whom we had seen in such strength an hour or two before in occupation of the place ? The suburb is passed. At the entrance of the city (Como) is a dense mass of figures with torches. Lights rapidly appear in all the windows, and instead of a storm of Austrian bullets the troops were met with a deafening shout, " *Viva Italia !* " " *Viva Garibaldi !* "

' The people were wild with delight. Men with torches marched on either side of his horse, and old and young rushed forward kissing his feet and clothes. Old men with tears streaming down their faces, and young girls threw their arms round our necks and saluted us as their deliverers. The uproar was immense. The sound of the bells which were ringing in all the *campanili*, and music of the bands were drowned by the cheering of the crowds that were assembled in the large Piazza. Marshal Urban, with eight battalions,* a battery of guns, and some squadrons of Uhlans, had evacuated the city about an hour previous to our arrival.'

It was indeed a happy night. Even the men whom Bixio had too often cursed and beaten with the flat of his sabre, came to tell him they loved him after having followed him in battle that day.

Urban was in full flight. Como and Camerlata were both abandoned in such haste that large stores of arms, provisions, and money fell a prey to the victors.

' Not only,' writes General Hohenlohe, the famous author of *Letters on Strategy*, ' was Garibaldi allowed to occupy Como, but the Austrian flank and rear were so threatened that the entire first Corps was ordered to Milan, where it was to arrive a few days later. . . . Thus Garibaldi with 3000 partisans contained nearly three brigades of Urban's and the whole of the first Army Corps.'

---

* He had not really eight battalions in Como itself, but he had eight at Como and Camerlata together.

Garibaldi was well aware that Urban would shortly be able to rally his two defeated brigades at Monza and Milan, join them to the brigade Schaffgotsche and return against him in overwhelming numbers. Meanwhile he had secured two or three days' respite by his victory of May 27, and he resolved to turn the breathing space to account. After conceding a needful day of rest at Como, he led his men back on the 29th through Varese, leaving the defence of Como city and lake to the local patriots and a detachment of *Cacciatori*. His objective was a secret from his own men ; he gave out that they were going to meet the small mountain battery which Cavour had sent after them. But when these guns had been found safely arrived at Varese, it appeared that the real object of the march was the capture of the port of Laveno on Lago Maggiore. Laveno was the base system of Austrian navigation which still secured the waters of the western lake for the black and yellow flag, while on more eastern Como the red, white and green already held the waters and both the shores. On the night of May 30 the Garibaldini attempted to surprise the little fort defended by 590 men, and the steamers in the port below. One of the columns lost its way in the darkness and the surprise failed. The morning after this repulse from Laveno, the unwelcome news arrived that Urban, with his three brigades complete—over 11,000 men —was in front of Varese, whither Garibaldi was retreating. All that he could now do was to go up into the skirts of the mountain called Campo dei Fiori—an Alpine 'Field of Flowers' 4000 feet high—which overhangs the city. Descending as far as S. Ambrogio, he remained there to protect the inhabitants of Varese, who had fled for refuge to the high perched village and pilgrimage shrine of S. Maria del Monte. From that point of vantage the unhappy citizens watched Urban bombard their empty houses in Varese, as a punishment for the way in which they had received their liberators.

Garibaldi had before him the prospect of being once

more, as in 1849, hunted like a partridge in the mountains,
though on this occasion the superior *morale* of his small
force would enable him indefinitely to protract the campaign
in the fastnesses of the Alps. It would be a sort of war
which he was eminently fitted to conduct, but 3000 men
could hardly be expected to defeat 11,000, unless Urban
constantly repeated the error of dividing his force, now
nearly fourfold that of his adversary. For the moment,
posted as Garibaldi was within a few miles of Varese, he
was in imminent danger of being overwhelmed. So, by a
rapid and secret march over mountain tracks on the first
night of June, he carried back his force to Como city, which
had remained in the hands of the patriots. But at the same
time Urban received orders partially to retire. For on
May 30 Victor Emmanuel and General Cialdini had tri-
umphed at Palestro. Urban, though recalled from the close
pursuit of Garibaldi, was not brought down to the main
scene of operations, and his 11,000 men were useless on
the decisive day (June 4) when Napoleon crossed the Ticino
and won a 'soldiers' battle' at Magenta. After the hard-
won victory of the French, Gyulai evacuated Lombardy
and fell back on the Venetian Quadrilateral, for which his
unadventurous soul had been yearning during the days
when he should have had no thought but to advance on
Turin.

Some time on June 5 the news of Magenta reached
Garibaldi at Como. Grasping at once the new situation
created by the great battle, he started on again that very
night, his men acting as the detached left wing of the allied
advance across Lombardy. During June 6 steamers crowded
with the *Cacciatori* passed along the shores of the most
beautiful lake in Europe, while the peasantry shouted and
waved greetings of wild delight from the water's edge and
from chestnut woods high overhead. Rounding the point of
Bellagio, the boats discharged their freight at Lecco before
nightfall, and Garibaldi was thus already across the Adda,

while the main army was only just across the Ticino. From
Lecco he pushed on to Bergamo and Brescia by a most
dangerous route, parallel with the Austrian main army as
it retreated towards the Quadrilateral. But he used his
fifty mounted scouts with the same ability and vigour with
which he had used his cavalry in the retreat of 1849.
He cleverly out-manœuvred the Austrians at Ponte S.
Pietro, and fought a spirited little action at Seriate, where
a single company under Narciso Bronzetti drove in rout
a whole battalion of Hungarians.* In this way he arrived
safely, first at Bergamo and then at Brescia, the twin sub-
alpine cities which shared the reputation, earned by terrible
sacrifices in the evil years gone by, of being the most patriotic
of the Lombard towns.

On June 11, in Garibaldi's headquarters at Bergamo,
Giovanni Visconti Venosta, brother of Emilio the Royal
Commissioner, witnessed a curious and characteristic scene.
Half a dozen Austrian officers, captured in fight, were
brought before the General. They came into the presence
of the ' red devil ' with the constrained resolution of men
prepared for death. The troops whom they commanded,
the ignorant peasantry of Croatia, used to tell their Italian
captors how they had seen ' Garibaldia ' in the thick of the
fight at Varese and Como, with the bullets leaping off his
coat like hailstones, and how they knew he ate the flesh of
his prisoners.† Their officers did not share these supersti-
tions, but they fully expected that the fierce guerilla, whom
they had hunted to the death with his wife and friends
in '49, would order to instant execution every Austrian

---

* Bronzetti's extraordinary feat at Seriate, in defeating about 800
Hungarians with 100 *Cacciatori*, may be partly accounted for by the political apathy of the Hungarians for the Austrian cause. Signor Marchetti
tells me that they found the Croats in this campaign always held out longer
than the Hungarians. In the Italian war, 1915–18, the opposite was
usually the case, for obvious political reasons.

† The Austrians called him the *rothteufel* in 1859, although he
wore no red shirt in this campaign. The name, I suppose, referred
partly to his hair, and partly to their recollections of the red shirt in
1848–49.

whom he caught. When, instead, he rose to shake each
of the six prisoners by the hand, with a word of commen-
dation for their courage and of pity for their misfortune,
Venosta saw their faces change to profound surprise and
gratitude. (See henceforward Map VI. end of book.)

On the night of June 12–13 a dangerous forced march
was made, in order to reach Brescia. While Garibaldi,
skilfully avoiding Urban's columns, was winding his way in
the darkness by a small track along the slopes of Monte
Orfano, he suddenly drew rein and began to listen intently
—for the distant sound of horse hoofs or of cannon, as his
staff supposed. But, in fact, a nightingale had just broken
into song over his head, and in a moment he had been rapt,
in that moonlit hour, into another sphere where the inner
life of his soul was spent,

> ‘ Some world far from ours,
>   Where moonlight and music and feeling
>   Are one.’

He sat long motionless, in a trance from which his followers
were at last fain to wake him. In the morning they safely
entered Brescia, after one of the most hazardous marches
of the campaign.

At Brescia Garibaldi's independent command came to
an end. During the approach of the allied armies to the
southern end of the Lago di Garda, he continued to act as
their advanced left wing, but under Victor Emmanuel's
orders, no longer on his own responsibility. On the night
of June 14–15, he was instructed from headquarters to
advance on Lonato, and informed that he would be followed
on the road by four regiments of cavalry and two horse
batteries. Proceeding next day to carry out these orders,
he found the Austrians threatening his right flank, but
no sign of the promised cavalry. Pressing on himself with
a portion of his force to Lonato, he was obliged to leave
another part under Cosenz, Medici, and the rebel Hungarian
Türr to defend the line of communications at Tre Ponti.

This rearguard was shortly afterwards attacked, but after a successful defence it advanced and drove the enemy southward for two miles along both banks of La Lupa canal, until, arrived at Ponte S. Giacomo, it found itself in the neighbourhood of larger bodies of Austrians. Cosenz very properly ordered a halt, but Türr pressed on and became unnecessarily involved with a whole Austrian brigade. The gallant Narciso Bronzetti, the hero of Seriate, one of the finest of Garibaldi's officers, fell mortally wounded. A hasty retreat began, and Garibaldi, galloping up to the firing from the direction of Lonato, met some of the men in full flight along the canal. His terrible anger soon recalled them to their duty, but though the battle was renewed with success as a defensive operation on the Tre Ponti ground originally occupied in the morning, the counter-attack successfully begun from that position had ended in failure owing to Türr's rashness. The belated arrival of the regular cavalry removed all danger from the situation. At this battle, as at Varese and Como, the Austrians admitted a loss of between one and two hundred men, but at Tre Ponti the Italian loss, counting prisoners, was certainly not less than theirs.

Garibaldi was next sent to Salò, standing on a deep bay of the Lago di Garda. Here, in full sight of the Veronese Alps and the heights of Rivoli across the lake, he made naval preparations for the passage, expecting to march through Venetia, as he had marched through Lombardy, the advanced left wing of the allied armies. His forces now first began to increase rapidly, and in a short month they rose to 12,000 volunteers. But before they had reached that number his high hopes had been dashed to earth, by an order from headquarters received at Salò, on June 20, to carry his force out of the seat of war into the remote Valtelline. Whatever the motives of those who gave the order, the *Cacciatori* were furious at being thus sent to the rear, at the first moment when they were becoming formidable in numbers. The Austrian invasion of the

Valtelline was a chimera, as Garibaldi rightly supposed, and as the men who sent the order perhaps themselves suspected.* The hostile force occupying the Italian foot of the Stelvio Pass did not require 12,000 *Cacciatori* to check its advance down the valley. In the first days of July, Medici with the vanguard easily drove them out of Bormio, and Bixio, following them up the pass, formed a chain of posts on the eternal snow, where during the brief remainder of the war the Italian and Tyrolese patriots stood watching each other on the vast white boundary, at the point where, until 1918, Austria, Italy and Switzerland marched with one another.

Giovanni Visconti Venosta, himself a native of the Valtelline, who had been named as Local Commissioner for the valley under his brother Emilio, had opportunity to observe there certain phenomena which soon became common throughout Italy.

' When Garibaldi passed through a village,' he wrote, although he was not now wearing the red shirt, you would not have said he was a General, but the head of a new religion followed by a crowd of fanatics. The women, no less enthusiastic than the men, brought their babies to Garibaldi that he should bless and even baptize them. To these crowds that thronged him, Garibaldi would speak with that beautiful voice of his which was a part of the secret of his charm—" Come ! he who stays at home is a coward. I promise you weariness,

---

* I do not know whether the order was given in good faith for genuine military reasons, or to get rid of the Garibaldini from motives of political or professional jealousy. In February 1910 I asked Marchese Emilio Visconti Venosta, who had been` the King's Commissioner in Alpine Lombardy in 1859 (see p. 99 above), what he thought was the motive of sending the Garibaldini to the Valtelline in June. He replied that when the order was given the larger number (12,000) of Garibaldini were only just being enlisted, and were still undisciplined, and the force was therefore in a state of flux, not the compact 3,000 with which the campaign had begun. The idea of sending them to the Valtelline was that they would be disciplined there, and then used for some greater purpose elsewhere. But, he added, there also was a military theory that the Austrians could come over the Stelvio, which they had made as a military road, though in fact local and physical conditions made a debouchment thence in great force impossible, and a much smaller force than the Garibaldini would have sufficed to guard the upper Valtelline.

hardship, and battles. But we will conquer or die." These were not joyful words, but when they were heard the enthusiasm rose to its highest. It was a delirium. The crowd broke up deeply moved, commenting on what the General had said : many had tears in their eyes.'

The mountaineers of the Valtelline, who were no mere shouters like some of the more southern populations over whom he threw the same spell, enlisted in crowds,—400 from the small town of Morbegno alone. But Garibaldi himself was no great organiser. Venosta records how when certain contractors came to the General for his signature to their contracts he broke out :—

' What ! These rascals who have the honour to clothe our brave young men who are giving their lives for their country, while they themselves are playing the coward at home, dare to ask for contracts, agreements, signatures ? Is not my order enough ? Send them to the devil ! If they are not enemies, they certainly are not patriots.'

They got their contracts, but the scene depicts the nature of the man.

The Garibaldini, on their way to the Valtelline, had heard news of the great battle of Solferino, in which they thought they might well have been allowed to take part. The Austrians, who had retired beyond the Mincio, suddenly recrossed it, and on June 24 fought a last fierce battle for the recovery of their Milanese possessions. After a terrible carnage, they retreated once more and for ever out of Lombardy. But the French and Italians had suffered scarcely less than they, and the advance against the fortresses of the Venetian Quadrilateral was delayed. A fortnight later came the news which crushed the hopes and roused the fury of Italian patriots from the Garibaldini in the Valtelline to the farthest Sicilian conspirators : the Emperors of France and Austria had met at Villafranca and arranged terms of peace.

Garibaldi and his volunteers had played no decisive

part in the war of 1859, which had been won by the regular armies on the battlefields of the Lombard plain.   But the spirited little campaign in the wooded mountains round Varese and Como is a story dear to all true Italians, for it moves in that unmistakable atmosphere of the pure poetry of the Risorgimento.   Nor is it wanting in technical interest, for it shows how far Garibaldi and his men were a match for the best Austrian troops under one of the most distinguished Austrian generals, and how far his detractors are right when they say that he could only defeat Neapolitans.   The impartial student may well agree with the Prussian military historian in his admiration for the leadership which enabled 3000 young volunteers, with old muskets and no cannon, to defeat twice the number of highly trained Austrians, excellently armed and fully equipped with artillery, and thereby to draw away from the main seat of war three whole brigades amounting to over 11,000 men.*

Yet the Alpine campaign is perhaps of most importance as being the field where the guerilla chief trained that small and peculiar force with which he accomplished the work of the following year.   It was in the Alps of 1859 that the Garibaldini acquired those fighting qualities and that unbounded confidence in themselves and in their leader which enabled them in 1860 to conquer Sicily and Naples.

---

* *Hohenlohe,* ' Letters on Strategy,' i. 206.   He speaks indeed of Garibaldi's ' 3000 mountaineers and riflemen,' but the 3000 were in fact neither riflemen nor mountaineers.

CHAPTER VI

VILLAFRANCA AND AFTER

Peace, peace, peace, do you say ?
    What ! With the enemy's guns in our ears ?
    With the country's wrong not rendered back ?
What ! While Austria stands at bay
    In Mantua, and our Venice wears
    The cursed flag of the yellow and black ? '
        MRS. BROWNING. *First News from Villafranca.*

NAPOLEON III. cannot justly be blamed for making peace
after the battle of Solferino.   If, indeed, the whole strength
of France and Piedmont could have been devoted to the
expulsion of the Austrian armies from the Venetian Quadrilateral, there would have been a good prospect of success
after a bloody and protracted campaign.   But whatever
odds might be taken as to the result of a fair fight there
was grave reason to fear that the ring would not be kept.
Prussia was considering whether she should seize her opportunity and invade the Rhine frontier of France.   Russia,
whose friendship to France had hitherto held Prussia in
check, had been alienated by the popular risings in Tuscany
and the Romagna, which gave the war a revolutionary
character, and by the conspiracy of Napoleon, Cavour and
Kossuth to raise the Hungarian nation in arms.   For the
fortunes of Hungary, which the troops of the Czar had
helped Austria to suppress in 1849, always affected the
political barometer in Poland.   The clerical party in France
were growing openly restive at the course of events in Italy,
particularly at the encouragement given to the rebellion
of the Pope's subjects in the Romagna.   The French
soldiers were discontented with the small amount of assist-

ance obtainable from the newly liberated provinces of
Italy. Napoleon knew that he might lose his throne as
the result of a single defeat, and even if he had been ready
to risk that personal loss, he surely had no right to expose
France to Prussian conquest, in pursuance of schemes
which, however generous, interested himself and Italy rather
than France herself. Unnerved by the heat of the Italian
summer, conscious that his own bad generalship had hitherto
escaped punishment only by the worse generalship of
Gyulai, horrified at the carnage he had witnessed on two
hard-won fields, he had none of the self-assured and callous
fortitude of the victor of Eylau and Borodino. Napoleon III.
determined to avoid his Leipzig and Waterloo while there
was yet time.

But if the wisdom of making peace can hardly be chal-
lenged, the terms hastily and secretly agreed upon at
Villafranca by the two Emperors were monstrous. By
those terms, not only was Austria left in possession of the
Venetian territory still occupied by her armies, but the old
Ducal and Papal despotisms were to be restored in Tuscany,
Modena and the Romagna. These provinces had, during
the last three months, one by one revolted and established
orderly provisional governments under the protection of
Piedmont. The foolish, kind, old Grand-Duke Leopold of
Tuscany had never been forgiven for allowing the Austrian
occupation in 1849, though he had managed to bring it to
an end seven years later. When, in 1859, he refused to
join in the national war, his subjects sent him off in a
carriage to the frontier with good-humoured cries of ' a
rivederci in paradiso,' ' good-bye till we meet in heaven.'
That was at the end of April ; in June, after Magenta, the
fiercer despots of Modena and Parma fled from their territories with the Austrian garrisons, and the simultaneous
withdrawal of the white-coats from Bologna was the signal
for the rising of the Pope's Romagnuol subjects. The
proposal of the signatories of Villafranca in the following
month to restore the old rulers involved the return of the

armies of Austria, for a liberticide conquest of Florence and Bologna by French troops under the liberator of Milan was hardly to be contemplated. The treaty further mocked the aspirations of Italy by a proposed Federation of Italian States under the presidency of the Pope, in which Austria would clearly exercise a dominating influence. ' Perhaps,' wrote Napoleon's shrewd and cynical friend Prosper Mérimée, ' perhaps peace was necessary, but we ought not to have begun so well merely to leave Italy in a worse mess (*gâchis*) than before.' If Piedmont had accepted these terms as final and satisfactory she would have gained Lombardy and perhaps Parma, but would have forfeited her headship of the patriotic movement, and the reversion of the rest of the Peninsula.

When Cavour heard that the French and Austrian Emperors had made, without consulting or even warning him, so cruel a settlement of Italy's claims, a life-time's habit of self-restraint fell from him like a disguise. The astonished world had a vision of the nether fires in the man, the furnace that drove the smooth and perfect engine, and learnt that the heart with which he loved Italy had been fashioned on the same scale as the brain with which he served her. For a few hours Cavour was more obstinate and frantic in the face of accomplished facts than Garibaldi in his most headstrong mood. He advised the king to reject the treaty and to carry on the war single-handed. When Victor Emmanuel refused thus to commit national suicide he flew into a rage, and after a violent scene between the two men, who always admired but never loved each other, he left the royal presence gesticulating wildly, his face ' red as a furnace,' his lips trembling, ' a singular and terrible spectacle ' to his friends. Victor Emmanuel, though bitterly mortified by Villafranca, kept his head during the perilous days of Cavour's madness. With a juster perception of what Napoleon had sacrificed and risked for Italy, he continued till the end of his life to feel a personal obligation to the man who had crossed the Alps to fight for him against

Austria.*   Knowing that it was impossible to continue the
war alone, he put his signature to the treaty, but added the
significant words of reservation—' so far as concerns myself '
(*pour ce qui me concerne*).   He thus made it clear that while
he consented to peace and took Lombardy as the price of
peace, he did not guarantee the clauses which provided
for the return of the despots to the revolted provinces.

Meanwhile Cavour, still in the heat of fury, had mastered
himself enough to be turning that fury to account.   He
had gone back to Turin, where on July 14 he met Kossuth.
The two patriots had an equal right to complain of the
peace, for Napoleon had sprung it on them both after
fostering far other hopes.   But the Hungarian was overwhelmed by the Italian's passion and carried away an
undying recollection of the terrible emphasis with which
Cavour had exclaimed :—

' This treaty shall not be executed.   If need be I will take
Solaro Della Margherita† by one hand, and Mazzini by the
other.   I will become a conspirator ' (striking his breast), ' I
will become a revolutionary.   But the treaty shall not be
executed.   No !   A thousand times no !   Never, never ! '

When Cavour said ' Never,' the negative prophecy that falls
so easily from the mouth of smaller men was likely to be
fulfilled.   He had already sent in his resignation, but while
the king was seeking a man to take his place, he continued
to organise by advice and encouragement the resistance
set up by Tuscany, Modena, and the Romagna against the
return of their old rulers.   The newly-liberated States had,
according to French accounts, been lukewarm or at least
ineffective in sending troops to the front during the war.
Modena and the Romagna, which had got rid of the Austrian
garrisons only in June, had not had time to levy troops,
but the charge was in some measure true in the case of

---

* In 1870 he wished, out of sheer gratitude for 1859, to go to war for
Napoleon against Prussia.   Here we have the chivalrous and even quixotic
knight-errant, whose family had ' held its head high for 850 years.'

† Leader of the Clericals in the Piedmontese Parliament.

Tuscany, where the population was not warlike and the conscription was unpopular with the peasants, as it had been in 1848. But the inhabitants of all three States were prepared to fight rather than take back the old *régime*. The Romagnuols, under the Piedmontese Commissioner D'Azeglio, began to organise at Bologna a force to repel the Pope's Swiss mercenaries, who threatened to reconquer the province for their master. Cavour's friend Farini put Modena in a similar posture of defence, and declared that if the Duke tried to return he would be treated as a public enemy; on July 17 he received the following telegram from Turin,—' The Minister is dead, but the friend greets you and applauds your decision.' At Cavour's personal instigation he remained at his post in spite of the orders of recall which as Piedmontese minister Cavour had been forced to send in accordance with the terms of Villafranca. Cipriani soon succeeded D'Azeglio as Governor of the Romagna. Neither he nor Farini were now Piedmontese Commissioners in name, but as Dictators they upheld the national flag until the time should come round when Piedmont could venture on annexation.

Tuscany adopted the same policy in close alliance with Modena and the Romagna. Soft Tuscany needed a man to hold her firm, and she found for the purpose her own ' iron Baron,' Bettino Ricasoli, one of the half-dozen titanic men produced by the Italy of that period. Not unlike a Republican of our own Puritan Commonwealth in his personal, religious and political temper, he was as a rock planted, and Tuscany clung to him for ten months till the long-wished-for day of annexation and union came at last.*

Thus Cavour, before quitting office, had seen to it that Central Italy would continue, under strong but moderate leaders, to maintain liberty and order, and to demand unswervingly from diplomatic Europe nothing short of union with Piedmont. With the help of Ricasoli and the people

---

* A fine personal account of Ricasoli can be found in Countess Martinengo Cesaresco's *Italian Characters*.

of the Central Provinces, he had in a week laid down the lines of passive resistance to Villafranca, along which it was easy for his successor to continue during the next half-year.

This done, Cavour retired for five months into private life. He spent the greater part of August 1859 in the quiet home of his friends the De La Rives, above the southern shore of Lake Geneva, where he soon recovered all his old sagacity and calm. ' His normal state came quickly back, and with it came oblivion of the past now useless to contemplate, new hopes, new designs, a new policy, another plan of campaign.' So wrote his friend, William De La Rive, who, watching and listening day by day, heard Cavour foretell two coming developments of policy, by which Villafranca could be turned from a curse into a blessing. ' England,' he said, ' has done nothing yet for Italy ; it is her turn now.' And—' I shall take Naples in hand.'

It was indeed England's turn now. Jealousy of France, which had damped our pro-Italian ardour during the war, after Villafranca urged us to outbid Napoleon for Italy's gratitude now that he hung back, and to help build up an Italian State strong enough to be independent of his protection. It so happened that just a month before Villafranca there had occurred a change of ministry in England which enabled her to adopt the new policy fitted to the new situation. A general election had been held in May 1859, but the result of an appeal to the country in those days was not always apparent till Parliament met, because many members in that easy-going period were independent of party ties, and could make and unmake ministries by the exercise of their private judgment. The war was still raging, and the precise nature of England's neutrality was open to question, owing to the Austrian proclivities of the Derby cabinet, which still held office pending the vote on the Address.* Hence not only England but France,

---

* One of the last acts of the Conservative ministry was to send Henry Elliot to Naples with orders to dissuade the King of Naples from joining Piedmont in the war against Austria.

Italy and Austria waited anxiously to hear the result of
young Lord Hartington's amendment to the Address, and
when in the small hours of the morning of June 11, a majority
of thirteen for the amendment was declared to a crowded
house of over 630 members, the Piedmontese minister,
waiting ' with some other foreigners ' in the lobby,

' threw his hat into the air and himself into the arms of Jaucourt,
the French *attaché*, which probably no ambassador, or even
Italian, ever did before in so public a place.'

When old Lord Palmerston appeared, grimly radiant, the
Italians ' redoubled their vociferations.' Their conduct
wounded the feelings of the defeated ministers, and it
certainly was neither proper nor considerate. They had
forgotten where they were. They were not thinking of the
' ins ' and ' outs ' of Westminster, but of a tragic land of
which only a few of that great crowd of free and comfortable
Englishmen had any notion ; where but to think was to be
suspect, to speak was ruin, and to act was death, where
the talk at every table was hushed by the terror of priests
and spies and foreign soldiers, where statesmen were chained
to convicts, where women were flogged and men were shot.
They were thinking of Italy, poor fellows, and so when
they saw ' Pam ' they gave him a cheer. For there was
the man who in his own rough, brutal way had so often
told the kind of truth which statesmen and diplomats
generally conceal, and now he was coming into power once
more. In the doubtful twilight of that summer morning
in the heated lobby they spied a dawn of hope for their
country. And indeed she had won by that division more
than they knew, more than ' Jaucourt the French *attaché* '
guessed or wished. That had been the parting embrace of
Italy and France.

A month later came the news of Villafranca. By that
time the new Liberal ministry was well in the saddle. The
' Triumvirate,' as it was called, of ruling spirits in the
Cabinet consisted of three remarkable men, seldom united

except about Italy, which was now their chief thought. Lord Palmerston, Lord John Russell, and Mr. Gladstone were each personally predisposed by generous Italian sympathies to the new course which interest and circumstance mapped out for our country after Villafranca. In the game of stealing the gratitude of Italy from the French who had shed their blood for her, England started with three great advantages over her rival—she hated the Pope, she desired no territory, and she wished to see a really independent State in the Mediterranean. The Queen and Court and most of the fallen ministers were ranged in active hostility against the pro-Italian policy of the ' Triumvirate,' and the majority of the new Cabinet was indifferent to its leaders' enthusiasms. But the bulk of middle-class opinion was strongly pro-Italian, and so was the more influential part of the press. The *Times* came right round in the middle of 1859 to strong and lasting Italian sympathies.

When Pio Nono heard of the new ministerial arrangements in England, he said to Odo Russell in his mild, half-humorous, plaintive way—

' Well, of course, you belong to his party, but, *Poveri noi !* what is to become of us, with your uncle and Lord Palmerston at the head of affairs in England ? . . . Then again, Mr. Gladstone, who allowed himself to be deceived about the Neapolitan prisoners.'

Lord John Russell, the new Foreign Minister, was destined during the next eighteen months to be one of the principal instruments in the making of Italy. His part in that work, next to his part in the great Reform Bill, stands as the principal achievement of his life. Sir James Hudson, our minister at Turin, felt with joy a new hand on the rudder, and knew that the home government would now at last co-operate with him and listen to his sage advice for the good of Italy and for the honour of England. After Villafranca Lord John at once took up the cause of Tuscany,

Modena, and the Romagna, and opposed the restoration of their old rulers. During the half-year of Cavour's retirement the diplomatic struggle went on. 'The policy of Her Majesty's Government,' Lord John laid down, ' was not to interfere at all, but to let the Italian people settle their own affairs.' In consequence of our protest against French or Austrian interference with the doings of the populations of Central Italy, the terms of Villafranca could not be enforced. The gratitude of Italy was up for auction, and England ran up the bidding. Throughout the autumn of 1859 Napoleon became ever less subservient to the Pope, and more angry at his Holiness' refusal to make the slightest concession in the Romagna or elsewhere. The restoration of the old rulers in Central Italy receded into the region of the impossible, and the struggle shifted to this question, whether the revolted provinces should remain independent or be united to Piedmont. On this point Napoleon, fearful of any large step towards the union of Italy, still held out, declaring that he would never allow annexation. But Ricasoli, Farini, and the people whom they ruled would accept nothing else. Even in Tuscany, with its strong provincial tradition, the passion for national unity became almost as deep as the passion for freedom, thanks in no small degree to the insulting terms originally suggested at Villafranca. The deadlock continued all the autumn and winter of 1859, the Italian populations showing a firmness and patience which do not always go with exalted patriotism, and which, without the presence of Ricasoli and the support of England, would have degenerated into some form of weakness or violence.

In the middle of this long period of ferment and inaction an important incident occurred in the life of Garibaldi. In August 1859 a close military union was formed between Tuscany, Modena, and the Romagna, and the forces of the League were placed under the command of Fanti, a Modenese exile who had risen to the rank of General in the service of Piedmont. Fanti named Garibaldi as his second-in-com-

mand.   The primary object of the army of the League was
defensive.   In June, before the peace of Villafranca, the
Papal troops had reconquered revolted Perugia and so kept
down Umbria and the Marches, and they now threatened,
in close alliance with the armies of the King of Naples, to
invade and reconquer the Romagna.   The need for Central
Italy to defend herself was therefore obvious, but the
question which everywhere divided the counsels of patriots
that autumn was whether the army of the League was
merely to guard the frontiers ; or whether it was to invade
the Marches where the smouldering insurrection might at
any moment break out, and thence to sweep over the Papal
and Neapolitan dominions with the irresistible impulse of a
national revolution.   Passionate hopes were aroused when
it was known that Garibaldi was Fanti's second-in-command
and had been stationed by him in the region of Ravenna and
Rimini, on the banks of that ' Rubicon ' which now again,
it was said, divided the two Italies.*

Garibaldi brought with him from the Valtelline Cosenz,
Medici, Bixio, and large numbers of his volunteers, eager to
continue in the Apennines the war which had been cut
short in the Alps.   The Garibaldian programme, wrote
Benedetto Cairoli on September 25, was ' not local defence,
but national war.'   And the patriotic ardour of the Northerners was further stimulated by contact with the Romagnuols.   That fierce population welcomed with transports of joy the man who had owed his life to their courage
and fidelity.   He had said in 1849 that he would return in
ten years, and now he kept his word, for in September 1859
he drove through the pine forest and the marsh lands of
Ravenna to visit in their cottages the peasants who had saved
him and who had attempted to save his wife.   He entered
the farm where he had watched Anita die, and the neighbouring chapel where she now lay buried.   Surely the

* The ancient Rubicon was either the Uso or the Fiumicino ; in either
case it was really some fifteen miles north of Cattolica, the border town
which actually divided the Marches from the Romagna. See Map V.

time had come to avenge that day worthily by carrying the flag of freedom into the heart of the Papal provinces. The Romagnuols and the volunteers gathering round him from all parts of Italy called on him to lead them across the border. Mazzini, who had come to Florence in disguise, sent friends to urge him forward, and collected English money to buy arms for the impending invasion. The great conspirator was prepared to keep himself in the background, and even forego the proclamation of the Republic, if only Garibaldi would advance and make Italy.

At first Farini* and General Fanti lent themselves to the forward policy. On October 19 Fanti sent written instructions to Garibaldi that in case any province or city of the Papal dominions rose and asked for help, he was to cross the border at once. But Ricasoli from Florence, and Cavour's successor Rattazzi from Turin, represented that an attack on the Papal territory at this moment would mean war with France, or Austria, or both, and the ruin of Italy. Farini and Fanti withdrew their support from the forward policy, and urged the same prudent course on Garibaldi. The struggle in his mind was terrible, and with the weakness which he usually showed before coming to one of his iron resolutions, he changed his mind from hour to hour under the influence of those who had been with him last. On the night of November 12, Farini and Fanti, in earnest conclave, extracted from him a promise not to invade. A few hours later they received a telegram from him, ' The revolution has broken out in the Marches ; I must go to help it.' He was actually on the march, though the news of the ' revolution ' was an unverified, and in fact a false, report. Farini and Fanti, with a fine promptitude, successfully countermanded the invasion.

Victor Emmanuel, indispensable on these occasions, sent for Garibaldi, and persuaded him of the necessity for

---

* Farini this autumn became Governor of Parma, Modena, and the Romagna, united under the title of Emilia, because the Via Æmilia ran through all three.

patience.   He laid down his command and retired to Genoa,
issuing a manifesto in praise of the king as ' the soldier of
national independence,' and in dispraise of the ' vulpine
policy ' of his ministers.   Medici, Bixio, and about a thousand
volunteers retired with their chief, but his strenuous appeal
prevented a general disbandment.   The king, at their
parting, offered him his shot-gun and a generalship in the
Piedmontese army.   Garibaldi gladly accepted the symbol
of the hunter-king's friendship, but he refused the generalship, though it would have relieved the poverty of his life
as the gardener and shepherd of Caprera.   By refusing any
longer to wear the king's uniform, he left himself free for
the great enterprise of his life in the following year, which
could not have been undertaken by a royal officer.

' The man,' wrote Mazzini when he heard the news of
his surrender, ' is weak beyond expression ; and by sub-
scribing himself " your friend " or patting his shoulder, the
king will do anything with him.'   It was fortunate that it
was so.   If Garibaldi was as weak in the presence of Victor
Emmanuel as Chatham in the presence of George III., there
was this happy difference, that Victor was generally right
while George was generally wrong.   Italy had narrowly
escaped disaster.   It was impossible to attack the South
before Tuscany and the Romagna had been annexed with
the acquiescence of France.   With the French armies not yet
withdrawn from Lombardy, it was madness to defy their
master and the Austrians at the same moment.   But since
Piedmont was not in a position to support an invasion of the
Marches, her statesmen obviously should not have allowed
Garibaldi to take command of a revolutionary force on the
banks of the ' Rubicon,' a river which he could seldom
resist the temptation to cross.   The error of sending him
there can be compared to the error of choosing Gordon to
effect the evacuation of the Soudan.   The English and the
Italian hero, as one who knew them both once said to the
writer, closely resembled each other in many of those
characteristics which set them apart from common men.

Inextricably mixed with those high qualities was a tendency to obey the call of the spirit rather than the cautious orders of any mundane authority. Such men should be sent. to the front only when the orders are to advance, and when those orders are not going to be recalled.*

Indeed, it appears that at one moment Victor Emmanuel himself had contemplated permitting the guerilla to invade the Marches on his own responsibility. Although, on second thoughts, this plan was judged too dangerous, it may perhaps account for the original mission of Garibaldi to the Romagna. No doubt, too, his exemplary conduct during the last ten years had given the Piedmontese government a false sense of security in their dealings with him, for ever since the autumn of 1849 he had been so uniformly wise, moderate and obedient, that they had forgotten his earlier history. But Villafranca had destroyed his confidence in statesmen, and he now believed that he himself must sometimes take the initiative. From the moment of this quarrel in the autumn of 1859, the long honeymoon of Garibaldi and the cabinet of Turin was at an end. There reappeared the more dangerous and intractable Garibaldi, whom only Cavour had the ability at once to use and to control.

But it must not be supposed that the policy common to Mazzini and Garibaldi of pushing the revolution southwards was mere folly. It is true that the year for liberating the Marches, Umbria, and Naples by force of arms proved to be 1860, and not 1859, and that the best starting-place was Sicily, not the 'Rubicon.' But Mazzini had reason on his side when he wrote from Florence in August—' the revolution that stops in one place is lost.' He and Garibaldi were right in saying that Naples and the Papal territory should be attacked before the revolutionary ardour now raging throughout the Peninsula had been allowed to cool down. Garibaldi's great name held together a number of

* Anyone knowing the history and character of Garibaldi, and his relation to the Italian people and Government respectively, who reads chapter xxii. of Lord Cromer's *Modern Egypt* will be struck by the parallel.

different parties, classes, and persons all bent on this forward policy, and without that policy and the union of men vowed to accomplish it, Italy would never have been made by the diplomacy of the Turin cabinet alone.　No one was more convinced of this than Cavour.　Already in August he had said to his friend De La Rive, ' I shall be accused of being a revolutionary, but before all else we must go forward, and we will go forward.'

CHAPTER VII

NAPLES, 1859–MARCH 1860

'It appears that in the Kingdom of the Two Sicilies the authority of the law is entirely set aside, and nothing prevails but that vague and uncertain arbitrary power which is justly said to be the sign of a miserable servitude.'—LORD JOHN RUSSELL to the British Minister at Naples, November 28, 1859.

'Que voulez-vous faire avec un Gouvernement comme celui de Naples, qui s'obstine à ne pas écouter aucun conseil?'—NAPOLEON III., May 1860.

ALTHOUGH the slight wound inflicted on Ferdinand II. of Naples by the fanatic Milano in December 1856 did not, as has been sometimes alleged, cause the painful disease of which he died, yet the shock to his nerves and mind aggravated during the last two years of his reign the morbid fancies of fear and superstition. He appeared less than ever in public, the police system became more and more repressive, and he showered on the Church privileges which aroused resentment among even the most loyal of his lay subjects.

Meanwhile he steadily refused to alleviate the lot of the political prisoners at the request of the English Conservative ministry, who desired, if only he would meet them half-way, to compose Lord Palmerston's quarrel with him and resume diplomatic relations. At length, in the winter of 1858–59, the rumour of the coming Franco-Austrian war in Lombardy frightened him into a grudging concession. A chosen batch of sixty-six Neapolitan prisoners, including Poerio, Settembrini, Spaventa, and Castromediano, were put on board an old sailing vessel to be taken across to America and there set free as exiles for life. The chances were not great that they would all finish that long journey alive, in a craft no less ruinous and unsavoury than their old dungeon at

5

Montefusco. Fortunately Settembrini's son, Raffaele, came on board in disguise as scullion to the negro cook, raised a mutiny, and turned the vessel's head to the British Islands, where the whole party landed early in March 1859. The reception of the men whose names Mr. Gladstone's letters had made household words amazed and melted them after ten years of brutal usage. In the shouting crowd that thronged them in the streets of Bristol a poor girl thrust her last shilling into the hand of a very old man whose grey hairs had moved her pity ; it was the Baron Vito Porcaro, and he forced back upon her his own last piece of gold. Their arrival in London occurring just before the outbreak of the war, when British feeling wavered between fear of Napoleon's success and hopes for Italy's freedom, was of real weight in the balance. ' *Make the most of it*,' was the expressive English phrase used by Cavour in his letter to the Piedmontese minister in London. That spring the Italian cause became fashionable in society. Ladies of high position learnt the language and studied the history and literature of Italy, while their husbands from Westminster met the exiles at the great Whig houses, and found them to be as fine fellows as Mr. Gladstone had painted them. The most important of the many links which the Neapolitans formed during their brief residence in England was the close friendship that grew up between Poerio and Braico on the one hand and Lord and Lady John Russell on the other—a friendship destined to have its influence on the crisis of the following year, when the fate of Naples was decided in large measure by Lord John.

King Ferdinand's policy had been more purely Neapolitan and less subservient to Vienna than that of his predecessors, but he knew the value of the friendship of Austria, and was especially anxious to bequeath it as a support to his foolish and feeble successor, his eldest son, Francis. He therefore determined to marry him to the Emperor's sister-in-law, Maria Sophia, daughter of Duke Max of

Bavaria. It was her sister, Elizabeth, the most beautiful of a beautiful family, who had by her recent marriage become Empress of Austria.

And so Maria Sophia of Bavaria and Francis, Duke of Calabria, heir to the throne of Naples, were married at Munich on January 8, 1859, the bridegroom being represented by proxy. The bride was wisely prevented from seeing her husband, her new home, or her new relations, until it was too late to repent, for the two were as ill-assorted a couple as reasons of State ever brought together in matrimony. She had been bred with her four sisters in a simple, free and happy home life, partly in the Bavarian Alps, where they rode and climbed the hills, and partly in Munich, where it was their custom to walk unattended on their own errands. A girl so brought up might have been happy in England, but never in Naples. A dashing horse-woman, gallant and free in all her ways and speech, of heroic temper in war, as she was soon to prove before admiring Europe, she was no mate for the half idiotic youth whom Garibaldi was to dethrone, whom twenty-three years of hot-house education by Neapolitan priests and a jealous stepmother had deprived of any rudiments of sense and manliness that he may have inherited from his Savoyard mother. Judged even by his father's standard of strenuous tyranny, Francis was but a foolish Ishbosheth.

The young wife was brought down the Adriatic in the Neapolitan war-vessel *Fulminante* from Trieste to Bari in Apulia, where she was to see her husband and father-in-law for the first time. They, meanwhile, journeyed from Naples to Bari to do her honour, crossing the mountains in mid-winter, over the bad roads covered by unusually deep snow, with the result that the king fell dangerously ill. It was a sorry welcome for the gay Bavarian bride to land on that shore of a dead civilisation, amid the fawning, suspicious crowd of priests and doctors, courtiers and police, whispering round the royal sick-bed their base conjectures of poison, and their sycophantic hopes and fears of coming change. The dying king sought and won the affection of his new daughter, but she had little satisfaction from a husband whose chief outward characteristic was ' the peculiar expression of lifelessness that made him rather give the idea of an image than of a man. It was a wooden, not a marble statue, that his features called to mind.' He could hardly utter a word to her, still less make any lover's advances, and seemed tied to the apron-strings of his step-mother, Maria Theresa. That formidable dame was not long in conceiving an aversion for Maria Sophia, with her freedom and her laughter. She ordered the girl to observe etiquette more strictly, to attend the religious services more often, and forbade her ever again to ride a horse—an accomplishment of which her husband was innocent. In growing misery they waited some weeks at Bari, till it was decided to return by sea to the neighbourhood of the capital, where the king could more easily be cured or more conveniently die.

It was a tragic shipload that sailed on board the *Fulminante*. The unrepentant tyrant, dying in the agonies of a loathsome internal disease, lay in a cabin heaped with relics, images, and superstitious quackery of all kinds, gathered at his earnest desire from all over his kingdom, in the belief that they might help him where nature and the doctors had failed. Above on deck, in the air and the sunlight, the lovely girl of seventeen sat all day long on a gun-carriage, paying little heed to the feeble attentions of her husband, but gazing at the sea, at Etna and Aspromonte and all the passing pageant of the coast, steeling her heart to the knowledge that she was caught and caged for life.

At length these unhappy people reached their royal palace at Caserta, fifteen miles north of Naples, and there, on May 22, 1859, Ferdinand II. was gathered to his fathers. His last instructions to his son, which had an undue influence on that conscientious and dependent nature, were to enter into no belligerent alliance either with Austria or Piedmont in the war then beginning in North Italy, to continue the existing policy of repression at home, and if a time of desperate crisis should arise to trust to General Filangieri, the conqueror of Sicily, as the ablest man in the kingdom.

On the occasion when the new king received the homage of the grandees, a significant incident occurred.

' As the lieges passed before him they kissed his hand, which he did not take the trouble to raise, allowing it, when they had kissed it, to fall back by his side as if it had been the hand of a doll. . . . One very infirm old man caught his foot in the carpet and fell flat on his face to the feet of the king, who neither stirred to help him nor allowed a muscle of his face to move while the poor old fellow, awkwardly and with difficulty, scrambled up and passed him without a word from the king of condolence for his mishap or inquiry if he was hurt.'

The scene left a painful impression on the Neapolitan loyalists in the room, and the British Minister, Henry Elliot, turned and said to his neighbour, ' That young man will finish badly.'

On the death of *Bomba*, England and France at once resumed diplomatic relations with Naples, and their representatives, Elliot and Brenier, vied with each other for the ear of the new monarch. Mutually suspicious and hostile as were the two diplomats, they at least combined to urge amnesty and reform as the only means of saving the Bourbon throne. Piedmont also was at hand with a proposal which —were it possible to imagine it loyally accepted—might have led to a free Italy of two States instead of one. On May 27, 1859, five days after Ferdinand had breathed his last, Cavour dispatched Count Salmour to the court of Naples, with written instructions to negotiate an offensive alliance against Austria for the purposes of the war then raging in Lombardy. He was to point out that this adoption of the national cause in foreign policy would imply a change of system at home, an amnesty, and adherence to the constitution of 1848, which had been long ignored but never repealed. Cavour recommended that the internal changes should not go too fast, and that only men devoted to the dynasty should be employed.

The news of the battle of Magenta on June 4 soon followed, to lend weight to these diplomatic offers. The hopes aroused in the South by the victories in Lombardy took shape in demonstrations to which the streets of Naples and Palermo had long been unaccustomed. The time of crisis had already come, and Francis II., mindful of his father's dying words, at once sent for Filangieri and made him President of the Council and Minister for War. But unfortunately the views of the new Prime Minister were entirely inconsistent with the other parts of the late king's ' political testament,' for he recommended the introduction of a Liberal constitution which would enable the dynasty to lean on France instead of on Austria. The young monarch, thus called on to decide for himself which part of his father's self-contradictory advice he should prefer, stood in helpless distraction, pulled this way and that by his various advisers, male and female, while the system of government in the two Sicilies remained as he had found it, and forces both within and without the frontiers gathered head for the final explosion.

The chief personalities whose opposing efforts kept Francis for so long in this fatal state of equilibrium were Filangieri, Brenier, and Elliot * on the side of reform and the alliance of Naples with the Western Powers, while on the side of Austria and reaction were the Queen Dowager, Maria Theresa (herself an Austrian by birth), and the whole court camarilla headed by Troja. That party were encouraged by a visit of Count Buol, the late Austrian Minister for Foreign Affairs. Buol told Elliot that he found the people perfectly contented, that there were no grievances, and that he had been delighted to find that, after all, the miracle of the blood of St. Januarius was genuine. The

---

* Elliot had originally been sent out by the Conservative government, in May 1859, to prevent Francis from allying himself with Piedmont, but next month the advent of Russell to the Foreign Office reversed our policy on this matter.

credulity of this man, supposed to be one of the most experienced diplomats in Europe, is a testimony to the school that bred him. But the English diplomatists, as the dispatches of men like Elliot and Hudson show, were of a very different type, and were not accustomed to believe what they were told by foreign governments until they had tested it for themselves by some knowledge of classes and parties outside the walls of the palace. These admirable public servants poured into Downing Street from all the courts of Italy a constant stream of valuable information and just comment.

The young queen, Maria Sophia, was a Liberal influence, and urged her husband to grant a constitution. But she was not a politician, and on coming to the throne was glad chiefly because she could now ride as much as she liked, laugh when she was amused at public ceremonies, and defy Maria Theresa's stepmotherly advice. With better treatment and greater freedom she was able to feel some dawn of affection for her husband.

In political affairs the Queen Dowager retained over her stepson a great part of her old influence, although she had been strongly suspected of an intrigue to place one of her own sons on the throne in his stead. Her sinister figure presides over the ruin of the dynasty and of the ancient kingdom ; Maria Theresa finished what Mary Caroline and Lady Hamilton had begun. With the help of Austria and the court camarilla she persuaded Francis to refuse both the constitution and the alliance with Piedmont.

Like other weak rulers, Francis still hoped to please both parties. He still clung to Filangieri's person, while rejecting his policy. General Filangieri, Prince of Satriano, was by far the greatest subject in the kingdom. He had fought with honour in Napoleon I.'s great campaigns, he had served Murat well, and the restored Bourbons no less faithfully. He had reconquered Sicily ten years before, and had subsequently, as Governor of the island, attempted to introduce a milder *régime*, until the late king had quashed the attempt. The dynasty could still have been saved, and Filangieri was the man who could have saved it. But the new king refused to adopt his programme of reform. He thereupon offered to resign, first in July, and again in September 1859, but as Francis would not accept his resignation, he had the weakness not to press it. He actually retained office without performing even its ordinary administrative functions, which were deputed to others, while he shut himself up in his villa near Sorrento and refused to be seen. Only in March 1860 did he at length receive his formal demission.

During this long ministerial interregnum of the autumn and winter of 1859–60, while the man who was nominally chief minister had retired from public life, and the king was in his usual state of helpless distraction between opposing counsellors, the police governed the country on the established lines. The remonstrances of Brenier and Elliot against the continued misrule availed nothing, but the stories which they sent home incensed Napoleon and Lord John Russell respectively against King Francis, and thus prepared the diplomatic pathway for Garibaldi's invasion.

A royal decree for the relief of the tens of thousands of *attendibili* under police supervision was promulgated on June 16, 1859, but Elliot discovered that it had been followed a few days later by a secret letter to the prefects which made it practically inoperative. The police terrorism had never been worse than at the end of 1859 and the opening of the new year which was to see the downfall of the system. Members of respectable families unconnected with politics disappeared mysteriously—having been snatched away to secret prisons merely in order to create abject fear. And indeed no one dared to complain. ' In the centre of the typhoon of terror ' there was a ' dead silence.'

It might be thought that a government so unscrupulous in its use of arbitrary power would at least deal effectively with real crime. But the *camorra* was no less feared than the police, who themselves cringed before the dreadful society.

'If a petition,' wrote Elliot, 'was to be presented to the Sovereign or to a Minister, it had to be paid for ; at every gate of the town *Camorristi* were stationed to exact a toll on each cart or donkey-load brought to market by the peasants ; and, on getting into a hackney carrosel in the street, I have seen one of the band run up and get his fee from the driver. No one thought of refusing to pay, for the consequences of a refusal were too well known, anyone rash enough to demur being apt to be found soon after mysteriously stabbed by some unknown individual, whom the police were careful never to discover.'

The Neapolitans crouched before their two masters, the *camorra* and the police, who, as yet, acted in harmony. The distant Calabrian and Sicilian provinces, where alone the spirit of rebellion was serious, were controlled by the army, now fully large enough to secure the Bourbons against the impotent hatred of their subjects.

It will be well here briefly to describe the composition and character of the Neapolitan army, since the tale of its destruction is to play so large a part in these volumes. In 1848 it had numbered 40,000 in reality, and 60,000 in name. But in the early spring of 1860, some 90,000 men were under arms, and the total force, if the reserves were called out, would reach 130,000. This increase was due to the policy of Ferdinand II., who had found in the creation of a large army a safeguard against his subjects, and an occupation for his leisure hours. Although the chances of battle and the hardships of war had no charms for him, as he showed at Velletri, the pomp and circumstance of the parade ground continued to delight *Bomba* from the cradle to the grave. As a boy he had been found one day by his grandfather, Ferdinand I., studying a new uniform for the troops : 'Dress them how you like,' said the cheerful old man, 'they will run away all the same.'

This kingly utterance may stand as a criticism of the younger Ferdinand's lifelong efforts at military organisa-

tion. His troops made a creditable appearance at reviews.
The uniforms were good, the horses fine, the weapons
excellent. In the army that obeyed his son in the spring
of 1860, rifles vastly superior to the Garibaldian musket
were the ordinary weapon of the infantry. The cavalry were
not only well mounted, but well rehearsed in the art of
galloping up within forty yards of the enemy and wheeling
smartly round again.

Indeed, the only part of military discipline really enforced
was the drill. But a form of discipline not usual in camps
held good in this establishment—the discipline of confes-
sion and of religious practice. *Bomba* was as careful of his
men's souls as Cromwell, with this difference among others,
that as morality was not a necessity to salvation in the
Neapolitan scheme of things, the soldiers were too often
accomplished rascals as well as hypocrites. Although the
military floggings were of an unusually cruel and humiliating
character, the men were kept little within the bounds of
discipline in time of peace, and in civil war they were
encouraged to fight by the promise of free looting. In
Sicily it was not an unknown thing for a soldier to take
advantage of his excellent rifle to hold up a quiet English
tourist and relieve him of his money. The inhabitants
could not, like the Englishman, get redress for such outrages.
But, when all is said, the Neapolitan rank-and-file were not
without natural courage, and on occasions when they were
led with any spirit, as by Filangieri and Bosco, they showed
themselves worthy of those Neapolitan troops whom Napoleon the Great had praised for their valour in the battle of
Lutzen.

But spirited leadership was rare. It was commonly
said that the inefficiency of the Bourbon army was greater
in each rank than in the one below, till it culminated in
the total incompetence of the generals. Non-commissioned officers were found with great difficulty, owing to
political conditions and to the system of enlistment. The
conscription for a term of four years with the colours and

four more in reserve was so unpopular that it was not enforced at all in Sicily, and even on the mainland the middle as well as the upper classes were allowed to buy themselves out. The peasantry who were unable to escape service were among the most grossly ignorant in Europe, and it was difficult to select from them sergeants who could read and write. The non-commissioned officers, therefore, either were very ignorant, or else came of the middle class, and were liable, as such, to Liberal sympathies. It was observed in June, 1860, that 'three-fourths at least' of those who came over to Garibaldi after the taking of Palermo were 'corporals and sergeants.'

The same difficulty was experienced in obtaining commissioned officers. The nobility was partly too effeminate and lazy, partly too Liberal, to take pleasure in military service like the nobles of Piedmont. The better men could feel no pride in belonging to such an army. It was not a national but a dynastic force. Its object was less to protect the country against foreigners than to police it against rebels. So complete a breach had been made with the fine military traditions of the Napoleonic period, that the men and the families who represented them were now almost all outside the service and frowned upon as malcontents. The spirit cultivated by *Bomba* in the army which he brought up with his own hand, was that of monks and police spies, not of soldiers. In other services besides that of Naples professional efficiency has not always been the road to promotion, but scarcely anywhere else has the commonly accepted standard of military honour and spirit been positively discouraged. In 1848 a young officer who wished to go to the front a second time was introduced to the king : 'You have been to Sicily and come back with a whole skin, and now,' said his Majesty with undisguised astonishment, 'you want to go and risk it again ! Madonna help you !' The difficulty of obtaining enough good officers under such conditions was insuperable, and the difficulty of obtaining enough officers of any kind was great. Consequently many

had to be raised from the ranks, and they were not selected
on any wise principle.   There were officers who could not
read and write, and some who had been common thieves.
The average age of the service was far too high.   A captain not grey-headed was quite an exception.   The generals,
if we exclude Nunziante, Pianell, and a few more, were in
their dotage, and seemed to have been selected on account
of their notorious incompetence.

In this force, conscious of its unpopularity with the
inhabitants of the land, there was not even that internal
harmony and sense of comradeship often bred by such
isolation.   Court favouritism and personal intrigue, carried
on in the Neapolitan fashion, destroyed mutual confidence.   While merit and zeal were neglected, ' the greater
or less favour of superiors or of the sovereign ' was all in
all.   ' Egoism, envy, jealousy, intrigue,' writes Cava, a
faithful adherent of the Bourbons who saw it all from
inside the general staff, ' bore rule instead of the spirit of
mutual support.   Criticism degenerated into backbiting,
and thence into calumny.'   And not only were there division
and mistrust between man and man, but in a marked degree
between the various ranks and branches of the service.
Jealousy and ignorance kept apart artillery, cavalry,
infantry, engineers, and staff in mutually exclusive worlds.
Privates, sergeants, and officers were ' three castes, separate
and inharmonious.'   Besides the divisions of army rank,
there were the divisions of social status.   The middle
class, which might have held the whole together, was
insufficiently represented.   The nobles wrapped themselves in aristocratic pride, and yet the peasants had—
naturally enough under the circumstances—none of the
British soldier's contentment at being led by ' gentlemen.'
Against such an army a thousand picked men, moving with
a common impulse under a chief for whom each would gladly
die, might achieve astonishing results.

In the year that intervened between the death of the

old king, in May 1859, and Garibaldi's expedition, the Neapolitan army was brought up to its full complement by fresh levies, but on the other hand it was weakened in two important respects. In the first place contempt for the new king encouraged the revolutionaries to push their propaganda in the army, so that at the beginning of 1860 lists of officers supposed to be well inclined to Italy were circulated among the patriotic committees : the artillery and engineers were the most disaffected branches of the service. Secondly, the Swiss regiments, the best in the army, were disbanded.

These foreign troops were an integral part of the Neapolitan as of the Papal system of government. Monarchs who could trust few of their own subjects thought they could depend both on the loyalty and on the courage of Catholic herdsmen and mountaineers of the same breed as those immortal mercenaries commemorated by the Lion of Lucerne. The Swiss had, in 1848, taken a leading part in the successful operations in the streets of Naples and Messina. They were treated as a separate force with special privileges, and their pay exceeded by two-thirds that of the native soldier. Three of their regiments kept guard over the capital, while a fourth held Palermo in awe. But at the time of the accession of Francis the Swiss Federal Government, grown ashamed of the connexion between their free State and the worst tyrannies in Europe, requested that the cantonal crests should be taken off the banners of Swiss troops in foreign employ. When this unwelcome change was announced to the Swiss in Naples a thousand of them, more proud of their native land than of their paymaster's service, and fearful of the abrogation of their other privileges, rose in mutiny on the night of July 7-8, 1859. They were quelled with promptitude by General Nunziante, with a loss of nearly a hundred killed and wounded. All four regiments were thereon broken up, and their actual departure from Naples and Palermo in August raised the hopes of the revolutionists both in Sicily and on the mainland.

The Swiss had been disbanded at Filangieri's advice, but during the autumn and winter, when he had ceased to attend to affairs, the court devised a means of replacing them which he would heartily have disapproved. A conspiracy was formed by Naples, the Pope, Austria, and the expelled rulers of Modena and Parma, to attack and destroy Piedmont and the League of Central Italian States. The Government of Vienna ordered the Tyrolese authorities to give every assistance to the work of recruiting in their valleys for the Neapolitan army; and Austrian soldiers who had served out their time, were sent by sea from Trieste to Ancona and the Neapolitan ports, and drafted into the armies of Pio Nono and Francis II. They were not, in Naples, accorded the old privileges of the Swiss, but became part of the regular army. They were known as the ' Bavarian ' regiments, a diplomatic euphemism for ' Austrian,' which would have been the more correct description of a large number of the men.

This combination against the newly-won freedom of Upper Italy made it the urgent duty of the rulers of Piedmont, in self-defence if for no other reason, to destroy the Papal and Neapolitan kingdoms now leagued with Austria for their destruction. Neither party, given its principles, can be blamed for being the first to provoke a conflict now truly inevitable. Italy could not remain cleft in two by the Rubicon, 'half slave and half free.' It was the same problem of ' a house divided against itself ' then becoming visible in the United States of America, where Abraham Lincoln had recently prophesied that one or other of two irreconcilable systems must extinguish its rival. ' The revolution that stops in one place is lost,' wrote Mazzini, and the advisers of Pio Nono and Francis II. applied the same rule to reaction.

While the influence of Filangieri diminished daily, and the Neapolitan government drifted ever further into violent measures at home and abroad, the statesmen of Piedmont were closely on the watch. Their agents kept them well

informed as to the real possibilities and difficulties of the
situation in the South. On August 29, 1859, the Piedmontese Minister at Naples wrote home at great length,
exposing the decadence of the Bourbon government since
Ferdinand's death, and the relative ease with which it could
now be overthrown by an attack from without. But he
denied the probability of an unaided revolution from
within. The people, he wrote again on November 26,
were ' cowed and disunited,' though hostile to the government ; the recall of Garibaldi from the ' Rubicon ' had
delighted the court, ' but not the country, which puts
its hopes in him, lacking confidence in its own power to
revolt.'

In January 1860, the Rattazzi ministry, seeing that
Naples was becoming the storm centre of Italian politics,
sent thither one of the ablest of Piedmontese statesmen,
the Marquis Villamarina. The instructions which he took
with him were to draw King Francis into a nationalist
alliance with Piedmont against Austria, on a basis of moderate Liberal reforms at home. It was the same offer
which Count Salmour had made at Cavour's bidding seven
months before, and it was equally unsuccessful. The
Bourbons refused to repent while there was still grace. The
time was fast approaching when they should sue to Piedmont for this same alliance, and sue in vain.

The mission of Villamarina was one of the last acts of
Rattazzi's ministry. In January 1860, Cavour returned
to power, to the intense joy of Italy, of England, and of
Liberal Europe. The hour had come and the man. The
curtain was rising on the second act. All was now ripe for
the forward policy which would have been madness a few
months before. Cavour, in his retirement, had watched
the ripening of events—the passive resistance of Italy
to Villafranca, so impressively and patiently prolonged, the
help rendered by England, and the alienation of Napoleon
from the Pope. The *non possumus* attitude of Pio Nono
towards revolted Romagna, and his ostentatious alliance

with the most rabid Legitimists in Europe, and particularly with those of France, were rash acts of hostility to the French protector of Rome, who was primarily a usurper and a child of the revolution, even if he required the Clerical vote to consolidate his power. At Christmas 1859, Napoleon punished the Pope and the Clerical party by the publication of the 'inspired' pamphlet, *Le Pape et le Congrès*, which proposed in veiled terms to confine the Papal territory to Rome and the surrounding province known as the Patrimony of St. Peter.

And so Cavour, even before his return to office, had often exclaimed, ' Blessed be the peace of Villafranca,' for he saw rising the hope of an Italy larger and more independent than that which the Emperor had promised him at Plombières.

At the beginning of 1860 Napoleon had moved so far as to be ready to sell his consent to the annexation of Tuscany and Emilia (Parma, Modena, and the Romagna). The price would be Savoy, and perhaps also Nice, the territory of which the cession to France was to have purchased Venice according to the unfulfilled terms of Plombières. Cavour was, therefore, fully determined that the first great step of his new ministry should be to annex Tuscany and Emilia at once, at the price of Savoy. In relation to Naples, his policy was less definite. He would wait on opportunity. But unless Francis accepted Villamarina's offer of alliance, he would certainly have no scruple in overthrowing the Bourbon dynasty if he could find the means. In a few weeks it appeared that Villamarina's offer was refused, and Cavour also became aware that Naples was forming an offensive alliance with the Pope and Austria. At the same time he secured the long delayed annexation of Tuscany and Emilia, confirmed by a plebiscite of their inhabitants, and he thereafter felt free, as he had never while that matter was still unsettled, to hope for adventures farther south. And so in March 1860, the attitude of Piedmont towards the Bourbons underwent a final change

for the worse, clearly revealed to posterity in Cavour's
secret correspondence with Villamarina.

On March 30 he writes to Villamarina at Naples :

' Evidently events of great importance are preparing in the
south of Italy. . . . You know that I do not desire to push the
Neapolitan question to a premature crisis.   On the contrary,
I think it would be to our interest if the present state of things
continued for some years longer.   But . . . I believe that we
shall soon be forced to form a plan which I would like to have
had more time to mature.'

He therefore asks a number of questions as to the relative
strength of parties in the Bourbon kingdom.   The just an-
alysis of the situation in Villamarina's reply of April 14,
1860, contains the significant words, ' The king has the army
on his side.   I have written to you and I repeat, the government is strong, very strong for the purpose of keeping down
the people.'

Such was indeed the case.   Force from outside was
needed to defeat the Neapolitan army.   But since the
Powers of Europe, particularly France and Austria, would
prevent Cavour from sending the Piedmontese regulars,
the external force to be applied must be that of revolutionary bands, and there was only one man in Italy who
could with any prospect of success lead a revolutionary
raid against 90,000 regulars armed with good rifles and cannon.   Fortunately that man, unlike some of the advanced
Democrats who followed him, was stubbornly faithful to
the programme of union under the Monarchy of Victor
Emmanuel, and while the fame of his romantic deeds and
character would serve to disarm much European indignation against acts of international piracy, the unbounded
enthusiasm which he aroused in England would ensure the
benevolent neutrality of the Power who could open or close
at her will the pathway of the Sicilian waters.

CHAPTER VIII

THE REVOLT OF APRIL 4, 1860—ROSOLINO PILO AND THE HOPE OF GARIBALDI'S COMING·

' Fratelli miei, la causa propugnata da me e dai miei compagni d'armi, non è quella di un campanile, ma quella dell' Italia nostra, da Trapani all Isonzo, dal Taranto a Nizza. Dunque la redenzione della Sicilia è la nostra, e noi pugneremo per essa con lo stesso ardore, con cui pugnammo sui campi Lombardi !

' My brothers, the cause fought for by me and my comrades in arms is not the cause of a parish, but the cause of our Italy, from Trapani to the Isonzo, from Taranto to Nice. Therefore the work of the redemption of Sicily is the work of our own redemption, and we will fight for it with the same zeal with which we fought on the Lombard battlefields.'

GARIBALDI's letter to the Sicilians, September 29, 1859.

THE island destined at this supreme crisis to be the starting-point for the making of united Italy, has a racial and social character of its own. Besides the early ' Sicani and Siculi,' of whose origin little is certain, the elements that compose the Sicilian people have come in historical times from the opposite extremities of Europe, from Africa, and from Asia. The inhabitants of the eastern end of the island are in part descended from the ancient Greek colonists, whose pastoral lives and loves inspired the muse of Theocritus. The western end—especially the district between Palermo, Trapani, and Marsala, the scene of the exploits of Garibaldi and the Thousand—has been largely peopled from North Africa and from Oriental lands. For that north-western angle of Sicily, where Phœnician colonists were settled at the dawn of Mediterranean history, remained as the last stronghold of Carthage in its struggle for the island against the Greeks and Romans. Possibly the Phœnicians left little behind them. But the Arab occupation of the Dark Ages, which succeeded to the rule of the decadent Byzantines, has left in that district its lasting impress not only on architecture and irrigation, but on the music, the customs, the faces, and the character of the common people.

In the ninth century Sicily was divided between the Mohammedan and the Byzantine-Greek religions. But as a result of the Norman conquest which took place not many years after the similar event in our own island, the Roman Catholic Church gradually won ground. In modern times Sicily has remained ardently Roman Catholic, and if the revolution of 1860 had come thither with the anti-clerical programme which it avowed in North Italy, it would have received but little support. The movement against the Bourbons was shared by many of the monks, priests, and bishops, for it was the rebellion of one of the most insular of peoples against the foreign domination of the Neapolitans.

The origin of this feeling against foreign mastery of the island goes back far into history, to the days of the Sicilian Vespers, that fierce event of which the memory was invoked with pride in the commonplaces of patriotic oratory. Brought up to believe that they had in all ages been wrongfully subjected to strangers—Byzantine, Saracen, Norman, Angevin, Spanish, Neapolitan—the Sicilians had something of the Irishman's inherited quarrel with fate and government. They were *frondeurs* born and bred. The aptitude of the leaders for weaving nets of close and subtle conspiracy, and the secret understanding of the whole population for the purpose of baffling the authorities, were even more marked than in the Italian States of the mainland. At times of crisis, as in 1820, 1848, and 1860, they took to the more open methods of street fighting in the cities of the coast, and prolonged guerilla war on the hills of the interior. But they had a hatred for regular military service in barracks or in the field, whether under the flag of the oppressor or of the liberator. ' Better a pig than a soldier,' was a Sicilian

proverb of the time. The Neapolitan kings dared not en-
force the conscription on their island subjects, so that in
1860 hardly more than a tenth of their army was composed
of Sicilians. Consequently the garrison in the island was
Neapolitan, hated as a foreign force in much the same way
as the white-coats in Lombardy.

This universal hatred of the alien government prevented
social discord among the natives themselves. Though
feudalism had been nominally abolished in 1812,* a system
of *latifundia*, with all the disadvantages and none of the
advantages of the similar system in England, kept the
peasants in abject misery. But many of the great proprietors joined with their tenants in the national movement, and were highly respected when they led against a
common foe the popular feeling which has in later times
been largely directed against themselves. Until after 1860
there were no purely agrarian troubles, and the social question was scarcely posed. For although the poverty of the
island was noticed then as now by every traveller, it was
regarded by the inhabitants either as inevitable and natural,
or else as the result of Neapolitan rule.

The revolutionary programme in 1848 had, in spite of
some Mazzinian influence, been essentially insular. The
expulsion of the Neapolitan troops after the street fighting
in Palermo in January of that year had been followed by
a declaration of the independent sovereigny of Sicily,
and the empty throne had been offered to a younger son
of Charles Albert of Piedmont. His refusal, necessitated
by the Austrian reconquest of Lombardy, left the Sicilian
patriots to carry on a provisional government as best they
might, amid increasing difficulties, such as the rooted antip-
athy of the population to military service, the cry of ' the
Church in danger,' the unsuppressed crime and disorder
throughout the island, and the administrative inability of
the high-minded men at the head of affairs. When at

---

* Large farms in Sicily are often called *ex-feudi*. Before 1812 they
were *feudi*.

length Filangieri entered Palermo at the head of his victorious Neapolitan troops on May 15, 1849, though he was hated by all as a foreign conqueror, he was accepted by many as a restorer of social tranquillity.

That able soldier and statesman, the surest prop of the Bourbon dynasty, if it had only been content to lean on him, was made governor of the island which he had subdued, and he might, if left with a free hand, have done something to reconcile the Sicilians to their fate. But he was subjected to the control of the Minister for Sicilian Affairs at Naples, because the House of Bourbon, ever since 1816, pursued the fatuous policy of treating as a subject province the island kingdom which had been so loyal to their shrunken fortunes during the Napoleonic period. Filangieri found himself thwarted at every turn. He meditated a scheme for giving to Sicily—not railways indeed—but roads. There were, in 1852, just 750 miles of carriage-road in the whole island. Even the two chief cities, Palermo and Messina, were not linked by any continuous highway, for the middle part of the connexion was a mule track 42 miles long. Travellers, therefore, went from the east to the west of the island by sea, except a few of the richer and more adventurous English tourists, who rode over the rough tracks, taking their own tents and provisions, for the food and lodging that could be obtained from the natives appear to have been more intolerable than they are to-day. Filangieri wished to amend this state of things, but his intentions were frustrated from Naples, and road-making was postponed till the Piedmontese era.

At length, in 1854, completely undermined by Court intrigues, he threw up his governorship and retired in disgust.

But he had temporarily succeeded in one part of his policy of conciliation. Although his troops had shown great barbarity during the war, particularly at Messina, no unnecessary reign of terror accompanied the restoration of absolute rule. Mr. Gladstone could not, in 1851, have

written of the Sicilian trials and prisoners as he did of the
Neapolitan, for the principal leaders of '48 in Sicily escaped
with the lighter penalty of exile. These men, worthy
as a whole of the high moral and intellectual standard
set by Amari and Ruggero Settimo, had been too simple
and inexperienced to govern with success, but they had
scorned to enrich themselves when at the head of affairs,
and now endured the miseries of banishment in London,
Paris, Turin, and Malta with an unselfish fortitude and
faith that won the respect of all who knew them.

With Filangieri's departure went the last hope of recon-
ciliation. His successor in the governorship was Castelcicala, a man without a policy. From 1854, till the crash,
the authorities gave no thought to anything except the
routine of repression, and the real ruler of the island was
Maniscalco, Director of Police. This public-spirited officer,
whose ability Filangieri had discovered and rewarded with
promotion, made himself the terror of the Liberals and of
the criminal population, who were too often associated in
the unquiet mountain districts of the interior, owing to their
common persecution by government. Maniscalco formed a
useful force of Sicilian mounted police, mostly ex-brigands,
known as the *Compagni d'armi*, better fitted to catch their
old friends than were the Neapolitan regulars.

The country was effectively gagged. No newspaper
was allowed to circulate except the official *Giornale di
Sicilia*. The real news had to be obtained by borrowing
the foreign papers from the Consuls of other countries, who
alone could receive them,* or by assembling cautiously in
parties of two or three at the chemist's, the usual meeting
place of the Liberals. The scorn of even the Austrian
authorities was aroused against the Southern police, who
hindered or prohibited journeys of Italians in Sicily, who
shaved off men's beards and seized their black Lombardy

---

* Colonel Tedaldi tells me that his father had him taught English
in order that he should be able to read the *Morning Post* of the British
Consul.

hats as seditious, and interfered with music parties of five or six persons. Of the upper class, some were passively on the side of Government, but another and more active section put themselves at the head of the artisan and peasant classes, who were universally hostile to the Neapolitan rule. There was no reactionary party among the peasants as there was on the mainland. ' When shall we be rid of this infamous yoke ? ' was constantly ejacu· lated.

It may seem strange that the Unitarian party among the Sicilians should have been able to use the outraged insular pride of their fellow-countrymen as the means of creating popular enthusiasm for absorption in the larger Italy and annexation to the crown of Victor Emmanuel. But the experience of 1848 had taught the Sicilians that, since they would not themselves become soldiers, they could not hope to effect their own permanent emancipation from Naples. They therefore began to look to Garibaldi to deliver them, and to the Piedmontese armaments to protect them from reconquest. Neither were men like Amari, La Farina, Crispi, and the educated classes in general, exclusively insular in their ideas. They held that annexation to the new Italy would satisfy their desire to participate in the wider Italian culture, which was after all the most valuable element in modern Sicilian civilisation, and the real influence that had since the Middle Ages fused into one the different races inhabiting the island. They rightly supposed that union with Italy would give that culture room to expand when freedom of press and person had once been established ; that it would yield them, at least in some degree, the sense of being masters in their own island ; that it would bring roads and railways, attract capital and commerce, and put them in touch with the outside world shut off from them by the Bourbon police system. And not a few wrongly supposed that these benefits would be obtained without higher taxation and military burdens, and would at once relieve the moral and economic poverty of the land. But the desire to be united to Italy did not become general until 1859.

From 1850 to 1858 the threads of conspiracy throughout the island were in the hands of the partisans of Mazzini. In proportion as his influence was superseded in Northern Italy, he directed the efforts of his remaining friends to the Sicilian field, neglected by other parties. His Unitarian and Republican ideas inspired Bentivegna, who gladly gave away his life in the winter of 1856 by raising a hopeless rebellion near Cefalù. Mazzini's principal agents for the affairs of the South were the Sicilian exiles, Crispi and Pilo, and the noble-minded Modenese, Niccola Fabrizi. Ever since 1837 Fabrizi had made Malta his headquarters, and there devoted his life to guiding the movement against the Bourbons in the direction of Italian unity. Early in the fifties he laid in a secret store of ammunition and hundreds of bad, old muskets—some saved from the wreck of the late revolution in Sicily, others purchased for £500 by Mazzini in England. Though such an armoury was illegal in Malta, the British authorities, benevolently neutral to *Bomba's* enemies, made no effort to find it. The rumour of its existence gave Fabrizi importance among all Sicilian parties. The government at Palermo kept spies round him, who periodically reported his doings. There was a constant passage of conspirators from Sicily, Genoa, and England centering at Malta, and thence threatening the Bourbon rule.

Owing to this ceaseless activity of the Mazzinians during the years when other parties were content to wait for better times, the idea of United Italy came to be closely associated in the Sicilian mind with the idea of revolt against Naples. When, towards the close of the fifties, the islanders began to hear tell of Cavour's policy, supported by the National Society under its secretary, La Farina—himself a Sicilian exile—their minds were already prepared by Mazzini for the idea of amalgamation with Italy. Nor can it be said that either Mazzini or his agents actively opposed the abandonment by their Sicilian friends of the Republican part of the old programme. Fabrizi himself, following Garibaldi, gave in his adhesion to the main principle of the National Society, union under Victor Emmanuel's crown.

At length, in the summer of 1859, the news of the victories over Austria in the Lombard plain brought about a united movement of all classes and parties in Sicily. The aristocracy of Palermo had not, as a whole, taken part in Mazzinian agitation and conspiracy, but Magenta and Solferino kindled their patriotic enthusiasm. On the night of June 26, 1859, a few young men improvised an illumination in the 'Nobles' Club,' opposite the fine statue of Charles V. in the Piazza Bologni. At first the lights in the windows puzzled the ignorant populace, who, on being told that the nobles were celebrating 'Solferino,' stood whispering ' *Chi è stu sufrareddu?* '—'What is this Solferino?' The Neapolitan sentry at the foot of the statue looked at the bright lights and laughed gaily, not knowing, poor fellow, that they were the beginning of many sorrows for him and his comrades. But the authorities soon explained matters. Maniscalco himself, hot with passion, stalked into the Club at the head of his police, put out the lights, shut up the house, and in the next few days arrested a number of young men of the first families in Palermo. These undignified and violent proceedings aroused against him the whole aristocracy of the capital, and drew together all classes from highest to lowest, in a tacit conspiracy against the government, which never abated during the momentous year that followed. The enthusiasm was infectious : young men of family, who had hitherto had no idea of using life except to partake of its less active pleasures, were ready to do anything in order to be marched off to the great Vicaria prison, which was 'considered the place where one received the baptism of patriotic regeneration.'

The movement at once turned men's thoughts to Garibaldi. The conspirators invited him to come to Sicily and

lead the revolution, and on September 29, 1859, he replied
from Bologna with great good sense :

' Unite yourselves to our programme—*Italy and Victor
Emmanuel*—indissolubly ! If you can do it with any chance
of success, then rise. But if not, work at uniting and strengthening yourselves. As to my coming to Sicily, I will come
with pleasure, with joy. But ere that we require a more
intimate communication between you and me ; we need
stronger connections and we must find means for this and make
them effective, because nowadays we must not risk what is
secure.'

His correspondents replied, again asking him to come over
and lead them, or if he could not come himself, to send a man
enjoying his confidence, because all parties and classes in the
island, however much they quarrelled among themselves,
would rally round the name of Garibaldi. There the matter
was left, but Garibaldi's advice and his conditional promise
to come had done much to unite and encourage the Sicilians.

Meanwhile, in August, a gentleman in spectacles, going
by the name of *Manuel Pareda*, from the Argentine, was
travelling through the island as a tourist. He duly climbed
Etna and looked down the crater in company with some
English officers, who found the American singularly well-
informed about Sicily. *Pareda* was in reality the disguised
Sicilian, Francesco Crispi, afterwards the celebrated Prime
Minister of Italy. At this time he was forty years of age,
and already appeared to some who knew him in London to
surpass his fellow-exiles both in ability and in the spirit of
personal ambition. But he had sacrificed to the Mazzinian
cause all ordinary prospects in life, had been expelled even
from Malta and from Piedmont, and now ventured this
dangerous journey in disguise through his native island
in order to bring the conspirators of Messina and Palermo,
always suspicious of each other, into communication for
a projected rising. The departure of the Swiss regiment
from Palermo served as an encouragement, and it was

agreed that the revolt should begin at the capital on October 4, 1859. But when, after a return to England, Crispi came back to the island in a fresh disguise on October 11, he found the plan had missed fire. Mazzini and his friends believed that Piedmont had sent counter orders through La Farina to prevent a rising in Sicily before the Central Provinces had been safely annexed. But more certainly the Sicilians were themselves afraid to strike, because the police had got wind of the plot, and arrested several of the leaders. A local rising at Bagheria, ten miles outside the capital, led by the impetuous patriot Campo, was easily put down. The whole conspiracy had failed.

On November 27, Maniscalco was stabbed at the door of the Cathedral of Palermo, whither he had gone with his wife and child to hear Mass. The disguised assassin escaped, and it is not known whether he had accomplices. The Director of Police soon recovered, but the revolutionists were encouraged by the temporary disablement of the man whom they most feared.

During February of the year 1860, a Piedmontese visitor, named Benza, was the observed of all observers in the best society of Palermo. He bore secret messages from La Farina, the representative of Cavour, to the effect that the Sicilians should rise if they were sure of success, that owing to the attitude of Europe, Piedmont could give no help until after the revolution was accomplished, but that she would protect against reconquest a Sicily already set free.

Mazzini gave the same advice. On March 2, 1860, he wrote his famous letter to the Sicilians :

' Brothers, I confess I no longer recognise in the Sicilians of to-day the men who flung down the challenge in '48. . . . First of all I repeat to you our declaration of two years ago : *It is no longer a question of Republic or Monarchy ; it is a question of National Unity, of existence or non-existence.* . . . If Italy wishes to be a monarchy under the House of Savoy, let it be so. If, at the end, they choose to hail the King and Cavour as liberators or what not, let it be so. What we all require is that Italy should be made. . . . Wait ? For what ? Do you

really think Napoleon or Cavour is coming to set you free?
. . . Dare, and you will be followed.   But dare in the name of
National Unity ;   it is the condition *sine quâ non*. . . . Garibaldi is bound to come to your help.   I believe I can say that
your initiative would be followed by the advance of the forces
of Central Italy.'

This letter, read in conclave by the revolutionary
Committee of Palermo, made no small impression on men
already ashamed of their own inactivity.

Urged thus by Cavourians and Mazzinians alike to act
first for themselves and then look for support to Piedmont,
the Sicilians at length began their revolt.   But it is doubtful
whether they would have screwed their courage to the
sticking place but for one man, Francesco Riso, a master
plumber and mason.   To Riso, in spite of his faults, Italy
owes a great debt, for, at the cost of his life, he set on foot
the local rebellion which drew Garibaldi into the field, and
so led in eight months to the liberation of Sicily and Naples,
Umbria and the Marches, and the creation of the Italian
kingdom.

The conspirators had only a few hundred firearms in the
whole of Palermo with which to attack a garrison of nearly
20,000 men.   Under such conditions it is easier to meditate
than to begin revolt.   Baron Riso * gave ' constant balls ' to
the aristocracy of Palermo ' on the first floor of his beautiful
palace in the Toledo,' where ' dancing served as a cloak to
meetings of patriots on the floor above, men in evening dress
slipping upstairs between a gay valse or contredanse ' to
help in the making of cartridges and bombs for the coming
revolution.   In another house seditious fly-leaves were struck
off on a small printing-press made to pack into a metal box
that fitted into a flower pot, and was covered with earth between whiles.   The gentlemen who laboured at the press and
manufactured the bombs were acting with courage, but a
more reckless daring was needed to go out into the street
and be shot down by the soldiers, and this was found only

* Not to be confused with Riso, the plumber.

in Riso the plumber and the few score workmen whom he inspired.

In March the two sections of conspirators, plumber Riso and the workmen, and Baron Riso and the aristocrats, drew together. Baron Riso and his committee supplied the workmen with the bombs and with means to acquire some firearms. The plumber brought into the town a little wooden cannon and a meagre store of blunderbusses and muskets, hidden under cartloads of material for his own trade, and stored them in the Terrasanta, a building annexed to the old Gancia convent. He had hired the Terrasanta for his purposes, under cover of repairing his own house, which stood opposite the Gancia. That fine building, and the network of old, narrow and romantic streets surrounding it, remain to-day, like so much else in Palermo, exactly as they were when the Italian Revolution of 1860 began in their midst.

Under strong pressure from Riso, who was fiercely determined on action, the Committee consented to April 4 as the day for the rising. On April 2, Riso told his friends of the Campo family that he did not expect that the nobles would actually join in the fighting or that the capital would rise, that he expected to perish, but that if he survived he would take a bloody vengeance on the Moderates and the aristocracy for having failed him at the crisis.

On the eve of the appointed day this desperate man and seventeen followers sat up all night over their pile of arms in the Terrasanta waiting for dawn. As the morning of the 4th of April grew grey upon the windows they heard the trampling of patrols in the street, which told them that their plot was discovered. They had not been betrayed by anyone, least of all by any monk of the Gancia convent, though both patriotic and Bourbon legend has often said so. The plot, known to large numbers of people, was almost common talk in Palermo, and came to the ears of some persons of governmental sympathies, who were justified in telling Maniscalco. 'We have gone too far now,' said

Riso when he heard the patrols, ' we have no choice but to face the enemy with courage.'   At five o'clock they issued from the Terrasanta, arms in hand, crying *Viva l'Italia*, *Viva Vittorio Emanuele*, and exchanged shots with the *compagni d'armi* and soldiers in the alley between the Convent and Riso's house.   Men fell on both sides.   Riso's party, joined by a few other rebels from a neighbouring centre of the conspiracy, retreated into the Gancia itself, where the soldiers besieged them.   In vain they rang the tocsin in the bell-tower to call the frightened town to rise ; in vain they hurled the bombs, which failed to explode. The Neapolitan troops blew open the doors with cannon and rushed into the Convent, killing some and seizing the rest as prisoners, including Riso himself, who had fallen mortally wounded near the door.   Wrongly supposing that the monks, who were known to have popular sympathies, had participated in the revolt hatched in the *annexe* of the monastery, the soldiers bound them in couples, and gutted and sacked their church.

It had been part of the plot that two other parties of rebels—fifty-two and thirteen men strong—should start from two neighbouring arsenals of the revolt, and find their way through the streets to join Riso, but they had been intercepted by the troops and very few had reached the Gancia.   The authorities, forewarned, were in such complete military occupation of all points of the town, that, as Riso had prophesied, neither the populace nor the aristocracy took part in the fight, although Baron Riso and other nobles went about the streets urging people to rise, and promising the aid of an armament from Piedmont. By eight o'clock all was over.

In the suburbs shots were fired at intervals until nightfall, and the Neapolitan troops seized the excuse to burn and pillage wherever they chose, and to murder unoffending women and children.   The *squadre* (as the bands of rebel peasantry from the mountains of the interior were called) had failed to carry out the difficult part assigned them by the committee of the conspirators, namely, to force their way into the heart of the town and join Riso. But some of them came down armed into the Conca d'oro, the marvellous plain wherein Palermo lies, and fought there in the streets of the suburbs, and in the surrounding groves of lemon and orange. From April 4 until the entry of Garibaldi, parties, varying from two or three up to a dozen vagabonds, hiding by day in the immense fruit forest, prowled about every night and let off their guns around the sleeping city.

But the real strength of the *squadre* lay, not in the seaward plain, but on and behind the steep wall of beautifully shaped mountains which holds the Conca d'oro in its arms. Behind that barrier stretches southwards a high undulating plateau of open cornland, broken here and there by precipitous hills and rock-ridges, on the summits and beneath the shadows of which nestle the upland towns— Corleone, Calatafimi, and others of less note. In such colossal villages of 5000 to 20,000 inhabitants the Sicilian peasants have from time immemorial congregated for safety at night, walking and riding out by day to distant labours in the vast open cornfield that once fed Imperial Rome. This strange country, the heart of Sicily, little known to foreigners then or now, had never been occupied in an effective manner by the Neapolitans or by the Spaniards before them. The Arabs of old had built castles in the interior, but the races who succeeded them in the possession of the island kept no garrisons except in the coast towns. Under the Bourbons, while Palermo and Messina, Trapani and Girgenti, were always full of troops, and were constantly being searched for arms, the population dwelling inland had seldom seen a brigade of soldiers even in the largest towns, and still possessed their sporting guns and blunderbusses.[*] So now, at the signal of the Gancia revolt, the more ad-

---

[*] See Maps III., IV., and VI., below. I think that the only Neapolitan garrison up country in 1860 was that of Caltanisetta. Certainly there were no troops permanently stationed in Piana dei Greci, Alcamo, Calatafimi, or Corleone.

venturous or patriotic—and in some cases the more criminal
—of the young peasants in the north-west of the island
followed their landlords into the field, inspired by a last
after-glow of the old feudal attachment.   Until the coming
of Garibaldi these bands, wandering about in the mountains, sometimes coming into the villages to sleep, skirmished
with the flying columns sent out after them from Palermo.

During the fortnight following April 4 continual en-
counters with *squadre* of a few hundred men each took
place on the mountains overlooking Palermo, at Monreale,
Gibilrossa, and elsewhere.   The royal troops were usually
victorious, and the result of the final conflict at Carini on
April 18 bade fair to disperse the last of the bands

Piana dei Greci, an Alpine village in a small fertile
plain enclosed by a circle of magnificent mountains, was the
hearth of freedom in Western Sicily.   Though only ten miles
from Palermo as the crow flies, the intervening mountain
barriers rendered it remote and relatively free from interference.   It had been peopled at the end of the fifteenth
century by Greek-Albanians flying from trouble in their
own country, many of whose descendants preserved in this
fastness of the hills not only their Greek religion but the
sturdy and independent character acquired by their ancestors
in Balkan warfare.   Hither, on April 19, the Albanian leader
Piediscalzi returned with a small and dispirited remnant
from the Carini fight, intending to disband his followers
and to emigrate.   This would have meant the end of the
revolt, for when the Albanians laid down their arms no
other community was likely to continue the struggle for
long.   But on the evening of the next day hope suddenly
revived.   Rosolino Pilo, a Sicilian of noble family, who
had taken a leading part in 1848, and had since been one
of Mazzini's closest friends in his English exile, unexpectedly
appeared in Piana dei Greci, and announced himself as the
herald of the coming of Garibaldi.

Pilo and his companion Corrao had left Genoa in a small

sailing boat on March 25, and after many dangers and delays landed near Messina on April 10. Hearing that the insurrection was in progress at the other end of the island, they travelled its whole length to Piana dei Greci, rousing the villages through which they passed to demonstrations of patriotic enthusiasm, and everywhere promising the speedy advent of Garibaldi. Towards the close of their romantic journey, in the wild and solitary oak-forest of Ficuzza, they had fallen in with the *compagni d'armi*, who gave chase and captured their guide.

The news of Garibaldi which they brought safe through so many perils to Piana dei Greci prevented the total extinction of the movement initiated on April 4. Pilo was playing a game of bluff : he had gone to Sicily to keep the insurrection alive in the hope that by doing so he would induce Garibaldi to follow and take over the lead, but he found that the only means of keeping it alive was to announce Garibaldi's coming as a thing already certain. The Albanians at once sent word round to the patriots of the Sicilian townships to take the field again, and, although their own village was speedily occupied by royal troops, they put themselves under Pilo's leadership and marched off once more to the other side of Monreale. There, establishing his rough camp on the Inserra mountains, Pilo, at the head of the partially revived insurrection, watched Palermo in the plain below until the actual coming of Garibaldi relieved him of a heavy responsibility.

Pilo's arrival as earnest of the approach of the *deus ex machinâ* entirely changed the political atmosphere. In spite of the failure of the revolt, it was the Sicilians who exulted, the soldiers who were gloomy and anxious. During the last fortnight of April and the first few days of May, the authorities at Naples and Palermo were perpetually alarmed by false reports sent them by the Cardinals in Rome and by their own agents in Genoa and Turin, to the effect that Garibaldi had already sailed.

The confidence of the Sicilians of all classes that he

would come and that he would conquer was irrational and unbounded ; 'this belief,' wrote the Governor Castelcicala, on May 3, 'is universal, and has spread to the remotest villages of the island.' In Palermo the secret press was often taken out of the flower-pot to print off little handbills, beginning *Fratelli vinceremo* ('Brothers, we shall conquer'), and signed *Il Comitato* ('The Committee'). The excitement had been tense ever since April 7, when Baron Riso and five other nobles of the first families in Sicily had been marched through the crowded streets to the Castellamare fortress, bound together as common felons. 'The Committee' organised impressive demonstrations of the unanimity of the capital and its obedience to orders. One day a vast crowd of many thousands appeared suddenly in the mile-long Toledo street which divides the town in half, and gave one universal shout of *Viva Vittorio Emanuele* before the astonished police knew what to do. Every day there were smaller demonstrations and numerous arrests. The shutters were often put up and commerce was at a standstill. The Vicaria gaol-fortress in the northern suburb was crowded by hundreds of political prisoners, who cast in the teeth of the gaolers that '*Piddu*' (Giuseppe Garibaldi) was coming.

Amid the gathering of these thunder-clouds, so soon to break over Palermo in the deluge of the final catastrophe, a strange melodrama was being enacted round the death-bed of Francesco Riso. On April 14, thirteen of the Gancia rebels had been executed on a piece of waste ground near the port, now known as the '*Piazza delle* 13 *vittime.*' Among these victims was Riso's aged father. A few days later Maniscalco came to the bedside of the son, who lay dying from the wound received at the Gancia, and offered to spare the life of his father if he would reveal his accomplices. Riso, full of pity for the old man, whom he thought to be still alive, and perhaps not unwilling to expose the nobles whom he held to have deserted him, made long statements on April 17 and 22, in which he named Baron Riso

and others who were already under arrest, and Mortillaro
and Pisani who were still at large. When it was too late
to repent of his weakness, he learned from the Chaplain of
the hospital that his father had been shot several days
before. He procured, by the help of the sympathetic
Chaplain and of a medical student in the hospital, a pistol
with which to avenge himself on Maniscalco, and hid it
under his bedclothes. But he was too weak to use it, and
on April 27 he died, in no Christian frame of mind.

None of the conspirators whom he had named came to
grief, but the revolt which he had set on foot continued and
spread until it became the Italian revolution. While he
was breathing his last, his countrymen whispered to each
other as they passed in the streets, ' He is coming ! '
' Garibaldi ? '   ' Garibaldi.'

CHAPTER IX

THE ORIGINS OF THE EXPEDITION—NICE OR SICILY ?

> ' Such ties are not
> For those who are call'd to the high destinies
> Which purify corrupted commonwealths ;
> We must forget all feelings save the *one*,
> We must resign all passions save our purpose,
> We must behold no object save our country,
> And only look on death as beautiful,
> So that the sacrifice ascend to heaven,
> And draw down freedom on her evermore.'
>
> BYRON. *Marino Faliero*, Act II., sc. 2.

THE expedition of Garibaldi, that led in six months to the liberation of the whole of Italy, except Venetia and the district round Rome, was not the work of one party, but of all the elements of Italian patriotism. Mazzini and his friends instigated the expedition ; Garibaldi and his followers accomplished it ; the King and Cavour allowed it to start, and when it had begun to succeed, gave it the support and the guidance without which it must inevitably have failed midway. It is true that the fiercer adherents of each party vilified their allies, denying to them their just share of credit. But these partisan and personal jealousies have at least helped forward the investigations of the historian, by inducing controversialists, like Bertani and La Farina, to give to the world documents that can be trusted better than the opinions of their editors, while moderate men like Sirtori, Medici, and Bixio, regretting these unseemly squabbles, have come forward with reliable statements of what they themselves saw and heard.* The whole truth is

* A good example of this will be found in the report of the important retrospective debate in the Chamber on June 19, 1863, in which Bertani, La Farina, Bixio, and Sirtori all took part.

not yet clear, especially as regards the motives that prompted Cavour's action up to the time of the sailing of the Thousand, but it is now possible to give a fairly accurate though not a complete narrative of the origins of the expedition, and of the preparations made for its armament and departure.

The idea that Garibaldi should go to liberate Sicily was as old as March 1854, when Mazzini had suggested it to him in London at the moment of his return from America on board his coal-ship. In September 1859, the Sicilians had themselves invited him. On both occasions he had replied that he would gladly go, but only if the Sicilians were already in open rebellion, to which he declined to incite them on his own responsibility. Since he always adhered strictly to this formula, it became the task of the Mazzinian party to stir up revolt in the island in order to hold him to the terms of his promise.

In December 1859, Mazzini's agent, Crispi, returning from his unsuccessful attempt to promote a rising in his native Sicily, repaired to Tuscany and Emilia, the newly-liberated States of Central Italy, which were not yet annexed to Piedmont, but still under the provisional government of the Dictators Ricasoli and Farini. Here he sought and found Fabrizi, revolutionary agent in Malta for the affairs of Sicily and Naples, then on a visit to his native Modena after an exile of some thirty years. The two friends agreed that since the invasion of the Papal States had been vetoed from Turin, the time had come for an attack on the Bourbon kingdom. Emilia and Tuscany were filled with Garibaldi's volunteers, unemployed and discontented since their chief had, a few weeks before, been recalled from the ' Rubicon.' Let these men, said Crispi, be drawn off from a district where they are only a source of embarrassment to the authorities, and let them sail under Garibaldi to the liberation of Sicily. Thence the revolution would spread to Naples and from Naples to the Papal States taken in the rear.

Crispi, introduced by Fabrizi, laid the plan before Farini, the Dictator of Emilia, who was residing in Modena. Farini entered eagerly into the plot, and sent Crispi on to Turin to obtain the consent of the Piedmontese Government.

Rattazzi was still Victor Emmanuel's Prime Minister, but was already tottering to his fall. Between December 15 and January 3 he had several interviews with Crispi, and listened with sympathy to his proposal. The project was also laid before the Sicilian La Farina, Secretary of the National Society and Cavour's confidant, whom Crispi found more disposed than the Prime Minister to raise objections. Early in the new year the Rattazzi government fell, and Cavour came back to power (January 20, 1860). One of his first acts was to drive Crispi out of Turin under the old order of expulsion still hanging over his head. Cavour as yet only knew of Crispi as one of Mazzini's most violent followers, and he was moreover determined to enter upon no adventures in the South until he had secured the actual annexation of Tuscany and Emilia by a bargain which he was now on the point of negotiating with Napoleon.

Meanwhile, during the last days of 1859, Garibaldi came to Turin, bent on obtaining some employment for himself and his volunteers. He was not yet thinking of Sicily, though Crispi and Rattazzi were at that moment discussing the possibility of sending him there. He asked for a free hand to organise the National Guard in Lombardy as a force under his own command. Through the influence, probably, of Cavour, this was refused, although the king as usual treated Garibaldi with the greatest kindness, and sent him away from the interview with unshaken confidence in the *Re galantuomo*. His anger was entirely directed against Cavour. While he was in Turin, the ministerial crisis came to a head, and the baser friends of the falling Rattazzi government tried to save the situation by using Garibaldi's name against their great rival. ' Our poor Garibaldi,' wrote his wise and faithful follower Medici, who had thrown up his own commission in order to be at his service,

> ' Our poor Garibaldi . . . allows himself to be persuaded by discredited men to go to Turin ; he comes with most noble intentions ; but Garibaldi in alliance with Brofferio cannot succeed . . . he ruins himself in times of inaction ; he talks too much, writes too much, and listens too much to those who know nothing.'

Under these malign influences he resigned, on December 29, the Presidency of the National Society,* which was closely associated with Cavour through its Secretary, La Farina. On December 31, he proceeded to form a rival society of a more advanced tendency, to be called the ' *Nazione Armata.*' But the project failed to enlist support and was dissolved in ridicule. On January 4, 1860, by a happier inspiration, he issued an appeal calling on the Italians to subscribe instead to his ' Million Rifles Fund ' for the purchase of arms. Although the name betokened the ideal rather than the achievement, the Fund was destined to be of great importance in the history of the Sicilian expedition. The government consented to allow the purchase of arms by the Directors on condition that it was kept informed of the whereabouts of the armouries. To this Garibaldi readily agreed.

Cavour, having fought his way back to office in spite of the intrigues of his enemies, felt no resentment against the simple man whom they had made their tool, no pang of jealousy against the rival of his popular fame, and none of that contempt which clever people of the second order so often feel towards men of great but not strictly intellectual powers. ' Although,' he wrote, on February 10, ' Garibaldi allowed himself to be drawn into union with my personal enemies, Brofferio and Co., I recognise in him none the less one of the greatest forces of which Italy can avail herself.'

Indeed the main problem for Italy in the coming year was to avoid the wrong and to find the right outlet for the

---

* In which post he had succeeded Pallavicino in the middle of October.

pent anger and energy of the Garibaldini, now growing so
dangerous at home. The suggestion that they should be
sent to liberate Sicily, made in December by Crispi and
Fabrizi, was in January taken up by Garibaldi's own friends,
Medici and Bertani, who on January 19 wrote to tell their
secret to the confidant of all Italian patriots who sat in the
British Museum Library. ' English policy,' so they wrote to
Panizzi, ' will gain by the scheme : Medici and I will set to
work to persuade Garibaldi.' Bertani, who later in the
year was extreme in opposition to Cavour, in January still
understood the realities of the situation, which he himself
was doing much to develop in the right direction.

> ' To bring together Cavour and Garibaldi,' so he wrote,
> ' is now a difficulty but still more a necessity for our cause.
> Garibaldi has in his hands the people of Italy and the King ;
> Cavour could supply the intelligence and the guidance that
> both require through dangerous paths. Cavour with the King
> and Garibaldi can emancipate himself in great part from sub-
> jection to Napoleon. . . . You do not know perhaps how
> much Napoleon may fear and ought to fear Garibaldi, the
> only man able to disarrange his plans and force his hands.'

The history of the year was to be a remarkable fulfilment
of all these words.

On January 24 Garibaldi replied as follows to Bertani's
petition that he should go to Sicily :—

> ' You can assure your friends of South Italy that I am
> always at their disposition when they are willing really to act,'

and indicated that the weapons now being purchased by
his Million Rifles Fund might serve him to arm an expedition
against the Bourbons.

On the very day when he wrote this letter, which we may
regard as his first contribution to the correspondence of the
Sicilian expedition, he committed the most foolish act of
his private life in marrying the daughter of Count Raimondi.
At a critical moment in the Alpine campaign of the previous
summer, news of the Austrians had been brought to him

across the mountains by a young lady, whose handsome presence and daring deed appealed to his facile sense of the romantic. In the middle of December he became her father's guest at Fino, near Como, and after his political visit to Turin he returned there again in the middle of January 1860. That first month of his great year brought him little credit either in public or private affairs. Forgetting his fifty-two winters and her youth, and much else that it behoved him to remember, he proposed marriage and was accepted by her and her family. On January 24, 1860, the ceremony took place at Fino, but before nightfall a letter was put into his hand which proved that she was in the habit of favouring a younger man. Full of ' bad thoughts,' but ' terribly cool as to his demeanour,' he sought the house through till he came to his wife's room, and asked her if she had written the letter. She confessed it. ' Then see,' he said, ' that you do not bear my name ; I leave you for ever.'

In February he returned to dig at Caprera, bitterly mortified, and, as we may guess, craving to find oblivion of the present in deeds and adventures more worthy of things long past. As he moodily broke the soil in the cold February days he revolved letters and messages that came to the island, all urging him to go and liberate the South. Mazzini had written more than once calling on him to aid a simultaneous attack on Sicily and the Papal States, but apparently without obtaining an answer. In the middle of February Bertani sent to Caprera a certain Mignona, a Neapolitan exile of Mazzinian opinions, to arrange for an attack on the Bourbon power. Garibaldi agreed to help, on the condition that the movement was strictly monarchical, and wrote on February 20 to the effect that the money and arms collected by the Million Rifles Fund should be applied to this purpose.

It was in fact almost superfluous for Mazzini on February 19 and 28 to write from London beseeching Bertani, Medici, and Bixio to stir up Garibaldi. They had been

successfully at work upon him ever since January. But at
the end of February their efforts were seconded by the
arrival from London of Mazzini's Sicilian friend, Rosolino
Pilo, a still unreconciled Republican. On February 24
Pilo wrote to Garibaldi from Genoa, offering himself to go
to the South and raise a rebellion, provided that Garibaldi
would promise to come out then and take over the command. On March 15 Garibaldi wrote from Caprera in reply :

> ' Arrange with Bertani and the Directors of the Million
> Rifles Fund at Milan to obtain the arms and requirements.
> In case of action remember that the programme is *Italy and
> Victor Emmanuel.*
> ' I will not flinch from any undertaking, however dangerous
> it may be, where it is a question of fighting the enemies of our
> country. But at the present time I do not think a revolu-
> tionary movement opportune in any part of Italy, unless it
> has great probability of success.'

This famous letter is no more than a repetition of the conditional promise which he had made to Bertani, first on
January 24 and again in February at the time of Mignona's
visit. But his letter of March 15 was addressed to a man
who took him at his word and started off then and there for
Sicily to create the revolt for which he stipulated as the
preliminary to his own action. On March 25 Pilo, with
his companion Corrao, set sail in a fishing-boat from
Genoa.

But before their little storm-tossed bark could land the
two travellers on the Sicilian shore, the revolt which they
intended to stir up had broken out at Palermo on April 4
under the leadership of Riso the plumber. By the end of
the first week of April the news that the Sicilians had risen
reached Turin, at the moment when the representatives of
free Italy, from the ' Rubicon ' to the Alps, were gathering
there to watch the unequal Parliamentary duel between
Garibaldi and Cavour on the question of Savoy and Nice.

For now, after a year of waiting, Tuscany and Emilia
had been safely annexed, and the price of Napoleon's con-

sent to the annexation had been agreed to by treaty. On
March 24 Cavour signed away the provinces of Savoy and
Nice in the presence of the French Plenipotentiary. ' Now,'
he said, rubbing his hands together in a way that he had
when pleased, ' now we are accomplices.' Of two accomplices, one is certain to get the better of the other, and
Cavour rubbed his hands because he felt sure to get by the
bargain more than Napoleon intended to give. He had no
thought of being contented with the Central Provinces
alone. On March 30, six days after he had signed the treaty,
we find him writing to sound Villamarina at Naples as to
the practicability of a Neapolitan revolution. He would,
he wrote, have wished to postpone the attack on the South,
but that events were driving him forward. And indeed
the offensive alliance just formed by the King of Naples
with the Pope and Austria made it more dangerous for him
to sit still than to advance.

When, therefore, in the first week of April he knew that
the Sicilians were in revolt, his first thought was to send
them aid. He could hardly at that moment send them
Garibaldi, who had just arrived in Turin for the purpose of
denouncing him as the traitor who sold Nice. But on
April 6 the War Minister, General Fanti, wrote in Cavour's
name to General Ribotti, then in command of the royal
troops at Rimini, to ask ' whether if the revolution breaks
out in Sicily you would go there, first resigning your commission in the Army.' Ribotti, who had in 1848 commanded a brigade of Sicilian revolutionists, was a suitable
person to lead the insurgents, but, as we can now see, no
leader of irregular troops except Garibaldi would in fact
have had the least chance of success under the actual conditions in Sicily. Indeed, when Ribotti arrived at Turin,
eager to be sent on the expedition, he found Cavour and
Fanti already hanging back ; they expressed to him their
doubts as to the seriousness of the rising in the island, and
by that time, it must also be remembered, they knew for
certain that Garibaldi was preparing to go. Ribotti,

disgusted by the fickleness of statesmen, returned to his command at Rimini.

Garibaldi meanwhile, leaving Caprera on April 1 and visiting Nice on the way, arrived at Turin as one of the duly elected representatives of his native city to protest against the proposal to hand it over to France. In the blackness of his anger against the man who had 'made him a foreigner,' the great Nizzard might have carried his protest dangerously far, had not the news of the Sicilian rising on April 4 reached him in happy time, and thenceforth employed more than half his thoughts and energies. On April 7 Crispi and Bixio, who received the news at Genoa by a wire from Fabrizi at Malta, started for Turin to inform Garibaldi that Sicily was in arms. An hour before midnight they found him, and claimed that since the conditions of his often repeated promise were now fulfilled, he was bound to go to the help of the islanders. He consented at once, provided that his friend Hudson, the British Minister at Turin, would confirm the news. Next day (April 8), having, probably, been satisfied by Hudson, he wrote to the Directors of the Million Rifles Fund at Milan to send the arms and money to Genoa, where the expedition was to be organised. On the 9th he applied to his friend Fauché, the paid agent of the Rubattino Steamship Company at Genoa, to procure one of the Company's steamers—'either the *Piemonte* or the *San Giorgio*,' so he writes—' to take me to Sicily with some companions.'

These 'companions' were to be chosen principally from the volunteers of 1859. Many of them, including Medici and Bixio, had retired into civil life with their chief after his recall from the 'Rubicon' in November, and were therefore in a position to obey his summons at a moment's notice. But others were now in the royal forces, being chiefly congregated in the 46th regiment of the line under Colonel Gaetano Sacchi, a veteran who had followed Garibaldi in every campaign since 1842. Garibaldi's first idea when he heard the news of the Sicilian rising was to obtain leave to take with him Sacchi's regiment, and possibly the 45th as well. He saw Victor Emmanuel, who was sympathetic, but would say neither 'yes' nor 'no,' probably because he had not yet asked Cavour. Garibaldi thereupon called Sacchi to Turin, divulged the plan to him, and sent him off to sound the old Garibaldini among the officers of the 46th, who went nearly mad with joy at such a prospect. But a few days later the King, having consulted Cavour, not only refused to sanction this particular plan, but told Garibaldi that he must use every effort to preserve the discipline of the Army, and must not carry off either its regiments or its individual members, lest while he was conquering Sicily the country should be left defenceless to the attack of Austria, or to the now scarcely less dreaded protection of France. Garibaldi sent again to fetch Sacchi to Turin, and in the presence of Trecchi, the King's confidential aide-de-camp, told him the hard decision.

In this vital matter Garibaldi loyally obeyed the general spirit of the King's orders, in spite of great temptation to wink at desertions. Out of the Thousand who first sailed for Sicily, only five were royal officers ; but of these at least one, Bandi, was deliberately taken by Garibaldi because he required his technical experience on the staff, and he was not wrong in supposing that the King actually wished him to go. But great numbers of privates and officers were refused at every stage of the expedition, both by Garibaldi himself and by Bertani and the agents whom he left behind him to organise the reinforcements. In spite of the ardent desire prevalent in all ranks of the service to go to Sicily at every personal sacrifice of promotion or career, the combined efforts of the authorities and of Garibaldi's friends preserved very tolerable discipline in the Army, and so saved the country from disaster.

During the last five days of his residence in the capital (April 8–12), Garibaldi was torn between his duty to Sicily and his duty, as he conceived it, to Nice. A committee of

his fellow-townsmen had come to Turin and were urging him
to save them from France, while Crispi and Bertani worked
hard on the other side, telling him ' he ought now to think
of nothing but Sicily.'   The powerful advice of Sir James
Hudson was thrown into the Sicilian scale.   The British
Minister at Turin understood that Savoy and Nice were the
necessary price of Italian unity, and he made it his business
to prevent Lord John Russell and Garibaldi from ruining
Italy by useless resistance to Napoleon.   In England, then
nervous of every increase of French power, the feeling
against the cession of Nice and Savoy was very strong, and
Palmerston talked of war with France.   Lord John, as
Foreign Minister, loudly voiced the feeling of the country.
But Hudson, who saw in England's attitude a danger to
Italy, wrote, on April 6, to his friend Lady Russell a letter
which was certainly intended to be seen by her husband,
and is more artfully calculated to convince Lord John than
anything which its author could well have put into the
diplomatic language of a dispatch.   The abuse of Napoleon
III. may, in part, be set down to the desire of the writer to
win the confidence of his readers, and the rest of the letter
may still be read as one of the best statements of the
difficult case of Nice and Savoy.

'TURIN, 6 *April*, 1860

' MY DEAR LADY JOHN,
    . . . You mention in your letter the name of that scandal
to royalty—Louis Napoleon.   What can I say of him ?   Hypo-
crite and footpad combined.   He came to carry out an " Idea,"
and he prigs the silver spoons.   " Take care of your pockets "
ought to be the cry whenever he appears, either personally or
by deputy.
    ' But do not I beg of you consider and confound either the
King of Sardinia [Piedmont] or Cavour as his accomplice.   Think
for a moment on the condition of Sardinia, who represents the
nascent hope of Italy—think of the evil that man [Napoleon]
meant, how he tried to trip up the heels of Tuscany—establish
a precarious Vicarial existence for the Romagna, and plots
now at Naples ;   not to have surrendered when he cried " stand
and deliver," would have been to have risked all that was
gained—would have given breathing time to Rome—reinforced
and comforted Rome's partisans in the Romagna—have in-

duced doubt, fear, and disunion throughout Italy. Judging
by the experience of the last eight years I must say I saw no
means of avoiding the Rocks ahead save by a sop to Cerberus.

'But do not lose confidence in the National party. Cavour
or no Cavour, Victor Emmanuel or another, that party is
determined to give Italy an Italian representation. I regret
that the Nizzards (who have a keen eye to the value of Building Lots) are wrenched from us by a French filou—but I cannot
forget that the Savoyards have constantly upheld the Pope,
and have been firm and consistent in their detestation of Liberal
Government in Sardinia. I am not speaking of the neutral
parts, please remember.

Your most devoted servant,
'JAMES HUDSON.'

The writer of this letter was equally energetic in his
efforts to divert Garibaldi from Nice. We know from Crispi's
diary that Garibaldi consulted the British Minister in these
critical days at Turin, and Hudson himself used in after
years to describe how he had urged his friend to leave the
inevitable alone and to go where he was really wanted;
hoping to arouse his patriotic emulation, Hudson told him
that another expedition to help the Sicilians was being fitted
out by an Englishman.*

Whether this adventurous Briton was a reality or a bright
creation of diplomatic fancy, there was an Englishman of
flesh and blood at this time in the Piedmontese capital
deeply involved in another conspiracy. Laurence Oliphant,
the charming, witty and eccentric author of 'Piccadilly,'
who, when he was not shining in London society, was
seeking adventures wherever they were to be found, from
Nicaragua to Poland and Japan, managed on this occasion
to get into touch with the Nizzard Committee at Turin.
He helped them to persuade Garibaldi, who attended their
secret meetings, to make an interpellation in the Chamber;
but if that failed (as Garibaldi was angrily sure that it would
fail, having no faith in Parliamentary proceedings in times
of crisis), it was agreed that he should go to Nice and make
there some demonstration of a more practical kind. On

---

* I had this from Sir Cecil Spring Rice, who had it from Hudson's
own lips.

April 12 the famous interpellation took place before a large and excited audience. It was Garibaldi's first appearance in Parliament. He spoke calmly, repeating the constitutional arguments with which others had supplied him, but his best point was a well-founded complaint of pressure then being exercised by government on the people of Nice to induce them to vote in their *plébiscite* for annexation to France. He asked that the polling day at Nice should at least be postponed from April 15 till April 22, which was the date fixed for the vote in Savoy. Cavour answered courteously and effectively, assuring the House that to have refused to sign the Treaty of March 24 would have endangered the State newly formed by the annexation of the Centre, and would absolutely have destroyed all hope of further advance. ' Turn your eyes,' he said, ' beyond the Mincio and beyond the confines of Tuscany.' This somewhat broad hint was well understood, and the Chamber escaped from the subject by voting a non-committal ' order of the day.'

Garibaldi left the Chamber in a rage. ' I told you so,' he said to Oliphant : ' that is what your fine interpellations and Parliamentary methods always come to.' That night the Nizzard Committee met once more and, as Oliphant, who was there present, reports, a plan was decided on more suited to Garibaldi's taste. All knew that the *plébiscite,* manipulated by Government, would go heavily for annexation if taken on April 15. It was therefore decided that Garibaldi should ' leave Genoa in a steamer to be chartered for the purpose, with two hundred men,' and, sailing to Nice, should enter the town just after the vote had been taken, smash the ballot-boxes, and scatter the papers, so rendering a new ballot necessary. It was believed that this demonstration by Garibaldi, followed by an active canvass by the Nizzard Committee, would so change public opinion that when the new *plébiscite* was taken, the result might go against the wishes of the government. Garibaldi, for his part, having smashed the ballot-boxes, would sail for Sicily

—but with very little chance, after such an exploit, of support by Cavour or of toleration by Napoleon.

On the same evening (April 12), Garibaldi held another meeting in his own lodgings in the Via S. Teresa, with the Sicilian Committee, who strongly opposed the mad Nizzard project. There were present Bertani (who had come from Genoa on purpose), Medici, Bixio, and Finzi, one of the Directors of the Million Rifles Fund. It was agreed that Garibaldi should go to Sicily with 200 men armed with Enfield rifles, which Finzi undertook to supply from the armoury of the Fund at Milan.

Next morning (April 13), Garibaldi started for Genoa, with the Sicilian and Nizzard plans both in his head. Oliphant, who had no share in the secrets of the Sicilian scheme, travelled with him in a reserved railway carriage. They held scarcely any conversation on the way, because Garibaldi was engaged in reading an immense budget of letters received that morning. The Englishman observed him tearing each of them into little bits, until the floor of the carriage looked like ' a gigantic waste-paper basket.' Oliphant wondered at the time what all these letters could be, but afterwards learnt that they were answers to the call for volunteers for Sicily.

Arrived at Genoa, Oliphant went off, at Garibaldi's request, to charter a diligence in which a first batch of conspirators should go to Nice to prepare the way there for Garibaldi and his two hundred ballot-breakers. But when Oliphant returned from the coach office he found the whole plan abandoned, once and for ever, as being likely to jeopardise the more important Sicilian project.

' I repaired,' he writes, ' to the hotel which Garibaldi had indicated as his address, and which was a rough, old-fashioned. second-rate-looking place upon the quay.* There was no doubt

* I have no doubt this was the *Albergo della Felicità*, a picturesque old house still standing high above the quay on the top of the shops and the old arcade, nearly opposite the Palazzo S. Giorgio, in the heart of maritime Genoa. For Canzio told me that he well remembered Garibaldi coming

about the General being there, for there was a great hurrying
in and out, and a buzzing of young men about the door, as though
something of importance was going on inside. Before being
admitted to the General, I was made to wait until my name was
taken in to him. It was evident that precautions were being
taken in regard to admissions into his presence. After a few
moments I was shown into a large room, in which twenty or
thirty men were at supper, and at the head of the table sat
Garibaldi. He immediately made room for me next him;
and before I had time to tell him the result of my mission at
the diligence office, accosted me thus: " *Amico mio*, I am very
sorry, but we must abandon all idea of carrying out our Nice
programme. Behold these gentlemen from Sicily . . . I had
hoped to be able to carry out this little Nice affair first, for it
is only a matter of a few days ; but much as I regret it, the
general opinion is that we shall lose all if we try for too much." '

Garibaldi offered to take him to Sicily instead, and it
was afterwards the regret of Oliphant's life that, owing to
engagements at home, he refused the chance of representing
England among ' the Thousand.'

So Garibaldi accepted the cruel severance that henceforth divided his old home from his country, the haunts of
his boyhood and the house of his parents from the patriotic
ambition of his life. Those of us who have never undergone
this bitterness, and yet more those who have never had the
fortune to love one beautiful place out of all the world with
the love that is rooted in the memory of childhood, may
censure him because he thought too fondly of the little harbour with its seafaring folk that nestled close under the
rugged hill. The cosmopolitan wanderer who wearies of the
glittering esplanade at Nice, on the wrong side of that hill,
will not understand what his feeling was. Cavour no doubt
was right ; and Garibaldi could not see why, because he
did not understand European politics. And so he never
forgave Cavour, and misinterpreted all his actions in the
great year that followed. It was a pity. But his own
simple words, spoken to his aide-de-camp, Bandi, a few days

there on the day of his return from Turin, and, entering the inn, asking
him (Canzio), ' Will the Genoese Carabineers be ready for Sicily ? '

before they sailed together to Sicily, carry his condemnation or his apology according to the spirit in which we choose to read them :

'This man, you know, has sold my fatherland.   Poor Nizza !   Well, all the same I deal with him as a good friend and ask him to give me a thousand firearms, so that we can go and get ourselves cut to pieces in Sicily.   It seems to me not to be asking much, eh ? '

Of Victor Emmanuel, who for his part also had given up the mountain cradle of the House of Savoy, ' he spoke,' says Bandi, ' with much affection.' *

* Mrs. Browning put the pathos of the situation of Garibaldi and Nice into the famous poem, *Garibaldi*, in *Last Poems*, 1862.

CHAPTER X

THE VILLA AT QUARTO—THE PREPARATIONS

'Degno ei senza dubbio di essere comparato ai migliori romani, se in lui il senso umano non fosse più profondo e gentile che non potesse per alcune parti e per molte ragioni essere in quelli, se egli non avesse di più quell' istinto di cavalleresche avventure che è proprio delle razze nuove e miste.'—CARDUCCI, *Per la morte di Giuseppe Garibaldi.*

'Beyond doubt he is worthy to be compared to the best of the ancient Romans, were it not that in him the sense of humanity was more profound and tender than, for many reasons, it could be in them, at least on certain sides; were it not also that he possessed, in a higher degree, the impulse towards chivalrous adventures peculiar to young and mixed races.'

In the old district of Genoa that hangs crowded on the hillside above the port, the deep, sunless alleys, though too narrow for horse traffic, are cheerful with the life of an active and prosperous population. Here, in the centre of the maritime enterprise and democratic patriotism of Italy, Mazzini had been born and bred, and from his lands of exile he had long exerted over his native town an influence which now belonged rather to Cavour and Garibaldi. Much indeed had changed since Garibaldi himself, as a sea captain of twenty-six, had sought to head a rebellion in this very city against the House of Savoy, and after waiting in vain two hours in the open street for anyone to join him, had fled over the mountains for his life.

Genoa was Italy's port of departure for the liberation of the south. From Genoa the unfortunate Pisacane had sailed three years before, and Pilo in March of the current year. And now in mid April preparations were making for a happier enterprise. In the port lay the Rubattino Com-

pany's steamers, of which the agent Fauché had promised
one to Garibaldi ; and up the hill, in Bertani's house, sat
the men who were organising the expedition. Already
carefully picked volunteers from the patriotic cities of the
North were coming by invitation to report themselves to
the Committee and to take up lodgings assigned them in
the town. During the three weeks that elapsed before the
expedition started there was a constant increase in the
number of these strangers, and in the excitement of the
Genoese at the preparations known to be going on in their
midst. Secret agents, not only of Cavour, but of governments hostile to the Italian cause, were there to watch the
game, and between April 17 and May 1, the Neapolitan
Foreign Office was at least four several times alarmed by
premature reports of the departure of Garibaldi.

Within a day or two of his arrival from Turin upon this
busy scene, Garibaldi wisely withdrew himself from the gaze
of the curious to a villa at Quarto, some three miles outside
the town, along the eastern Riviera. The *Villa* Spinola, as
it was then called (now the Villa Cosci), rises within its own
little walled garden, at a place where two country lanes
meet. It stands in a district of vineyards and scattered
houses, a quarter of a mile from the rocky sea-coast, from
which it is completely cut off by the enclosed woods and
pleasure grounds of the *Palazzo* Spinola. The *Villa* Spinola
was in 1860 a yellow painted house of two floors above the
rez-de-chaussée ; * the first floor only was inhabited—by the
family of Augusto Vecchi. This veteran, one of Garibaldi's
dearest friends, was no longer able to follow him to battle,
but in 1849 he had kept close to his side through that fierce
mêlée, prolonged from midnight to summer dawn, when the
French had burst over the last defences of the Janiculum.
He now received no notice of Garibaldi's visit. He and his
son were leaning out of the window when they saw a carriage
drive up the lane from Genoa, and a man in the ordinary
black coat of civilisation descend from it at their door. It

* It is now painted red, and another storey has been added.

was the General himself, whom they rushed down to welcome with transports of joy.

From the northern bedroom in Vecchi's apartments on the first floor, where Garibaldi slept and held his consultations, he could see across the neighbouring vineyards the full sweep of the Genoese mountains, their lower slopes clothed in wood and dotted with white buildings, the upper ridges naked against the sky-line, crowned by the cross on the top of Monte Fascia, and by the old forts used in Massena's defence of Genoa, which had enabled the First Napoleon to free Italy at Marengo. Here for the three weeks before the sailing of the Thousand, Garibaldi lived secluded, often in the garden playing at bowls with Vecchi, or digging hard to ensure his health for the coming campaign. But he seldom went outside the wall of the enclosure, for all around lurked spies and busybodies, whom the General's younger followers from time to time chased down the lane, not without unseemly violence, especially when the prowler was a priest. But the Villa was often thronged with those who came and went on high matters. Day by day the organisers of the expedition appeared from Genoa; sometimes, too, a messenger from Sicily, and sometimes an emissary from Cavour.*

During the first days of his residence at the Villa Spinola, Garibaldi hourly expected to hear of the arrival at Genoa of 200 good Enfield rifles from the Million Rifles Fund at Milan. He was determined, when these had come, to start for Sicily with 200 followers in the small steamer *Piemonte*, and it can hardly be doubted, from what we now know of the real state of Sicily after the rebel defeat at Carini on April 18, that if he had gone with this little band, they would have perished in an almost unaided struggle with 20,000 regulars. But a chapter of accidents postponed their sailing from day to day

---

* My account of the villa and the life there in April–May, 1860, is partly drawn from notes taken on a visit which I made there with Canzio himself, not a year before he died. Since he was one of those who had admission to the villa during the preparations, he was able to tell me much.

and from week to week, till a somewhat fuller knowledge of
the real course of the Sicilian revolt, and the constant
stream of eager volunteers into Genoa, induced him to
charter a second steamer and to take with him a thousand
men, the bare minimum, as it proved, with which even he
could work that miracle of conquest.

The first of these lucky delays was caused by the non-
arrival of the 200 Enfields from Milan. Before leaving
Turin for Genoa Garibaldi had ordered Finzi, the Director of
his Million Rifles Fund at Milan, to send to Genoa rifles and
other accoutrements for 200 men. But from April 13 to 16
Finzi had deliberately refrained from obtaining the arms,
because the news from Sicily had been so bad that he thought
Garibaldi would change his mind and not go. But on
the 16th Garibaldi, deceived by false ' good ' news from
Sicily, was eager to start in ' four or five days.' Finzi,
therefore, on April 16, at length sent to the armoury of the
Million Rifles Fund to obtain the 200 Enfields, and great
was his astonishment when Massimo D'Azeglio, the Governor
of Milan, forbade any of the 12,000 firearms in the armoury
to be moved, even at the order of the Directors of the
Fund.

It has often been disputed whether D'Azeglio acted in
this matter on his own responsibility, or by orders from
Cavour. The Prime Minister had left the North for Tuscany the day before the incident took place. D'Azeglio
himself, who enjoyed a rare reputation for truthfulness,
writing to Rendu a month later and to Admiral Persano
two months later, states that he acted on his own judgment.
' I had in my hands,' he writes, ' 12,000 firearms (*fucili*) of the
Garibaldian Subscription, which I suspected would go into
quite other hands than his.'   The fear was groundless : Finzi,
the Director of the Fund, who made the application, was
a friend equally of Cavour and of Garibaldi, and certainly
his presence ought to have been sufficient guarantee against
any Mazzinian intrigue. But the Governor was in fact

taken by surprise and much discomposed by a responsibility as unexpected as it was grave.   Under these conditions, his own view of what Piedmontese policy ought to be, which differed profoundly from that of Cavour, swayed his decision in this sudden crisis.   An upright man before everything else, D'Azeglio felt a strong aversion, as he confessed in his letters, from the policy of arming guerilla bands against the Bourbons in Sicily while keeping up diplomatic relations with their court at Naples.   And therefore, as the representative of government on the spot, he felt bound not to allow the Director of the Million Rifles Fund to take the arms purchased by that Fund in order to attack a friendly power.*

Meanwhile the Committee at Genoa were growing impatient for the rifles, and on April 17 Bertani sent Crispi to Milan to inquire.   He found Finzi there on the 18th, and heard what had happened.   On the 19th Finzi and Crispi went together to Turin, and each had a separate interview with Farini, now Victor Emmanuel's Minister of the Interior. Farini had in December last, as Dictator of Emilia, shown sympathy with the idea of the expedition when Crispi broached it to him at Modena.   Now, however, he told Crispi that he disapproved an expedition to Sicily at this juncture of Italian and European affairs, especially since the *squadre* in the mountains round Palermo had been dispersed.   To Finzi, however, the Minister held a different language, suggesting that, although he could not in Cavour's absence take upon himself to overrule D'Azeglio, Garibaldi might obtain 1500 guns from the National Society, of which La Farina was Secretary.

Cavour, indeed, had already, before departing for

---

* D'Azeglio's letter to Rendu :—' Quant à moi, comme j'ai une réputation d'honnête homme à conserver, je fais à Milan ma politique *à moi;* j'ai refusé les fusils à Garibaldi . . . et j'ai notifié aux *Italianissimi* que, selon mon opinion, on pouvait déclarer la guerre à Naples, mais non pas y avoir un représentant et envoyer les fusils aux Siciliens.'   He repeats the same thing to Persano.   Now Cavour's policy all the summer was exactly that which D'Azeglio repudiates as dishonest.

Tuscany on the 15th, offered these arms of La Farina and
the National Society to aid an invasion of Sicily by Sicilian
exiles under La Masa.   La Masa himself was not a man
whom Cavour could have expected to lead such an expedition with success : a popular figure at Palermo in 1848, of a
somewhat theatrical type, he was devoted and active, and
had influence on the lower orders in the island, but he was
quite devoid of military talent.   It can hardly be doubted
that Cavour, when he told La Farina to act with La Masa
and supply him with arms, trusted the wit of the two
Sicilians to call in the only man who could save their
country.   They certainly acted at once on that assumption,
for on April 17th they both came to Genoa to concert
measures with Garibaldi.   On the 19th Crispi returned
with the news that there was no hope of obtaining the
Enfields of the Million Rifles Fund.   On the 20th a great
gathering was held in the Villa Spinola, a truce was called
to all personal and partisan feuds, La Masa and the Sicilians
gladly put themselves under the orders of Garibaldi, and
La Farina agreed to supply the weapons of the National
Society to arm the joint expedition.   On the same day
Crispi wrote in cipher to his friends in Sicily :—

'About the 25th of the month I with others under the command of Garibaldi, having arms in plenty, will come to Sicily ;
be sure to expect us between Sciacca and Girgenti.'

But again there was a fortunate delay.   The arms
ordered by La Farina, registered as cases of ' books,' did not
arrive at Genoa station until the 24th.   Then, by the com-
plicity of the Vice-Governor of Genoa, Pietro Magenta, to
whom Cavour had passed the word, some thousand of the
' books' were taken by Bixio from the station to the Villa
Spinola, where they awaited the moment of embarkation.
When Garibaldi saw the volumes unpacked at the Villa, he
was deeply disappointed to find how much they differed
from his fine library which D'Azeglio had sequestrated at
Milan.   They were smooth-bore muskets, rusty with age,

which had been converted from flint-locks into percussion, and finally sold as obsolete by the military authorities. They were, he bitterly exclaimed, so much ' old iron.' But since nothing better was to be had, he and his men were ready to face the Neapolitan rifles with the same inadequate type of weapon with which they had faced the Austrian rifles in the previous summer.

Meanwhile Victor Emmanuel was making a triumphal progress through his newly-acquired territories. At the moment of leaving Turin for Florence on April 15 he wrote, by Cavour's advice, a remarkable letter to his ' dear cousin ' of Naples :—

We have reached,' so wrote the Northern to the Southern King, ' a time in which Italy can be divided into two powerful states of the north and of the south, which, if they adopt the same national policy, may uphold the great idea of our times— National Independence. But in order to realise this conception, it is, I think, necessary that your Majesty abandon the course you have held hitherto. . . . The principle of dualism, if it is well established and honestly pursued, can still be accepted by Italians. But if you allow some months to pass without attending to my friendly suggestion, your Majesty will perhaps experience the bitterness of the terrible words —*too late*.'

Was this a serious offer of friendship, or an ultimatum to serve as the prelude to hostilities ? The King who penned the letter had, a few days before, heard Garibaldi's plans from Garibaldi's own lips, and had bade him only not to take the royal troops. The Minister who approved the latter had, nine days before, asked General Ribotti to head the insurrection in Sicily, and had yet more recently arranged that the muskets of the National Society should be used for a similar expedition under other leadership. Possibly if Francis II. had repented, Cavour and his master might have been glad to act in the spirit of their proposal. But they knew that he would not repent, that he was plotting for their destruction with Austria and the Pope, and one cannot help suspecting that the letter was composed rather for the satisfaction of their own consciences, and for the edification of Europe and of posterity, than for the benefit of the Prince to whom its wise words were so vainly addressed.

The reception by the Florentines both of Victor Emmanuel and of his Minister showed the warmest gratitude and enthusiasm. But Cavour had no time to waste in enjoying the sweets of a popularity which came to him late in life and which he valued chiefly as giving power to his hand. On April 21 he left the King in Tuscany, and sailed from Spezia on board Admiral Persano's flagship. Next day he landed at Genoa, where he stayed more than twenty-four hours to take stock of the situation.

During this brief residence in Genoa, the Prime Minister received an emissary from the Villa Spinola. Garibaldi was too angry with the man who had ' made him a foreigner ' to open negotiations himself. But he and his lieutenants recognised that their success depended on the permission and in some degree on the support of the government, and Bertani did not raise objections when Sirtori offered to go and call upon Cavour.

Sirtori is one of the most attractive figures in the Garibaldian epic. Having begun life as a priest, he had studied and doubted in Paris. Soon after 1840 he had become a layman and a philosopher, and in 1848 a soldier. He remained all his life a mystic and a Puritan. His emaciated form and sad, benevolent, ascetic face marked a man living apart from his fellows, and drawing from another and a purer world of thought and feeling the power which enabled him to dominate them in council and in war. He stands with Bixio, Medici, and Cosenz at the head of the Garibaldini for military talent ; and these four fine soldiers were moreover their General's best advisers in politics, on which they looked with less distorted vision than those civilians whom Garibaldi was accustomed to consult. Sirtori, who in his youth of dreams and noble illusions had been a more ardent Republican than Mazzini, now not only was a staunch Monarchist, but realised the necessity that his companions in arms should have the government behind them, if the slender chances of success which he predicted for the Sicilian expedition were not to vanish altogether.

Sirtori therefore visited Cavour and laid the whole of the plans of the party at Villa Spinola before him, emphasising their lack of means and the dangers of their course. He acknowledged that a twofold movement was designed : an attack on the Papal territories by way of Umbria and the Marches, and an expedition led by Garibaldi himself against Sicily. Cavour's reply, reported by Sirtori, is clear enough :—

' As to the expedition to the Marches, he said absolutely : " *No ; the government will oppose it by every means in its power.*" As to the expedition to Sicily, Cavour said exactly these words : " *Well and good. Begin at the south, to come up again by the north. When it is a question of undertakings, of that kind, however bold they may be, Count Cavour will be second to none.*" Those were his precise words. He said this naturally referring to all those means by which the government without compromising itself could help the expedition. He promised to help it, provided the responsibility of the government was completely concealed.'

Cavour then left Genoa for Turin, and next day (April 24) a note was sent after him by La Farina, in which the latter described the coalition of himself and La Masa with Garibaldi, and referred to the muskets which he was supplying for their enterprise. Yet although Cavour was prepared to arm the expedition in case it started, he was not eager that it should start, because he greatly feared its destruction. The melancholy Sirtori, who always told Garibaldi that he would go with him, but that he thought they would all perish, could not have described the chances to Cavour in very glowing colours. Neither was the Prime Minister deceived as to the collapse of the rebellion in Sicily, for Pilo and his compatriots were not sending to him those exaggerated reports with which they strove to draw Garibaldi to their island. Failure, then, was probable, and the scandal before a hostile Europe of an unsuccessful buccaneering expedition, coupled with the appalling catastrophe of Garibaldi's death, would, as Cavour fully realised, put back Italy's hopes for years to come. On April 23 and 24 he sent Frappolli and other agents to the Villa Spinola to try and persuade Garibaldi that the risks were too great, and that he would perish as Murat and Pisacane had perished before him. These warnings had some effect, and Crispi found the General hesitating and anxious after Frappolli's visit on the 24th. But, a day or two afterwards, the 28th was fixed for the departure, and the Vice-Governor of Genoa duly notified the fact to the authorities at Turin. Everything this time was ready. La Farina's muskets had arrived. Fauché had been induced to provide a second and larger steamer, the *Lombardo*, in addition to the *Piemonte*, and the volunteers chosen and enrolled in Genoa by now numbered 500. If the 'Five Hundred' had sailed on April 28, instead of the 'Thousand' on May 5, history would have had a sadder tale to tell.

But again fortune intervened with another propitious delay. On the morning of the 27th a telegram arrived from Fabrizi at Malta, a source of information more convincing to the inhabitants of the Villa Spinola than all the warnings of Cavour's emissaries. The telegram was deciphered as follows :—

'MALTA, *April 20*, 1860.

' Complete failure in the provinces and in the city of Palermo. Many refugees received by the English ships that have come to Malta.'

Fabrizi afterwards declared that a mistake had been made in deciphering, and that he had really written :—

' The insurrection, suppressed in the city of Palermo, main tains itself in the provinces.'

If so, the misreading represented the truth rather more nearly than the message.

That morning the Villa Spinola was crowded with

patriots, all bound in one agony of suspense. All eyes were watching the door of the little bedroom behind which Crispi, La Masa, and Bixio were expostulating with Garibaldi. The two Sicilians were ready to drag him to their island at any hazard. They were powerfully supported by Bixio, who, though he completely lacked their faith in Southern promises and Southern valour, was certain that Northerners under Garibaldi would not fail, even though the Sicilian rising had indeed been suppressed. But Garibaldi, when he saw Fabrizi's telegram, had said, with tears in his eyes, ' It would be folly to go.' The decision was his own. He well knew that the responsibility was his and not theirs ; that he had less right to throw away the fortunes of Italy and the lives of her bravest sons, than they had to offer him those lives for the sacrifice.

Before long the two Sicilians came out of the bedroom in despair. Bixio stayed on alone with the General, but at last he too burst out at the door, possessed by one of those fits of fury which made all men save one shrink from before him. The melancholy word was passed round ' *Non si parte più* ' (' We're not going '), and in a few minutes all had started back to Genoa, leaving the Villa empty save for its residents and half a dozen sea-captains who still lingered to bid a sad farewell to their chief. The day passed slowly in the house of Vecchi, in silence and in gloom. The meal, said one who shared it, was like a funeral. A dream, the fairest ever dreamed by patriots, had faded from the hearts of all who sat at the board.

After supper, a deputation of a dozen young men from the rank and file of the expedition appeared from Genoa, demanding to see Garibaldi. Bandi was sent into the bedroom to tell him. ' What do they want ? ' ' They say that if you won't go to Sicily with them, they are going without you.'

' I shall never forget,' wrote the aide-de-camp, ' the terrible expression in the eyes of the future conqueror of Palermo at hearing my words, and I could have bit my tongue off. " I am afraid, am I ? " he said, his face growing as red as a furnace, but in a moment he mastered himself and said in a calm voice, ' Show them in.''

'They came in. I was shaking like a leaf. I would not have been in their shoes for all the wealth in the world. The General was standing up, with his arms crossed. He nodded in reply to their salutations, and looked at them one by one. No one spoke for two or three minutes, which seemed to me an age. At last the youngest found his tongue—a Genoese tongue —and began to perorate. When he had done, another and then another held forth. Then they began to talk together. . . . When they had talked and shouted enough for ten, in God's own time they came to an end. Again for a short while no one spoke, while Garibaldi's eye spoke more than a hundred tongues.

'But when at last he opened his mouth, and began to speak to them in that voice of which the mere sound made men in love with him, the poor ambassadors began to grow pale, then red, then white as paper, and their eyes filled with tears. Neither did Garibaldi's eyes remain dry ; dismissing them with an affectionate wave of the hand, he turned round quickly and went to lean out of the window.'

Meanwhile at Genoa all was rage and confusion. Many of the volunteers were leaving for home, others crying out on Garibaldi's lieutenants to lead them in his stead. Partisans of Mazzini were heard saying ' Garibaldi is afraid.' Heated councils were held among the promoters of the expedition as to whether they should go without him. La Masa, who was least capable of conducting such an enterprise, offered to lead his fellow Sicilians to their native island. His compatriots were divided, some offering to follow him, others, like the fine soldier Carini, and Amari himself, who had collected money for Garibaldi's expedition, angrily refusing to have anything to do with such folly. Bixio in his rage offered to steer the ship for La Masa and his Sicilians, though if he had started, he would probably not long have remained subordinate under such a chief.

In this confusion of councils Crispi seems to have kept his head best. He induced his fellow Sicilians to wait a few days, clearly perceiving two things, that it would be useless to go without Garibaldi, and that Garibaldi would be only too glad to go if a ' new fact ' could be provided. Crispi set himself to obtain this ' new fact.' On the 27th, he sent a cipher telegram to his friend Agresta in Sicily :—

' Not having received by this courier any letters from you here, there is hesitation, and I fear I shall not succeed in getting the expedition to start. The news received by this steamer is no better, and for twenty-two days we have not got one letter from Sicily which gives any precise news. Here everything is ready, even the steamer. It is possible we may end in coming.'

On the evening of April 29 Crispi's ' new fact ' came to hand, in the shape of certain mysterious telegrams, letters, and dispatches. It has been said by some of his comrades in arms that he forged them, but the evidence is not deci- sive. Some say it was a telegram from Fabrizi, others that it was news from Crispi's correspondents in Sicily whom he had been so busily dunning for good news. In any case these documents described the insurrection as having revived in the mountains above Palermo, a statement to which Pilo's recent action after his arrival in Piana dei Greci gave some faint colour of truth.

With these papers in their hands, on the evening of the 29th, Bixio and Crispi in Genoa felt so sure of persuading Garibaldi when they saw him next day at Quarto, that they revived the preparations for the expedition, writing to Fauché at nine that night : ' We must see you. The news is good, and we resume business. Bixio.' Next morning Bixio and one or two of the Sicilians went to Quarto, and found their chief at the Villa Spinola, still of the same mind. He had already that very day written to the Directors of the Million Rifles Fund : ' By now you will know about Sicily. The expedition does not start.' But the ' new facts ' which Bixio brought in his hand took instant effect upon him. ' We will go,' he said, rising from his seat, his eyes flashing and his voice vibrating with sudden gladness. All remembered that it was the 30th of April, the anniversary of the day when he had defeated the French before the walls of Rome, and the Villa was decorated with laurels to celebrate the double occasion for rejoicing.

By 10.45 in the morning Bixio had sent off a note to Fauché, who was to supply the steamers :—

' I am returning at this moment from Quarto ; the General is coming to Genoa at once, and will be waiting to see you at Bertani's house as soon as you can get there.'

At this council of war, held in Genoa round the sick-bed to which Bertani's exertions had already confined him, the decision to go was formally taken. Only Sirtori opposed it, saying : ' No, I disapprove. I do not believe it will succeed ; but if Garibaldi goes to Sicily, with many or with few, I go too.' Medici next day expressed similar sentiments.

The whole machinery of organisation was set to work once more. Several days were required to reunite the volunteers, many of whom had left Genoa in despair, and it was now determined to raise the numbers to a thousand. For the next five days men worked as they work at the crisis of life. Bertani in his bed, his handwriting a mere scrawl, dealt with heap after heap of letters offering service of every sort from every part of Italy. Bixio, who had to prepare the embarkation, neither ate nor slept, but unconscious of all other objects, in a trance of sleepless activity, for once treated his family with the same brusque inattention with which he usually treated the rest of mankind.

Zeal in the work was by no means confined to the Committee in Genoa. Private subscriptions were organised in town after town by ' Committees for the succour of Sicily ' ; at Cremona and elsewhere they openly placarded the walls, and almost everywhere collected money in the streets. The Municipality of Pavia, the city of the Cairoli, voted a large sum out of the rates to the Million Rifles Fund to help the expedition. The Municipality of Brescia made a similar contribution direct to Garibaldi himself. At Pavia, at Milan, at Brescia, at Bergamo and elsewhere, officers of last year's *Cacciatori delle Alpi* were choosing out the best

7

young men of the place and sending them by train to Genoa.
At Bergamo, on May 4, the train that was to start with the
100 young Bergamasques for whom Garibaldi had asked
and whom Nullo had carefully chosen, was boarded by 300,
while 200 more, after a fierce struggle to get in, were left
broken-hearted on the platform. At Milan Nullo forcibly
got rid of another hundred of them, but not fewer than 160
from the little Alpine town landed among the Thousand at
Marsala.

A note from the diary of Abba describes some typical
experiences of a volunteer on the way to Genoa :—

PARMA, *May* 4.

' We are starting, seventeen strong, from here, mostly
students, some working-men, three doctors. Of these latter,
one, Soncini, is a veteran of the Roman Republic. They say
that in the train from Romagna we shall find other friends of
the best. They are coming from all parts.

' Great mystery is made of our departure. To hear some
people talk, not even the air knows. . . . Yet everybody is
aware that Garibaldi is in Genoa and is going to Sicily. As
we went through Parma they shook hands with us heartily
and wished us luck. . . .

(In the station at Novi.)

' There are some infantry here waiting for a train. Their
sub-lieutenant comes up to me and says : " Will you wire
me from Genoa the hour when you start ? " I remain silent.
The officer looks me in the eyes and says smiling, " Keep
the secret, but believe me I have not asked with any bad
intention." '

This young officer, named Pagani, deserted next day, came
on board under the false name of De Amicis, and was killed
fighting at Calatafimi. He was one of the five officers
who deserted and went with the Thousand. There would
have been many more if the organising committee had
allowed it.

The North was rising up to carry Garibaldi to Sicily.
There was no division of classes or of parties. Cavourian
Municipalities were voting money, the leisured class was as

forward in the movement as the working-men—the professional class perhaps most enthusiastic of all. Too rarely does an emotion like this, pure of self-interest and far above blind race-hatred, sweep along with it a whole people, lifting common men into an atmosphere which they seldom breathe, and never breathe for long. Those who remember the day speak of it as something too sacred ever to return. It was the supreme moment of the Risorgimento, and fortunately Italy did not waste it as she had wasted ' '48.'

The country was rising up; what would the Government do? Would it wish, and if so, would it dare, to stop Garibaldi? When, on the last night of April, Cavour heard that he had after all decided to start, was the news welcome to that anxious watchman? If Garibaldi had hesitated so long, Cavour could not be sanguine of success. The Prime Minister had no Crispis and Pilos to deceive him as to the real state of the Sicilian insurrection. He may well have thought that the chances were against Garibaldi, for indeed they never ceased to be against him until he had taken Palermo. The open preparation at Genoa had already brought down on Cavour a storm of diplomatic protest. Already he saw the threatening shadow of Austrian conquest, of French interference. Italy had but one strong friend in Europe, and British warships could not sail over the Lombard plain. Cavour, moreover, was in these very days trying to induce Napoleon to withdraw his troops from Rome, an advantage which it would certainly be worth sacrificing for a successful attack on the Bourbons, but not for the sake of a tragic fiasco with Garibaldi in the part of Pisacane. Furthermore, he rightly supposed that it was Garibaldi's intention, while himself attacking Sicily, to send a revolutionary force against the Papal provinces of Umbria and the Marches, a step only too likely to involve Italy with France.

On the other hand, as he had said to Sirtori at Genoa, if Garibaldi could indeed conquer Sicily, and thence ' come up again by the north,' it would prove the means of Italy's

deliverance.   And what other deliverance could he hope for
from the attack now threatened by the close alliance of
Austria with Naples and the Pope ?   He must strike ere he
was struck, and Garibaldi was the only weapon he could use
at once.   Lastly, whatever were the dangers of the expedition, there were immense dangers in trying to prevent it
from starting, with the country in this passion of enthusiasm.

In such a conflict of calculation, embracing perhaps
these thoughts, and doubtless others unknown to us, Cavour
ordered a special train to take him from Turin to Bologna,
there to find the king and decide once for all whether the
expedition was to be stopped or no.   The line was scarcely
finished in places, and the railway officials at Bologna were
surprised to hear that the Prime Minister was coming.   But
on May 1 he arrived in a solitary carriage behind the engine.

That same day the King drove with relays of horses
from Florence to Bologna, over the Pass of the Central
Apennines.   It had been raining in torrents, but as the
liberated people crowded the mountain road to see their
deliverer pass, he would not let the carriage be closed.   It
was the very road on which Garibaldi had been so nearly
caught in the wayside inn in September 1849, and no doubt
Teresa Baldini, whose courage and wit had saved the hero
from the Austrians, now saw her King drive past the door.*

So Cavour and Victor Emmanuel met at Bologna in the
rooms of San Michele in Bosco, to decide between them
whether the expedition should be allowed to start.   It is
universally agreed that the King was the more eager and
sanguine of the two, but no one knows what passed between
them.   A writer in a French review afterwards asserted that
witnesses of the interview had told him that Cavour offered
to go and arrest Garibaldi with his own hands, but that the
King would not allow it.   Since, however, no one has shown
who were these witnesses, or what reason there is to suppose that any third person was present at all, the historian
will do well to be sceptical.   All that is known is that

---

* *Trevelyan's Gar. Rome*, chap. xvi.   Teresa died in 1908.

at this interview the King and his Minister finally agreed to let Garibaldi go.

The great statesman had made one mistake of detail, which nearly proved fatal to Italy and to him. He let the Thousand start with La Farina's bad muskets, when they might have had the Enfields from the Million Rifles Fund. But two things are to be remembered. First, that in all probability Cavour did not know that the weapons of the National Society were bad, since even Garibaldi, who had been President of the Society, only found that out when he saw them unpacked, and the Secretary, La Farina, had most likely cried up his wares to Cavour. Secondly, that after the misfortune of D'Azeglio's sequestration of the Enfields, a fact widely known and commented on, it would perhaps have been difficult for Cavour afterwards to have removed the embargo without openly committing the Government to Garibaldi's expedition in the eyes of hostile Europe.

I have now given some account of Cavour's action in April 1860. I do not pretend to have fathomed his motives. Our knowledge of his correspondence and his conversation is still incomplete, and those of his sayings and letters which we already know contain, in the same week and even on the same day, such strange contradictions that it is folly to dogmatise as to the nature of his wishes and intentions up to the time of the departure of the Thousand. I will only venture to suggest that, until the moment the expedition had sailed, Cavour was, at least in some degree, an opportunist waiting on circumstance, and unwilling to commit himself or his country till the latest possible moment. Nor, in the terrible uncertainties of the case, can he be blamed for refusing to take a more decided part in thrusting Garibaldi out on an expedition where Sirtori and Medici thought he would fail, and Garibaldi himself could not at first believe in his own chances of success.

CHAPTER XI

THE SAILING OF THE THOUSAND

'Breve ne l' onda placida avanzasi
striscia di sassi.   Boschi di lauro
frondeggiano dietro spirando
effluvi e murmuri ne la sera.

     *   *   *   *

Italia, Italia, donna de i secoli
de' vati e de' martiri donna,
inclita vedova dolorosa,

     *   *   *

quindi il tuo fido mosse cercandoti
pe' mari.   Al collo leonino avvoltosi
il puncio, la spada di Roma
alta su l' omero bilanciando,

stiè Garibaldi.   Chieti venivano
a cinque a dieci, poi dileguavano,
drappelli oscuri, ne l' ombra
i mille vindici del destino,

come pirati che a preda gissero ;
ed a te occulti givano, Italia,
per te mendicando la morte
al cielo, al pelago, a i fratelli.'

                           CARDUCCI, *Scoglio di Quarto.*

'A short rock-rib that cleaves the placid sea ;
Behind, the leafy laurel thicket breathing
Odours and murmurs on the evening air ;
. . . Thence, Italy, thou queen of ages past,
Of prophets and of martyrs still the queen,
Famous, unhappy, widowed lady proud,—
Thence, Italy, thy faithful sought thee out
Across the sea.   Around his lion's neck
The puncio wrapped ; the sword that flashed at Rome
Across his shoulder balanced—so he came.
And silent came his shadowy companies,
By fives and tens, then vanished in the gloom.
The Thousand, destined to avenge thy wrong,

Like pirates to their prey they glided down,
Hidden from thee they glided, Italy,
Sea-beggars, begging death from sky and waves
And brethren, only for thy service sake.'
The Rock at Quarto.

IN order to secure the passive connivance of the authorities
in the departure of an expedition which they would be
forced to repudiate, in any event for a few days, and in case
of failure for all time, it was necessary to act with a formal
show of secrecy. The Government had taken steps to
indicate that the embarkation itself must not take place in
the port of Genoa. The plan of operations was therefore
drawn up as follows :—The two steamers were to be seized
in the port at midnight, and as quietly as possible, by a
picked body of seamen, under Bixio, who would take the
vessels empty out of the harbour. Then, as they sailed
eastward along the Riviera, they were to meet row-boats
from Foce and Quarto bearing the volunteers, the provisions, and the cases of arms. Finally, the bulk of the
ammunition would be rowed out from Bogliasco.* Men
and stores would be hauled up on to the steamers at sea, and
the voyage would begin.

Much of the plan was common knowledge in Genoa on
May 5, the busy day that preceded the night of departure.
The authorities duly kept watch at Cornigliano and S. Pier
d'Arena, to the west of the city, leaving undisturbed the
real places of embarkation to the east.† But one detail of
the conspiracy was still a secret. Except Bixio, not even
those who were to seize the ships knew which those ships
were to be. The truth was that the *Piemonte* and the
Lombardo were to be taken without leave from Rubattino
and his Company, according to a most secret agreement of
Garibaldi, Bixio, and Bertani with Fauché, the Company's

---

* For this chapter see Map VI., at end of book, route marked.
† There were indeed the usual two gendarmes in the crowd that
witnessed the embarkation at Quarto, but they confined their action to an
ineffectual protest against the cutting of the telegraph wires ordered by
Garibaldi.

agent. Although arrangements, afterwards liberally fulfilled, had been made to compensate the Company in case
of the loss or injury of the ships, it had been determined
not to confide in the timid patriotism of Rubattino and the
shareholders. It was a wise caution. For so little did
these men care for their country in proportion to the security
of their profits, that in the middle of June, when all Italy
went wild with joy over the taking of Palermo, they celebrated the occasion by dismissing Fauché because he had
enabled Garibaldi to go there. The expedition of the
Thousand owed nothing to the class of mind whose patriotism
consists in a calculation of the profit on shares. Cavour,
with that desire to do justice to the Garibaldini which
distinguished him from many of his followers, tried to
open to Fauché another career by way of compensation for
the excellent post which he had lost ; but Cavour died, and
with him perished the hopes of Fauché, and of many more.
Rubattino, who was erroneously believed to have given the
steamers, received the praise of historians for the deed of
the man whom he had ruined for doing it, and his statue
stands to-day on the quay-side whence the *Piemonte* and
Lombardo were taken so sorely against his will. Fauché
lived many years, rich only in the love of so poor a man as
Garibaldi, and passed away ' poor and forgotten in the
civil hospital at Venice.'

Before midnight on May 5, a party of men, chiefly
consisting of experienced seamen and engineers, had assembled one by one on board a hulk named the *Joseph* in
a remote corner of the port of Genoa, close to the eastern
lighthouse. At the right moment Bixio appeared among
them, and clapping on his head his *képi* of lieutenant-colonel,
said in his masterful voice, ' Gentlemen, from this moment I
am in command ; listen to my orders.' Only then did his
subordinates learn the identity of the vessels which they
were to seize. In a few minutes they were rowing in two
large boats towards the Rubattino steamers, which lay at
a pier in the most public part of the harbour, opposite the

main façade of the town. Bixio assigned the *Piemonte* to
one boat-load and the *Lombardo* to another. Swinging
themselves noiselessly on board, they roused the crews from
sleep, presenting their pistols for form's sake at the drowsy
men. As soon as they heard the name of Garibaldi all
gladly submitted, and some lent a hand in the work. The
'piracy' was regarded as a good joke by captors and cap-
tives alike. But several hours passed before the steamers
were ready to move. First the fires had to be lit and stoked.
Then it was thought necessary to wrap the chains in cloth
to prevent noise in hauling up the anchors, for the pirates
had still some fear of the government, and much more of
the Company. Their accomplice Fauché watched from the
balcony of his house, almost opposite the Rubattino pier,
sickening with suspense, as the night waned, and still the
two masses, motionless at their place, loomed clearer
through the melting shadows. Then it was discovered that
the engines of the *Lombardo* were out of order, and the
Sicilian engineer Campo had to be sent on board from the
Piemonte to aid his compatriot and brother-engineer Orlando
before that too was set right. And even then the *Piemonte*
had to take the *Lombardo* in tow to get her out to sea. It
was long past three in the morning before Fauché, with a
deep sigh of relief, saw the two dim shapes begin slowly to
move from the pier and vanish in the darkness of the harbour.

Meanwhile, in Bertani's house, high up the hill in the
heart of Genoa, the night had passed amid grave anxiety.
The money, without which the Thousand could not sail, was
to be supplied by Finzi out of the Million Rifles Fund, from
which Garibaldi was allowed to draw anything except actual
weapons of war. Besides large sums already spent in fitting
out the expedition, 90,000 *lire* were to be taken to Sicily, of
which 30,000 had reached Bertani's bed-side that day enclosed in a letter from Finzi, and the remaining 60,000 were
due to arrive by the last train from Milan about ten at
night, in the hands of Migliavacca. This officer reached
Bertani's house in good time with the money, but more than

half of it was found to be in the form of a draft on the Bank
of Genoa, which would be of little use in the hill-towns of
Sicily. Migliavacca was sent in haste to rouse some of
Bertani's rich commercial friends, while Nuvolari, who was
to take the money down to the steamers and go with the
expedition, waited at Bertani's with growing impatience as
the minutes passed. At length Migliavacca returned with
the change in so many hundred gold pieces in time for
Nuvolari to carry safely on board the whole of the 90,000
lire.*

Throughout the evening of May 5 the volunteers of the
expedition had been leaving Genoa by the Porta Pila and
walking, singly or in groups, to the appointed places of
embarkation. Some forty or fifty turned off to Foce, where
a few boats awaited them. All the rest followed the highway to the shore below Quarto. For the whole three miles
the road was lined by the people of the city, who stood
uncovered and in silence as they passed. There were no
chants de départ, no flags and folly, no vulgar revelry and
boasting. All were too deeply moved, too uncertain of the
event.

At Quarto, the large wooded grounds of the Palazzo
Spinola, dividing Garibaldi's residence from the sea, were
this night flung open for his use, and the Thousand, as they
arrived there, dispersed themselves in groups under its
trees, or sat on the rocks below, watching the cases of
muskets being piled into the boats. On the embanked
high-road of the Riviera, which ran close along the top of
these sea-worn rocks, stood a dense crowd of friends, parents,
wives, sisters, and sweethearts come to witness the departure.
Some kept their eyes fixed on the gate of the Spinola grounds
through which the figure of Garibaldi must soon emerge,
while others imparted in low whispers the last blessings and
farewells to those whom they only half expected to see
again. Not a few of the Thousand themselves, like the poet

---

* Out of this sum, 70,000 *lire* were spent on campaign up to the time
of the capture of Palermo at the end of the month.

Nievo, undauntedly shared Sirtori's view that they would none of them return alive. Medici himself, though he was of much the same opinion, came like the rest to embark, but on the shore at Quarto a letter from Garibaldi, couched in affectionate terms, was put into his hands. It began, ' It is better that you should remain behind, and you can be more useful so,' and asked the defender of the Vascello to absent him awhile from a soldier's felicity, in order to organise and dispatch reinforcements both to Sicily and to the Papal States.

A stranger, coming by chance upon that scene, would scarcely have been able to distinguish the men who were starting for the war from those who were there to see them off. The immense majority of the Thousand had no arms in their hands—for the muskets were to be dealt out during the voyage—and they were dressed in the peaceful garb of artisans, merchants, gentlemen, or students. A very few wore Piedmontese uniforms. It was only on the voyage that fifty red shirts were distributed, so that when they landed in Sicily one in twenty wore the famous dress that they all adopted after the taking of Palermo. The Genoese carabineers, about thirty-five strong, could be distinguished at Quarto because they already carried the rifles which were their own property ; some of them wore a grey uniform, but others were in plain clothes.

Meanwhile in the Villa Spinola a small group of men were waiting for the General to leave his bedroom. He was alone, effecting some change in the black garb of civilisation which, varied by the Piedmontese uniform in '59, he had endured for the last decade. At length the door opened and they saw him for the first time in the outfit which he wore for the rest of his life, whether at home, in Parliament, or in the field. Loose grey trousers of a sailor cut, a plain red shirt, no longer worn like a workman's blouse as in '49, but tucked in at the waist, and adorned with a breast-pocket and watch-chain, a coloured silk handkerchief knotted round his neck, and over his shoulders a great

American *puncio* or grey cloak, which he now wrapped about him as a protection against the night air. A black felt hat completed the figure which will be familiar to the Italian as the symbol of his country for long ages to come. His face was radiant and his bearing elate, for now that after long hesitations he had made up his mind to go, he at least had no shadow of a doubt as to what the issue would be.

Carrying across his shoulder his heavy sword with the belt attached to it, and followed by his staff officers, he stepped out of Vecchi's villa, crossed the lane into the grounds of the Palazzo Spinola, walked down the path between its trees and shrubberies where many of his men were waiting, passed through the little gate in the angle of the wall, and so emerged on the open road beside the sea. The crowd gathered there in the twilight gazed at him in silence as he crossed to the rocks, and descended by a little broken foot-track to the bottom of the cliff.* There he found himself standing on a rib of rock, beside a tiny bay a few feet deep and two or three yards long, into which boats could be brought one at a time. Here the embarkation took place.

It was about ten o'clock that Garibaldi and the first flotilla put out half a mile to sea to await the steamers. Many of the Thousand remained for the second journey, as there were not enough boats to take all at once. There was a swell upon the waters, but the night was calm, cold, and bright, and the string of boats could clearly be seen moving out in the track of the moonlight. The beauty of the night, the stars, the silence of men and Nature deeply affected every one. Garibaldi, wrapped in his *puncio*, sat in the boat immersed in silent joy. His whole being expanded once more, as on those nights on the pampas when he

---

* The foot-track is still clearly visible on the west side of the present memorial pillar. I had the honour of going down it with Canzio himself, a year before he died ; he said to me on this path, ' How many who came down here with me that night are now dead ! ' The silence and gravity of everyone during the whole of the dignified scene at Quarto was remarked on by eye-witnesses.

had ridden and slept with Anita under the stars they loved.

'O night of the fifth of May,' he writes, ' lit up with the fire of a thousand lamps with which the Omnipotent has adorned the Infinite. Beautiful, tranquil, solemn with that solemnity which swells the hearts of generous men when they go forth to free the slave. Such were the Thousand, . . . my young veterans of the war of Italian liberty, and I, proud of their trust in me, felt myself capable of attempting anything. . . . I have felt this same harmony of soul on all nights like those of Quarto, of Reggio, of Palermo, of Volturno.'

There had been another such moonlit night, scarcely to be forgotten in his meditations as he sat there off Quarto, floating on the tide that was to carry him at last to fortune. He must have well remembered that on such a night as this, eleven years before, on the upper waters of the Adriatic, the Austrian squadron had discovered Italy's last fugitives by the light of the August moon.*

But the midnight hours wore on, and still the belated steamers were not in sight. Among the men who had been four or five hours in the boats tedium succeeded to the first enthusiasm of embarkation, and even Garibaldi grew impatient and ordered his boat to be rowed on towards Genoa to find Bixio. The morning was almost grey, and the earliest peasant-girls were passing along the high-road to market in Genoa, ere the long-expected signal of lights in the national colours flashed across the western waves. As day dawned, the two steamers hove in sight, already having on board the small body that had rowed out from Foce. Then a wild scene began. Men and cases of arms were dragged up the ships' sides pell-mell, and as fast as each boat was emptied it plied back to the shore for a second load. It was a fierce

---

* *Trevelyan's Gar. Rome*, chap. xiv. Of the night of August 2, 1849, Garibaldi wrote—' The moon was full, and it was with a terrible misgiving that I watched the rising of the mariner's companion, contemplated by me so often with the reverence of a worshipper. Lovelier than I had ever seen her before, but for us, unhappily, too lovely—the moon was fatal to us that night. East of the point of Goro lay the Austrian squadron.'

scramble.   Men clung to the ship's ladder four or eight at a time and struggled as for their lives to get on board, for the long delay in port rendered it necessary to start at once, even at the risk of leaving a few comrades behind.   Garibaldi had no wish to be found near Genoa in broad daylight.   Good haste was made, but the sun was gilding the mountain tops before the *Piemonte* and the *Lombardo* moved off with their freight of men.   ' How many are we all told ? ' asked Garibaldi.   ' With the sailors we are more than a thousand,' was the reply.   ' Eh ! eh ! *quanta gente !*   What a host ! ' said this strange general, and set his aide-de-camp thinking.

One thing was not yet embarked—the ammunition. The bulk of the gunpowder and a few additional firearms had been entrusted by Bixio to a score of young patriots, who were to bring the precious cargo out from Bogliasco, a few miles east of Quarto.   Bixio had also appointed some local seamen as their guides, who proved to be a very bad choice.   The whole party had set out from Bogliasco early in the night, but the guides had insisted on rowing in front of the heavy ammunition boats in a light skiff of their own, showing a lantern in the stern.   After twenty minutes the lantern was extinguished and the rascals made off, in order to go smuggling on this propitious occasion when the authorities had deliberately relaxed their watch on the landing-places between Genoa and Portofino.   To this day no one knows whether the smugglers felt ill-will towards the expedition, the success of which their treacherous conduct imperilled.   They may perhaps have thought that the ammunition-boats could hardly fail to sight the steamers at daybreak, even without special guidance ; and indeed if the young men had been content to wait where they had been left in the lurch, off Bogliasco, they would almost certainly have been picked up by the expedition as it passed at eight or nine in the morning.   But they did exactly the wrong thing.   Not knowing that their comrades were several hours

late in starting from port, they rowed westward all night in
hope of meeting them, and were unfortunate enough to pass
them, unseeing and unseen, probably close off Genoa, in the
small hours. In broad daylight they saw with rage and
despair the smoke of two steamers far away to the east,
making round the promontory of Protofino.

Garibaldi, on the *Piemonte*, alarmed by the absence of
the ammunition-boats, waited half an hour or more, and then
held on his course, hoping to find that the *Lombardo*, which
had gone on in front, had taken the gunpowder on board
unnoticed. The *Piemonte* could soon overhaul its more
slow-moving companion. At Camogli, near Portofino
promontory, Canzio, of the Genoese Carabineers, was sent
ashore to obtain oil and grease for the engines of the two
steamers, and it was probably during this halt that Garibaldi hailed Bixio and ascertained that they had set out to
conquer Sicily and Naples without ammunition. ' Let us
go on all the same,' he said, and directed his course first
towards the Tuscan coast.

Nearly 1150 fighting men had boarded the steamers.
Garibaldi commanded the *Piemonte*, and Bixio the slower
and more capacious *Lombardo*. The decks were crowded,
and at first some could not even find room to sit down.
There was no food except a little water and biscuit. Garibaldi was radiant, feeling his foot on deck once more and
enjoying the management of the ship, and a large proportion
of Genoese and others were equally at home by land or sea.
But almost all the Milanese and the men from the Alpine
cities succumbed on that first day to the heavy rolling,
and not a plank of Italy's Argo but was occupied by the
prostrate forms of heroes in distress.

Garibaldi, while in the villa at Quarto, had determined
that as soon as he was out at sea he would run straight for
the coast of Tuscany, and that for three reasons. In the first
place, as early as May 1, he had warned Zambianchi that he
would detach him with a portion of the expeditionary force
to invade the Papal States by way of Orvieto and Perugia ;

with this end in view Garibaldi had caused to be printed at Genoa proclamations calling on the Pope's subjects to rise, and had brought them with him on the ship. In the second place, on May 2 he had given a *rendezvous* in the Straits of Piombino to a party of seventy-eight Tuscan volunteers, under Sgarallino, who were to come thither by ship from Leghorn. Thirdly, he had, we may suppose, foreseen the need for a temporary disembarkation, prior to the landing in Sicily, which might have to be made in the face of the enemy. It was necessary ere that to establish the rudiments of military discipline in a mob speaking all the dialects of the peninsula, to name the non-commissioned officers, assign the men to their several companies and captains, and hold one or two drills of the improvised regiment. This could not well be done on the crowded decks at sea.

But to these considerations was now added a new and supreme necessity. When they stood off from Portofino, there was not enough coal or food to take them to Sicily, and no ammunition with which to fight if they ever reached its shores.

Running through the Straits of Piombino, between Elba and the mainland, they found the little sailing-ship *Adelina*, with the Tuscan volunteers from Leghorn, which had beaten about near the straits for three days waiting for the steamers to appear. At dawn on May 7, the three ships passed along the wild coast of the Tuscan Maremma, whence, in September, 1849, Garibaldi had embarked in the fishing-boat at the end of his adventurous escape. A little after nine in the morning the *Piemonte* came to anchor off the miserable coast village of Talamone.

CHAPTER XII

TALAMONE AND THE VOYAGE *

' Success will stamp Garibaldi as a General and statesman of the highest rank; defeat, ruin, and death will cause him to be remembered as a Quixotic adventurer of dauntless courage but weak judgment, who has thrown away his life in a desperate filibustering attempt. The expedition to Sicily may in future be ranked with William of Orange's landing in England, or it may be ranked with Murat's landing in Calabria.'—*Times*, leading article, May 11, 1860.

' We know that our sympathies and the judgment of history will distinguish between the cases of the filibuster and felon and that of the hero and the patriot. We had once a great filibuster who landed in England in 1688.'—LORD J. RUSSELL in the House of Commons, May 17, 1860.

As the engines of the *Piemonte* stopped beside the quay of Talamone, Garibaldi went ashore to win over the official world, clad for this special purpose in his Piedmontese General's uniform. No sooner was he gone than the men were called together on deck to hear his proclamation read. At the same hour another copy was being read on board the *Lombardo*, still many miles behind along the coast. The proclamation, which identified the Thousand with the volunteers of the Alpine campaign of the previous summer, ran as follows :—

' The mission of this corps will be, as it always has been, based on complete self-sacrifice for the regeneration of the fatherland. The brave *Cacciatori delle Alpi* have served and will serve their country with the devotion and discipline of the best kind of soldiers, without any other hope, without any other claim than the satisfaction of their consciences. Not rank, not honour, not reward have enticed these brave men. They returned to the seclusion of private life when danger disappeared. But now that the hour of battle has come again,

---

* For this chapter see Map VI., at end of book, route marked.

Italy sees them once more in the foremost rank, joyful, willing, ready to shed their blood for her.   The war-cry of the *Cacciatori delle Alpi* is the same as that which re-echoed from the banks of the Ticino twelve months ago—

Italia e Vittorio Emanuele,

and this war-cry, from your lips, will strike terror into the enemies of Italy.'

These words inspired the hearers with sober enthusiasm and pride.   Only a small group of unreconciled Mazzinians heard with dismay the name of Victor Emmanuel.   They had hoped that when Garibaldi once got to sea in his red shirt, the old Republican instincts would revive in him, and that he would hoist the ' neutral banner,' the tricolour of Italy unstained by the cross of the House of Savoy.   In the eyes of their party, the object of the Sicilian expedition was, as Mazzini told Karl Blind, ' that the movement was to be continued up to and into Rome, and that then a Constituent Assembly was to be convoked there for the expression of the will of the nation,' which might haply be for a Republic.   Garibaldi's proclamation ran counter to these hopes. When, therefore, the belated *Lombardo* reached Talamone, a council of Republicans from both the ships was held on board her, to decide what they should do.   Antonio Mosto, the bearded Genoese who commanded the Carabineers, Crispi, Savi, and others decided to go on.   But Onnis and one or two more of the pure gospel refused to fight for a King, and walked off inland out of the page of history. Garibaldi, when he heard what had happened, expressed bitter resentment.   His dislike of Mazzini and the Mazzinians had not been diminished by his recent quarrel with Cavour.   Mazzini himself was at this moment hastening from London to Genoa, in the hope of going with the Thousand.   If he had come in time, it may be doubted whether Garibaldi would have consented to take him.

Except these few Republicans, the Thousand were far

too well pleased with their cause and their leader to join in debating his proclamation. They were more pleasantly employed ashore recovering from the miseries of the voyage. It was a clear spring morning. Some bathed in the sea, some searched the friendly but poverty-stricken village for eatable food, while many of that learned regiment admired the scenery and discussed the antiquarian and literary associations of the Maremma. Close at hand the coast ran southwards to Orbetello, through unreclaimed marshland and tangled brushwood. The low, desert shores of the Gulf of Talamone stretched thus for ten miles, bounded on the north by a high hill, on the spur of which Talamone and its old war-tower projected into the sea, and on the south by the promontory mountain of Argentario, on the side of which Porto S. Stefano was clearly visible. Among the lagoons dividing Mount Argentario from the mainland lay the fortress of Orbetello. The possibility of proceeding to Sicily depended on securing coal from the government store at Porto S. Stefano, and ammunition from the fortress in the lagoons.

At this crisis Garibaldi employed a wise and even artful diplomacy. He chose as his principal agent Colonel Türr, the Hungarian. Türr, who died in 1908 full of years and honour, began his career as patriot when, in January 1849, he deserted the hated Austrian flag at the persuasion of some Italian officers. During the war of 1859 Cavour, who, together with Napoleon, was in close negotiation with Kossuth as to the possibility of a Hungarian insurrection. had sent Türr to join the *Cacciatori delle Alpi* and represent among them the unity of the Italian and Magyar cause. Partly for his country's sake, partly for his own, he was treated with special favour by Garibaldi. With his long moustache, his fine person and carriage, his disinterested virtue and his inconsiderate valour, he was the perfect type of a Hungarian cavalier. He had not, perhaps, the military talent of Bixio, Medici, or Cosenz, but as a diplomatist he had no superior among the Garibaldini, and it might be

supposed that his connexion with the Court and the official
world would be known to the commandant of Orbetello.

That officer, Lieutenant-Colonel Giorgini, had the dull
round of his garrison life broken in upon at about two in the
afternoon of May 7 by a visit from Türr, who had driven
along the coast road from Talamone. The Hungarian presented his letter of introduction from Garibaldi, explained
the situation, told the story of the lost ammunition, and
asked for all the powder in the fortress. Never, perhaps,
was an officer who wished to combine his military with his
patriotic duty placed in a more difficult position.

' You are a soldier,' he said to Türr, and you know what
it means to give up the arms and ammunition of a fortress
without orders from one's superior officer.'

' But what,' answered the resourceful Magyar, ' if you get
the orders from the King himself ?   It will be enough for you
to send him this letter which I will write.'

Sitting down there and then, Türr wrote to Trecchi, the
King's Garibaldian aide-de-camp :

Dear Trecchi,—Tell his Majesty that the ammunition
destined for our expedition has been left in Genoa.   We beseech
his Majesty to order the Commandant of the fortress of Orbetello to provide us with all that he has in his arsenal.'

Handing this letter to Giorgini, Türr observed that as there
was neither telegraph nor railway, it might be a week before
an answer could reach the Maremma from Turin ; that it
was impossible for Garibaldi to wait at Talamone, because
in less than a week the European powers would have interfered and the Neapolitans would have completed their naval
and military defences against a raid which was already
known to have left Genoa.   Therefore, said Türr, Giorgini
must send the ammunition before he received the King's
reply.

' Colonel,' the other answered, ' you place me in a
terrible situation. But since you assure me that the
undertaking has started under the auspices of the King,

I put the arsenal at your disposal.' So saying, Giorgini went to Talamone and saw Garibaldi, who, dressed as a Piedmontese officer, heartily thanked his comrade for helping him at a pinch. The commandant of Orbetello was shortly afterwards arrested and brought before a court martial, by whom he was acquitted.*

Meanwhile several waggons were loaded up and the stores taken from Orbetello to Talamone. The ammunition was partly in the form of cartridges, partly of loose powder packed in pine-wood boxes. Even now there was not really enough ammunition for the muskets, and some of the Thousand went through the campaign from Marsala to Palermo with no more than ten cartridges a man. Other war-like supplies were added, including bullets used by the *Bersaglieri*, which proved a bad fit for the muskets of the Garibaldini, a hundred Enfield rifles, and lastly two bronze cannon cast in 1802, and an old culverin (*colubrina*) which had been out of date long before the era of Napoleon. These three, together with two more garrison pieces of like antiquarian interest found by Garibaldi in the old tower of Talamone, were taken to Sicily, mounted there on wooden carriages roughly put together, and so dragged about and occasionally fired as the field artillery of the Thousand. The fame of these five veterans, transformed by Southern imagination into twice as many ' rifled cannon ' carrying for ' four miles,' made the Sicilians take courage and the Neapolitan soldiers take thought, and had no small moral influence on the result of the campaign.

The 7th and 8th of May were busy days at Talamone. While the organisation of the main force destined for Sicily proceeded apace, sixty-one unfortunate men who had sailed with the rest from Quarto were formed into a separate company and sent, together with the Tuscan detachment

* This decision of July 5 was annulled on appeal on August 29 by the Supreme Military Tribunal, but this quashing was only a question of law and did not affect Giorgini's immunity from punishment.

from Leghorn, to invade the Papal States under Zambianchi. This expedition is called in Italian history ' The Diversion, because it was intended to attract the notice of the Neapoli- tan government away from Sicily to its northern border. But it was not intended merely as a diversion. It was part of the national policy of 1860, conceived by Mazzini in February, and carried out in the autumn by Garibaldi and Cavour, of placing the Neapolitan and Papal provinces ' between two fires,' kindled, the one in Sicily and the other in the Marches.

Zambianchi's expedition was not a mere diversion, be- cause it was meant to succeed. His men were armed by Garibaldi with good rifles, which would better have gone to replace some of the wretched muskets distributed among the Thousand. Zambianchi was to traverse the north of the Papal States eastward by way of Orvieto and Perugia into the Marches. Garibaldi had made inquiries about the Liberal Committees of those districts and believed that they would rise at the signal of Zambianchi's approach. The insurrection was then to be aided by Bertani and Medici, whom Garibaldi had left at Genoa, with orders to organise reinforcements alike for Sicily and for the Papal States. Zambianchi's orders were to place himself under the com- mand of Medici, if Medici came to his help. From the Marches he was to penetrate southwards into the Neapolitan kingdom. Rome was for the present to be left alone, though Garibaldi hoped to enter the capital of Italy at the end of the year, when he himself returned north by way of Naples.

The fate of this worse than foolish expedition under Zambianchi can be briefly told. He marched up country to Scansano and Pitigliano, where he waited several days. On the night of May 18–19 he invaded Papal territory and pro- ceeded a few miles towards Orvieto as far as Grotte di Castro, where he made his first halt. The men were taking their midday *siesta* in the houses of the town when the Papal gendarmes galloped past the sentinels into the market place.

A skirmish followed in the streets, and the Garibaldini repelled the attack. But they were now thoroughly disheartened, they distrusted and disliked their leader, who had shown neither sense nor valour in the fight, and they scarcely numbered 230 all told. Fearing the approach of the Papal army, they waited in Grotte till the evening, and retired by night across the frontier. Next day they were disarmed by the Italian government. They were not, however, placed under arrest, and were able to go out in the later expeditions to Sicily and share Garibaldi's victories at Milazzo and Volturno.

Only their leader, Zambianchi, was kept in prison until February 1861, and then banished to America; he died upon the voyage. He was a man of immense physical size and strength, probably a sincere patriot, but a bully, a ruffian, and if not a coward at least an incompetent blunderer. Garibaldi never in his life made a worse mistake, in every sense, than when he sent this man, whom he knew to have shot priests in Rome in 1849,* to invade the Papal States at the head of a totally inadequate number of Garibaldini who despised his military incapacity and want of initiative, and strongly resented being placed under the orders of a murderer. Luckily the whole scheme was so absurdly inadequate that it did not by partial success bring scandal and embarrassment on Italy and jeopardise the support which Cavour was able to give Garibaldi himself.

Meanwhile the organisation of the more fortunate Thousand who were destined for Sicily proceeded during May 7 and 8 by the seashore in and near Talamone. Their exact number was 1089. Thirty-three were afterwards officially classified as non-Italians, but this small foreign element comprised fourteen Italians of the Trentino, and Giuseppe Garibaldi of French Nice; the 'American' in the same list was his son Menotti, born of Anita on the Pampas in the war of the wilderness. Four, including Türr, were

* *Trevelyan's Gar. Rome,* chap. viii.

Hungarians. The greater part of the Thousand came from the cities of North Italy. Bergamo headed the list with 160, Genoa sent 156, including the Carabineers, Milan 72, Brescia 59, and 58 Pavesi followed Benedetto Cairoli. Among the exiles Austrian Venetia was well represented. Forty-six Neapolitans of the mainland, and about as many Sicilians, sailed to free their homes. Seven, including Lady Russell's friend Braico, were revered as being among the ' Neapolitan prisoners ' who had suffered for ten years in Procida or Montefusco. It was noticed that they spoke but seldom, and then with gentle utterance, seeming to desire victory not for the sake of vengeance, but in order to open the prison doors to the many thousands of innocent people who were still enduring the agonies that had darkened their own lives.

A large proportion of the Thousand were students from the Universities, not yet engaged in earning their livelihood. But those who have classified the Thousand according to professions which they followed in 1860 or embraced in later years, roughly estimate the result at 150 lawyers, 100 doctors (who used to fight until the battle was over and then tend the wounded), 100 merchants, 50 engineers, 20 chemists, 30 ship-captains, 10 painters or sculptors, 3 ex-priests, one lady (Crispi's wife), besides gentlemen of private means, government employees, authors, professors, journalists, and many small tradesmen such as barbers and cobblers. But perhaps half the whole number were workmen of the towns. There was hardly a single peasant. The average age was very young, but there were a fair number of veterans, and practically all the officers and the majority of the rank and file had fought in the Alps the year before, or in one of the earlier campaigns of Italian Liberation.

Such were the men whom Garibaldi now divided into eight companies of infantry, the staff, the artillery, twenty-three scouts (*guide*), who had to dispense with horses, and the Genoese Carabineers. Each of the eight companies had its captain named by Garibaldi, and each captain chose his own lieutenants and non-commissioned officers, subject to the General's approval. The territorial principle was largely observed in forming the companies and choosing the officers. The eighth company was entirely from Bergamo. The seventh, or ' students',' company, under Benedetto Cairoli, contained as many as fifty-two Lombard students, chiefly from his own University of Pavia, besides twelve merchants, thirty proprietors and civil servants, and thirty-six artisans and workmen, all men of intelligence and education, deeply devoted to the Cairoli family which had a wide influence in that part of Lombardy. The first four companies formed the first battalion under Bixio, the last four the second battalion under Carini, an able and daring Sicilian officer.

Thus rapidly organised, the little army was drilled on the sea-shore, and Garibaldi held his first review. On the night of May 7 they slept round their camp fires. But on the evening of the 8th, the second day ashore, an incident occurred, unimportant in itself, but highly significant of the difficulties overcome by Garibaldi in imposing the discipline of war and the authority of the officers on men who regarded themselves as free volunteers and in some sense the equals of everyone except their General. Some of the Thousand behaved rudely to the inhabitants, as they never did after they reached Sicily. When their officers interfered they refused to obey. These officers, of whom Nino Bixio could certainly not have been one, were unwilling to draw swords on their men in the streets of Talamone, and sent Bandi on board the *Piemonte* to fetch the General. When he heard what had happened, ' he glared at me,' says Bandi, ' with the eyes of a wild boar.' He went ashore and in speechless fury ordered the whole army aboard. The mutineers withered up at the sight of his anger, which was in fact the main safeguard of discipline throughout the expedition.

That night no one dared to approach his cabin, for his wrath was prolonged by the continued absence of his commissary Bovi, who had been sent to Grosseto to purchase food

for the voyage. Garibaldi chafed at the delay, for everything else was ready for their departure, and he knew that
the Neapolitan cruisers must every hour be strengthening
their watch against him round the coasts of Sicily. He
retired to rest, leaving orders that when Bovi appeared
he was to be thrown overboard. Just before daybreak he
arrived with the provisions. Garibaldi came out of his
cabin, while all held their breath to see in what temper he
had woken up. When he saw the culprit, he puffed at his
cigar and said, ' Good-morning, Bovi ; you made me very
angry last night.'   All breathed again, and the faithful Bovi,
who was in fact an excellent commissary, wiped his eyes
with his one remaining hand (for he had lost its fellow in
the defence of Rome), and explained the difficulties which
had caused the delay. The General heard him out, and
dismissed him with ' *Eh, va bene.*' If Garibaldi had not
been feared as well as loved, he could not have extracted,
as he always did, the utmost service that each man could
render to the cause.

The provisions were now on board, and between three
and four o'clock on the morning of May 9 the *Piemonte* and
Lombardo hauled up their anchors, while the inhabitants of
Talamone, who bore no ill-will for the incident of the previous night, cheered them and wished them luck as they
departed. They sailed across the gulf to Porto S. Stefano, at
the foot of Monte Argentario. There they landed again for a
few hours, to enable the steamers to coal. A deputation
was sent to the government coal store, with orders to
negotiate politely ; but as Nino Bixio was in the party, the
parleying was soon cut short, and the official in charge was
seized and shaken until he gave up the keys of the shed.
The steamers were next invaded by a large body of Bersaglieri who had deserted from the garrison of Orbetello, in
order to take part in the expedition. Garibaldi, though he
felt sorry for the *poveri ragazzi*, fulfilled his pledge to the
King and had them all hunted off the ship, except three or
four stowaways who succeeded in escaping the chase.

During the morning, the old muskets supplied by La Farina were distributed among the eight companies, and called forth general amazement at their extreme badness. It was difficult even to fix the ill-fitting bayonets securely on the muzzles.

Early in the afternoon of May 9 the two vessels finally stood out to sea and steered a course for the north-west corner of Sicily, avoiding the ordinary routes. The men had now been divided afresh between the two ships, in a more orderly manner than had been possible at Quarto. On the *Piemonte*, besides Garibaldi and the staff, sailed most of the artillery and the seventh and eighth companies from Pavia and Bergamo. The first six companies and the Genoese Carabineers, amounting to 650 or 700 men, were in the more capacious *Lombardo* under Nino Bixio. This Hotspur soon established his authority according to his usual methods. At a reply from a corporal which he considered impertinent, he threw a plate at the man's face, and summoning everyone on deck, addressed them with a ferocity of intention that subdued and even captivated his audience.

I command here. I am everything. I am Czar, Sultan, Pope. I am Nino Bixio. I must be obeyed like God. If you dare to shrug your shoulders, or to think of mutinying, I will come in my uniform, sabre in hand, and cut you to pieces.'

Everyone knew that he would be as good as his word, and liked him none the less. Loud cheers greeted this extraordinary speech. When the applause had died down, the Sicilian La Masa jumped up and began delivering a florid oration in praise of Bixio, in the style in which he so often charmed the crowd at the street corners of Palermo. But the northerners paid him scant attention, and Bixio strode angrily away, conceiving for La Masa a bitter contempt which grew steadily throughout the campaign.

Next to Garibaldi, Bixio was the chief cause of the success of the expedition. He well earned his title of ' the second of the Thousand.' For the danger of that little army, strong in individual valour and self-sacrifice, was the lack of constraining authority, and this want was filled up, mainly indeed by the veneration and fear felt by all for Garibaldi, but partly also by a wholesome terror of Bixio's half-insane but sometimes well-directed violence.

Meanwhile, on the *Piemonte*, the able Sicilian, Giordano Orsini, whom the General had put in command of the artillery, set up a laboratory on deck, where all took their share in casting bullets and manufacturing cartridges. At dawn of May 10 no sail was in sight. Only a shoal of dolphins followed the ships, while the work on the ammunition and the singing of the songs of '48 beguiled the hours on the lonely by-paths of the sea.

Garibaldi, who had once more discarded the Piedmontese uniform, which he had assumed at Talamone, for the red shirt and *puncio*, was in a mood of unalloyed and radiant happiness. The coming struggle for liberty was to be fought out alone by him and his chosen band, in the mountains of a romantic island almost totally unknown to the world, under conditions making real for once that poetry of war and patriotism after which his whole life was one long aspiration. His aide-de-camp Bandi found him in his deck-chair, spectacles on nose to mark the hour of literary labour. The verses which he was composing sang of tyranny and of revolt, though not in such melodious numbers as Carducci has often found for the theme. He told Bandi that he wished his young men to set his words to music and sing them as they charged on the battle-fields of Sicily. Bandi returned on deck with the General's poem, and soon collected in a circle the literary and musical talent of the *Piemonte*. All were in high spirits, and not incapable of poking fun—even at him. The concert proceeded, with strange sounds, to uncouth tunes, amid suppressed laughter, until Garibaldi's head appeared out of the cabin. ' What music is that ? Have you composed it ? ' ' No, General ! Not I ! ' ' Eh, *diavolo* ! '—and the head was withdrawn.

CHAPTER XIII

THE LANDING OF THE THOUSAND AT MARSALA

'He either fears his fate too much,
Or his deserts are small,
That dares not put it to the touch,
To gain or lose it all.'

MONTROSE.

WHILE Garibaldi was still at sea the diplomatic storm had broken over Cavour's head. Prussia, though she had held apart from the reactionary league formed against Piedmont during the winter, roundly declared that had she any vessels of her own in Italian waters she would herself stop the pirates. Russia held similar language, protesting that only her geographical position prevented her active interference. But Austria, the most formidable of the three, would promise no help to the government of Naples, though expressing the strongest sympathy. England for more than a fortnight gave no official sign, and Lord John's first communication on May 22 seemed chiefly concerned with the rumour that if Piedmont acquired Sicily or Naples, France would obtain Genoa or the island of Sardinia, as she had obtained Nice and Savoy, in return for her protection against Austria. When somewhat reassured on this point by a promise from Cavour, our Government allowed itself to take the same friendly interest in Garibaldi's chances of success as the British public had taken from the first announcement of his departure on so sporting an enterprise.

France was, in fact, the Power from which Cavour had most to fear. Throughout the revolution of 1860 Napoleon, with more than his usual uncertainty of purpose, was per-

petually vacillating between the desire to protect the
Neapolitan government against the movement for Italian
unity, and the desire to reform or overthrow it by some
Liberal revolution engineered in French interests. On
May 7, before any other Power had protested, his Ministers
sent a menacing expostulation to Turin, within a day
of Garibaldi's departure from Quarto. And they followed
up their protest by stopping the projected withdrawal of the
French troops from Rome. With revolution beginning in
the South, Napoleon could feel no certainty that Rome
would not be attacked before the year was out, and when
he had proposed to withdraw his own garrison, he had by
no means intended to allow the Italians to occupy the
Papal city.

On May 7, Cavour telegraphed to the Governor of Cagliari
in Sardinia :—

> ' Garibaldi has embarked with 400 volunteers on two
> Rubattino steamers for Sicily.   If he enters a port of Sardinia
> arrest the expedition.   I authorise you to employ, if required,
> the squadron commanded by Count Persano.'

Next day he sent a further explanatory telegram :—

> ' Do not arrest the expedition out at sea.   Only if it enters
> a port.'

Cavour afterwards declared that he sent the orders to arrest
Garibaldi because he heard that the expedition was to be
diverted against the Papal States. But in his telegram of
May 7, he had mentioned Sicily as being Garibaldi's destination, and it therefore seems more probable that his real
purpose in sending the message was to save his own position
in face of the diplomatic world, by enabling him to declare
that he had given orders for the arrest. He had little cause
to fear that Garibaldi would be so foolish as to sail into a
port occupied by vessels of the royal navy, and none to
suppose that the Piedmontese admiral would be ' strict in his
arrest.' Persano, indeed, received on May 9, at Cagliari,

these strange orders to stop Garibaldi if he met him in ... ort of Sardinia, but not out at sea. Suspecting, partly no doubt from the conditional nature of the order, that the arrest was not really intended to take place at all, he wrote on the same day (May 9) from Sardinia to Turin to ask Cavour if the message was seriously meant. In a few days the answer came back by wire that ' the Ministry had decided ' for the arrest. The Admiral, choosing to assume that this meant that Cavour differed from the rest of the ' Ministry,' telegraphed back, ' *Ho capito*,' ' I understand.' It mattered little what he understood, for by that time Garibaldi had safely landed in Sicily.

Late on the evening of May 10, Cavour, having heard that Garibaldi had put into the Gulf of Talamone, and therefore supposing that he had diverted his attack from Sicily to the Papal States, gave orders that a war vessel should go to Porto S. Stefano and arrest the Thousand if they were still to be found on the Tuscan coast. But, as we have seen, they had left Porto S. Stefano for Sicily that very day. Once assured of this fact, the government thenceforth used every unofficial means to secure the success of the expedition. Its policy was sketched out in a correspondence between the two greatest Italian statesmen, the Tuscan and the Piedmontese. On May 15, Ricasoli wrote to Cavour that it would be wrong as well as dangerous to oppose obstacles to the enthusiasm of the country for Garibaldi's patriotic enterprise.

' By as much as the Royal government ought to impede any attack on the Papal States at this moment, by so much ought it to tolerate and even support and help the aid given by Italians to the Sicilian insurrection, if that can be done covertly and at least without compromising ourselves too much. We cannot sufficiently proclaim before Europe the duty that binds Italians to help their compatriots who are subject to the bad governments ' (*ai mali governi*).

On May 23, Cavour replied to Ricasoli,—

' I entirely agree with you about Garibaldi's expedition.

I have nothing to add, except that we must save appearances so as not to increase our diplomatic difficulties. France has shown less displeas re than I expected.'

Already the ditors of the Cavourian press had hailed the expedition of Garibaldi as the rallying point for all sections. He had, they declared, by sailing with the war-cry of ' Italia e Vittorio Emanuele,' united the country, and put an end to party strife.

On the night of May 10–11 the Lombardo and Piemonte,* wholly cut off from the world which the news of their voyage had stirred to such conflicting passions, were plying their way through the darkness of the northern Sicilian waters. The ships' lights were extinguished, and all were on watch for the enemy. Garibaldi had gone ahead in the more swift-sailing Piemonte, in the hope of catching sight before sundown of the island of Marettimo, the outermost of the Ægades, visible in clear weather at a distance of sixty miles. Darkness fell before he could achieve his purpose, and he was fain to put about and sail back to find the Lombardo, cursing his own folly for having lost sight of the ship that carried two-thirds of his fighting force. Bixio meanwhile, in the gravest anxiety at losing touch with the Piemonte, held on his course as fast as his bad engines would allow, growing more and more doubtful whether he should ever see Garibaldi again. Suddenly, about ten at night, he was aware of a vessel coming to meet him through the darkness. All attempt to exchange signals failed, and Bixio, desperately resolving that it was one of the enemy's cruisers, ordered Elia to steer the ship against the intruder, and all hands to prepare to board. As he lay stretched over the prow of the Lombardo, sweating with excitement in his eagerness to be the first on the enemy's deck, he heard a well-known voice hail him across the waters, ' Captain Bixio ! ' ' General ! ' ' Why do you want to send us to the bottom ? ' So ended an incident which caused as much misery to the actors as

* For their route to Marsala see Map VI. at end of book.

any of the dangers from the real enemy which they afterwards encountered on land.   For on board the *Piemonte*
also the midnight assailant had for some minutes been taken
for a Neapolitan cruiser.   Garibaldi had seen the lights of
the enemy's squadron around him—so at least, he believed,
but whether rightly or wrongly it is impossible to say—and
for that reason had not dared to show the arranged signals
for Bixio's benefit.

If the two steamers had lost each other that night, they
would probably never have met again, for it had been
impossible to decide on a *rendezvous* where the disembarkation should take place.   Palermo, guarded by some 20,000
regular troops, was the objective of the campaign, and its
capture would mean the instant acquisition of the western
half of Sicily, possibly of the whole island.   Garibaldi had at
one time thought of running ashore as near to the capital as
the Gulf of Castellamare, but had abandoned the plan as too
hazardous.   A landing-place was required within a few days'
march of Palermo, but not so dangerously near it as Castellamare.   It had therefore been decided to land somewhere
between Trapani and Sciacca—most probably at Porto Palo
or at Sciacca itself.   But the place and hour of disembarkation would of necessity be determined by the position and
movements on the next morning of the dozen Neapolitan
cruisers guarding the coast-line of Sicily against the expected invasion, of which no fewer than four, the *Valoroso*,
the *Stromboli*, the *Capri*, and the *Partenope*, were patrolling
the thirty miles run between Trapani and Mazzara.

At dawn on May 11 the first beams of the sun touched
Ætna's cap, and all the Sicilian headlands one by one,
until in the west the ray struck on the bare rocks of Monte
Pellegrino that overhangs Palermo city, even as when
Hamilcar the Carthaginian made his strange encampment
on its summit ; and, last of all, Eryx, the famed acropolis
of Astarte and of Aphrodite, that looks out over the islands
of the Ægades and the baths of ocean.

8

The two ships that bore the fate of Italy were still far out
to sea, but drawing nearer and nearer to those guarded
coasts. Before daylight many of the Thousand crowding
on deck to catch the first sight of Sicily, mistook for land a
transitory bank of clouds. But with the rising sun appeared
the summit of the island of Marettimo, towards which they
were steering, and ere long Sicily herself was disclosed before
their eyes.

They sailed parallel with the coast from Cape S. Vito,
keeping out from Trapani, where were shoals and a Bourbon
garrison. Running through the archipelago of the Ægades,
' almost grazing Marettimo,' they left Favignana on the
east.* In the prison there lay Nicotera and the other
surviving leaders of Pisacane's expedition.† Garibaldi and
his men knew this well, and gazed at the island, thinking
how soon either they themselves would be dead or these
their forerunners and comrades be released. Nicotera
himself, when he saw two vessels go by flying no flag, wondered what they could be. ' Nevertheless,' as he afterwards
told his deliverers when he met them next month in Palermo,
' I felt in my heart I know not what, and a strange gladness
came over me. Then, when later I heard the cannon
[from Marsala], I suddenly remembered Garibaldi, and
guessed the secret of those two mysterious steamers.'

Garibaldi's first plan had been, on emerging from among
the Ægades, to keep well out to sea, half way across to
Cape Bon in Africa, in order to avoid the cruisers along the
coast,‡ and later in the day, when he had rounded the
western face of Sicily, to make a dash for Porto Palo or
Sciacca. Various persons, including Castiglia, the excellent
seaman who was captain of the *Piemonte*, claim to have

* Elia, who commanded the *Lombardo* under Bixio, writes to me that
they steered for Marettimo, ' leaving on their *left* the island of Favignana.'
Marettimo they left on their *right*, as Türr told me, and as all authorities
imply.

† See chap. iv. above.

‡ He must already, when threading the Ægades, have narrowly missed
falling in with the *Valoroso*, which was cruising ' among the islands of
Trapani ' that day.

been his advisers in the change of plan by which he determined instead to run straight from Marettimo to Marsala.

The sight of two war vessels anchored off the port of
Marsala caused only a momentary hesitation, for Garibaldi,
after examining them through his telescope, pronounced
them from their build to be British. In this belief he was
confirmed some minutes later by some Englishmen on board
a sailing vessel northward bound from Marsala, who, as
they passed the *Piemonte*, replied to inquiries that there
were no Neapolitan vessels at the port. As they sailed on
past the *Lombardo*, Bixio, after trying in vain to throw
them dispatches wrapped in a piece of bread, shouted to
them to give the news in Genoa that Garibaldi had landed
at Marsala. They answered with a cheer, and their well-
built craft shot on over the water.

At full steam ahead Garibaldi made straight for port.
On the way, about noon, he fell in with a large Sicilian
fishing-boat, which he took in tow, as it would serve for
the work of disembarkation. The master, a man named
Strazzera, came on board shaking with fear, but when he
had tasted a glass of wine, and heard his own language
talked by fellow-Sicilians, he recovered enough courage to
give what news he had. He believed that a battalion of
Neapolitan infantry had recently left the town, and he was
certain that the Neapolitan war vessels had quitted the
port some hours before, on a cruise towards Sciacca. These
vessels, indeed, were still visible not many miles away to
the south-east of Marsala, and were already turning back
to overhaul the new-comers. If they could return and
open fire within two hours, they would yet be in time to
stop the disembarkation and slaughter Garibaldi and all
his men. It was a race for more than life and death.

The modern city of Marsala, of Arab name and founda-
tion, was the successor of the Phœnician and classical
Lilybæum. The port of the ancient city had been on the
north side of the town, and the shallow modern harbour on

the south side, with its long mole and lighthouse, was an entirely artificial creation, due to the enterprise of successive generations of English merchants, who had settled down at this remote and half-civilised spot, to doctor the country-made wines of Western Sicily into their excellent ' Marsala.' The city, still in 1860 four-square within its mediæval walls, stood a few hundred yards back from the sea. But for the activities of the English merchants it would have had little claim to be called a port town at all. Beyond its walls, along the side of the harbour wharfs and further to the south, stretched for a mile or more the imposing *baglii* of the English—Wood, Woodhouse and Ingham—and of the one native wine manufacturer, Florio. A *baglio* at Marsala was a large space of ground, protected fortress-wise by high unscalable walls, within which were ranged the sheds for the manufacture and the vaults for the storage of the wine, besides in some instances a courtyard in the middle, and a well-appointed country house, where the comfort and hospitality of an English home stood entrenched in a foreign land. The imposing line of these mercantile fortresses, each flying the British flag in a time of danger and disturbance, was more prominently in view than the city itself to persons approaching Marsala from the sea.

When the news of Riso's revolt at the Gancia Convent in Palermo reached Marsala on April 6, a Liberal demonstration took place, the tricolour was carried through the streets and the Bourbon arms pulled down. But the news of Riso's complete discomfiture quickly succeeded, and a month of fearful expectation ensued, till on May 6 a column under the orders of General Letizia arrived in the town, imprisoned or drove away the leaders, and disarmed the inhabitants, including the British colony. But on May 9–10 the government, with incredible folly, transported Letizia's force from Marsala back to Palermo, in spite of the fact that they knew Garibaldi to have sailed, and expected him to land on exactly that part of the coast to the north of Mazzara. Indeed, on May 6, General Landi with

another force was sent from Palermo by land into the same
district to await Garibaldi, at the very time that Letizia
was being withdrawn thence to Palermo by sea.   Landi,
on May 11, had scarcely marched as far as Alcamo, so that
Garibaldi came to Marsala at a moment when there was no
force nearer than the garrison of Trapani.   This was the
first of the series of fatal military mistakes by which the
Governor Castelcicala and his successors succeeded in losing
the island to an armament ludicrously inferior to their
own.

The British colony in the *baglii* of Marsala, alarmed at
finding themselves deprived of their arms by a government
politically hostile, amid a population socially untrustworthy,
appealed for the protection of their own country.   For this
reason, and not, as was afterwards averred, out of collusion
with Garibaldi, H.M.S. *Argus* and *Intrepid* were detached
from the squadron at Palermo at nightfall on May 10, and
arrived at Marsala at ten on the following morning, about
three hours in advance of the *Piemonte* and *Lombardo*.*
The Englishmen found no other warships at Marsala, for
two or three vessels of the Neapolitan squadron had started
on their cruise towards the south so short a time before that
they were still visible in the offing at five or six miles'
distance.

The British officers anchored their ships well outside the
port, the *Argus* two or three miles out, and the *Intrepid*
nearer inshore, but still ' three-quarters of a mile to a mile
from the lighthouse at the end of the mole.'   From these
exterior positions they did not move during the exciting
events that followed, and consequently offered not the
slightest physical impediment to any operations which the
Neapolitans wished or could have wished to carry out.†

* The *Argus* is described as a steam-paddle sloop, six guns, and the
Intrepid as a gunboat.   The English warships at this period were wooden
ships of the old build with both steam and masts.

† Italian maps of the affair incorrectly represent the British ships as
nearer inshore.   But the separate evidence of the two British captains is
explicit and unimpeachable.

So little was Garibaldi or any other thunderbolt expected out of the blue of that calm and dreamy May noontide that the two commanding officers were on shore, being shown over the *baglii* by their fellow-countrymen, and hearing their complaints about the disarmament, when the party was called out from the wine stores to watch two strange steamers from the north-west running fast for port. Captain Marryat, of the *Intrepid*, noticed that the leading steamer, the smaller of the two, had a boat in tow. There appeared to be armed men on board the vessels, and as they approached they were seen to hoist the Piedmontese colours, the tricolour of Italy, but with the cross of the House of Savoy in the middle—not Mazzini's ' neutral banner.'

The sailors on board the *Argus*, who had a close view of the *Piemonte* as she passed under their stern, saw on board her, men in red blouses, ' which gave them somewhat the appearance of English soldiers.' The sympathetic Britons, alike on the ships and on the shore, now clearly perceived that it ' was a case of *Viva Italia*,' and an officer in a red blouse with a feather in his cap, standing on the bridge of the *Piemonte* beside the captain, was voted by some of those on board the *Argus* to be Garibaldi himself. The mouth of a cannon was noticed projecting from the bulwarks. The larger vessel that followed was seen to be ' literally crammed with men like herrings in a cask ; some in red, some in dark green like riflemen, but by far the greater part in plain citizens' attire.' They made straight for the port, the *Piemonte* anchoring safely inside the mole among a number of small English merchant vessels, but Bixio's *Lombardo*, of deeper draught, grounding on the shallows at the mouth of the harbour, within a hundred yards of the lighthouse.

It was now about 1.30 or 2 o'clock. The Neapolitan vessels had perceived their prey and were coming back in the utmost haste from the south. The sloop steamer *Stromboli*, after towing the sailing frigate *Partenope* some little distance, left her to follow, and made all speed for the scene of action. With destruction thus drawing near them

apace the Thousand began to disembark, making for a
point near the end of the mole.

Garibaldi sent Türr ashore first with a small body of men
to occupy Marsala. Their welcome was friendly but timid,
for the leading citizens had fled from the town during its
recent occupation by Letizia's punitive column, and the
remainder were frightened by the memory of that event and
by the approach of the Neapolitan war vessels. In the
centre of the town some junior officers of the *Argus* and
Intrepid were surprised as they sat eating ices in a café by
the appearance in the doorway of armed men in strange
uniforms ; shortly afterwards, in obedience to orders sent
them by their captains, the young men hastened back to
their ships. The invaders made haste to seize the telegraph
office, where they found a form filled in with a message
evidently just dispatched to Trapani, announcing the
arrival of two Piedmontese steamers with armed men on
board. From Trapani the news could be wired to Palermo.
The new-comers at once sent another message : ' My mistake ;
they are two of our own vessels.' Tradition has it that the
official at Trapani replied ' idiot ! ' (*imbecille !*), but in any
case the authorities at Palermo were not deceived, and while
the disembarkation was only beginning, had wired to Naples
to announce Garibaldi's arrival, and to ask that troops
should at once be dispatched from Naples to Marsala.

Meanwhile the main body of Garibaldini was disembark-
ing. The ships' boats and the fishing smack which they
had towed into port would not have sufficed for a rapid
landing, especially as the *Lombardo* had struck outside the
harbour. But the sailors of Marsala, induced by political
sympathy, by promises of high pay, and in some cases by
revolvers held at their heads, brought out swarms of small
boats to the rescue. The rapidity with which the disembarkation was effected roused the professional admiration
of many experienced English spectators.*

* ' Nothing could excel the able way in which the landing was effected.'
—Letter of English eye-witness in the *Times*, May 29, 1860. See also

When at length the *Stromboli* steamed up within shot, the *Piemonte* had discharged all its living cargo on the mole, but the *Lombardo* had still three-quarters of its men on board, to say nothing of the cannon and ammunition. A fairer opportunity for making an end of the expedition on the spot could not have been desired by a zealous and capable officer. But Captain Acton, of the *Stromboli*, though his family was British Catholic in origin, had the traditions of Neapolitan service ingrained through several generations of connection, honourable enough indeed, with the history of the House of Bourbon. The responsibility of that hour was too much for him.

'It was in his power,' wrote Captain Marryat, who was watching from the shore through his telescope, ' to place his steamer(s ?) within 200 or 300 yards of the Sardinian aground [the *Lombardo*], and in such a position that every shot fired by him would have raked her from stem to stern while the deck was crowded with men, and one may feel convinced that all landing by boats would have ceased. . . . So impressed was I with the idea that the Commander of the Neapolitan steamer would open fire an hour before he did that I advised the removal of English [merchant] vessels out of the port.'

This proved impossible because of a head wind, so that the merchant vessels remained in port to take their chance.

No account by Acton of his own motives has ever been given to the world, but we may perhaps deduce from his actions that his principal motive for hesitation was the very natural though quite unfounded suspicion that the almost simultaneous arrival at Marsala of the British warships and the invading expedition was the result of a dark English conspiracy. The Neapolitan Government and all its employees were rightly convinced of the hostility of Great Britain, but erred in supposing her capable of every kind of outrage. Terror of the British warships cruising ostentatiously and in large numbers round the island was one of the chief causes of Neapolitan miscalculation and

Times, May 25, another such letter : ' The landing was effected in gallant style, and with most extraordinary celerity and order.'

panic throughout this year of disaster. Probably Acton was no wiser than the government he served, and feared that the moment he opened fire he would be blown out of the water. His suspicions were the keener when he observed among the invaders a number of soldiers in strange red uniforms, which he took for British. He therefore sent a boat's crew to hail the *Intrepid* and inquire whether there were any English troops ashore. He was told ' No,' but that the Commanders of the two English men-of-war were on shore, and a few other naval officers. Even then he did not begin to fire, but sent again to the *Intrepid* to ask how he could find Captain Marryat. Meanwhile that officer, together with his colleague Captain Winnington-Ingram, of the *Argus*, who had known and admired Garibaldi fourteen years ago at Monte Video, rowed out from the wine stores to the *Stromboli* and interviewed Acton on board his own ship. Speaking in fluent English, but appearing ' excessively nervous and agitated about the affair,' Acton told them

' that he was obliged to fire, to which not the slightest objection was made, and nothing more passed than a request from us that he would respect the English flag, whenever he saw it flying, which he faithfully promised to do. Whilst we were on board, he continued his firing, and even offered a kind of apology for the shot going so low ; but he said he did not wish to fire into the town, only on the armed men marching from the mole to the city gate. As we left the steamer,' adds Captain Marryat, ' the frigate [*Partenope*, 50–60 guns] arrived under sail, and fired a useless broadside.'

The steamer *Capri* also appeared on the scene.

Garibaldi in his memoirs sums up the situation well. There was, he writes, no truth in the rumour that the British helped the disembarkation ' directly.' But, he adds, the presence of their ships ' influenced ' the Neapolitan commander in delaying the bombardment, and so

' the noble flag of England once more on this occasion helped to prevent bloodshed, and I, the Benjamin of these lords of the ocean, for the hundredth time received their protection.'

8 *a*

The bombardment, witnessed by the British captains from the deck of the Neapolitan steamer, was as badly aimed as it had been tardily begun. Having lost the opportunity of raking and sinking the *Lombardo* when the men were still on board, the three Neapolitan vessels, if they could have shot straight, had still the chance of inflicting terrible damage on the Thousand as they marched in column along the whole length of the mole,* and thence to the city gate. 'The patriots stood fire splendidly,' wrote Captain Ingram, ' and appeared to be altogether a fine body of men. But we only saw one man knocked over.' For the most part the missiles fell short in the open sea, but one or two passed overhead into the *baglio* Woodhouse, and nearly killed the English manager's wife. Garibaldi on the mole was in high good humour, chaffing those who showed any signs of nervousness. He himself remained one of the last outside the sea-gate of Marsala now called after his name ; as he stood beside it with Türr and young Giorgio Manin (the son of a famous father), a shell burst at their feet, covering the whole party with dust. When all were within the city gate, there was nothing more to fear. The total loss of the invaders had been one dog wounded in the leg and one man in the shoulder.

By 4.30 everyone was safe inside the town, except the Genoese Carabineers, whom Garibaldi stationed at the harbour to prevent the Neapolitans from landing. Nothing had been left on board the vessels. A quarter of an hour's excellent work had sufficed to land the five old cannon. The ammunition piled on the mole was all brought up to the town in carts and on mules, under a hot but ill-directed fire. Last of all, the sea-cocks of the two steamers were opened by Garibaldi's orders, in order to flood the ships and prevent them from being carried off by the enemy. The

---

* The landing took place at the end of the mole, not where the memorial stone has been erected. Now (1909) the mole has a high bulwark on its sea side, but then the bulwark was only a foot or so high, and no real protection. The mole was therefore rightly called ' *molo scoperto* ' by Castiglia.

Lombardo was thus rendered immovable, but the *Piemonte* was that evening salvaged and taken in tow by the Neapolitans. They clambered on her deck with cries of exultation and victory, vastly to the amusement of the Garibaldian and British onlookers, who had witnessed a previous attempt on their part to board her before she was quite empty ; on that occasion the boat's crew had thought better of it and ignominiously turned back half-way.

Safe within the walls of Marsala, Garibaldi summoned the *Decurionato*, as the municipal body was called. Its members, who showed considerable courage, readily obeyed his summons, and at the suggestion of Crispi, who from the moment of landing in his native island acted as the General's political secretary, they drew up and signed a document whereby they declared that the Bourbons had ceased to reign in Sicily, and called on Garibaldi to assume the Dictatorship in the name of Victor Emmanuel. ' I accepted the Dictatorship,' he writes, ' because I have always believed the way of safety lay there in times of crisis.'

A simpler demand made by Sirtori, the Chief of Staff, was less easily met. Before the expedition left Quarto the book-shops of Genoa had been ransacked in vain for a good map of Sicily—so little in those days was known of the island by North Italians. But it now appeared that Marsala was equally unable to supply the want, although the *Decurionato* produced a map of the lands of their *commune*, of which Sirtori at once set his officers to make three copies. The Marsalese, moreover, gave verbal descriptions of the geographical and physical position of Salemi, the nearest of the mountain towns. Relying perforce on such slight information, Garibaldi made his plan of campaign that night. He decided to march with all speed to Salemi, as the nearest defensible position, where he could defy a Bourbon attack from any direction, rest the Thousand, and gather round his flag the *squadre* of the upland districts, who could be trusted to show more martial zeal than the men of the coast towns. But he had no thought of waging for long a defensive or guerilla war in the hills. From Salemi it was his intention to march straight on Palermo.

Next after the intoxicating joy of having landed safely with all their warlike stores, the feeling that prevailed among the Thousand that night was disappointment at their first contact with the Sicilians. In the completeness of their ignorance, the Northerners had expected to find in the children of the ' land of the Vespers ' equal and like-minded comrades-in-arms. They found instead a race, whose language they could with difficulty understand, who were indeed politically friendly and not inhospitable (except for their habit of secluding the women of their families like Turks), but who seemed for the most part unwilling to fight, and were all quite unused to regular warfare. Garibaldi alone was contented and confident. ' Patience ! Patience ! ' he said next day to those who complained of the Sicilians, ' you will find that all will come right.' Indeed if he had felt the same irritation with his new allies as was felt by Bixio and most of the Thousand, he would not have won the confidence and adoration of the Sicilians in that extraordinary degree which proved one of the chief causes of his success. The quarrel of North and South was felt in the patriotic camp, to a greater or less extent, from the moment of the landing at Marsala, but it was not felt by Garibaldi, who remained the very personification of the idea of national unity, and succeeded, where a cleverer politician would have failed, in drawing North and South along together until the game was won.

His affectionate attitude towards the Sicilians was due to a mixture of shrewdness and simplicity, difficult to analyse, and highly characteristic of the man. The same may be said of his friendly attitude towards the Church in Sicily, resented in like manner by many of his Northern followers, and in like manner essential to the success of his enterprise. Even the first night in Marsala proved that in this strange island not only the priesthood but the great majority of the religious bodies were on the side of the revolution, though they pleaded the poverty of their convents as an excuse for supplying so few of their champions' wants. Garibaldi would allow no contribution to be forced from anyone except the reactionary and unpopular Jesuits, whom he soon afterwards expelled from Sicily. On this first night, the Jesuits of Marsala were obliged to disgorge their blankets, by throwing them unwillingly and gradually out of the window to the officer in the street below. But Sirtori, the serious and ascetic ex-priest, was sent round Marsala that night by Garibaldi to restrain the *mangiapreti* * among the Thousand from offering personal insult even to the Jesuits. Another member of his staff, devotedly attached to his person, Gusmaroli, an ex-priest of a different and coarser type, could not understand the point of a revolution in which the Church was spared. But the fear of the General lay heavy upon the wildest of his followers, and he continued to the end to receive the active support of priests, monks, Bishops, and friars. ' True they are enemies to modern ideas of progress,' he said to one of his followers next month, ' but above all they are enemies to the Bourbons.'

At dawn next morning, May 12, the little army started for Salemi.† Garibaldi, Bixio, and a few other officers were mounted on horses procured in Marsala, but some of the staff officers and some of the cavalry scouts had still to trudge on foot. It was a joyful scene outside the landward gate. The rising sun shone on Mount Eryx on the northern horizon, and on the sea where the baffled Neapolitan steamers were towing off the *Piemonte*, and on the crowd of Marsalese enthusiasts who had come to wish the Thousand God-speed. Out of a small body of the townspeople who actually enlisted, some ran off that same day with the firearms that had been lent them, while others remained to fight and bleed at Calatafimi. The British Consul, Mr. Cossins, rode some

* ' Priest-eaters.'
† Henceforward use Map III., Western Sicily, at end of book.

little distance at Garibaldi's side, and took charge of a bag of private letters to wives and families of the invaders, which he undertook to have delivered in the North.

All in the highest spirits, the Thousand moved off through the flat desert, or *sciara*, as it has been called since the days of the Arabs, that stretches for some miles behind Marsala. After that they entered on the green undulating sea of corn and bean-fields which, in alternation with uncultivated prairie, composes the interior of Sicily. Houses were scanty, for cultivators and shepherds dwelt in the distant and crowded hill-towns, and the Garibaldini with South American memories compared the scenery to that of the pampas. At rare intervals the large farm buildings of some *ex-feudo* afforded water from a well. The heat and thirst that day were terrible, and only Bixio, standing at the fountains revolver in hand, prevented the men from endangering their health, as it was supposed, by drinking too deep. At the farms of Chitarra and Butagana they made their midday halt and obtained wine and water. After that point the high-road ended abruptly, becoming a mere track very difficult for the carts that carried the yet unmounted cannon, which were brought along by the efforts of the sailors turned artillerists. Garibaldi marched a great part of the day on foot, talking cheerfully with the rank and file. At evening the Thousand, fairly exhausted with the heat, reached the *ex-feudo* and mediæval tower of Rampagallo, that stands in a solitary place amid low hills, a little aside from the rough path they were following. Garibaldi slept under a tent, and his army around him in the open. There was no wood with which to make camp fires, and in the middle of the night it came on to rain. The miseries of war had begun.

That evening at Rampagallo they were joined by the first of the genuine *squadre*—finely built farmers, horsed and carrying their guns across the saddle-bow. Some were led by Baron S. Anna, the territorial magnate of Alcamo, others by Don Alberto Mistretta of Salemi and Rampagallo. Garibaldi

soon won their hearts, and sent on La Masa the same evening
to Salemi to prepare the inhabitants for his entry next day.
La Masa, in his real element as a street orator and popular
leader in Sicily, whence he had been excluded for eleven
years, was actively assisted by the priests of Salemi in
rousing the popular ardour of the place. When next day
(May 13) the Thousand wound up the mountain track *
between sparse olive groves towards the high *piazza* outside the castle and gate of the old city, the bells of the
campanili rang out welcome, and the population came down
the hill with music to greet their deliverers, shouting for
Italy and Victor Emmanuel with a heartiness that removed
much of the impression of the timid reception at Marsala.

Safe on high-placed Salemi, whence the sea and the low
southern coast are viewed in panorama, Garibaldi had again
won the race against his tardy foemen. They should have
occupied the town before him, and so kept him down in the
lowlands. He had now opened up his connexion with the
centre of the island, roused the *squadre* of the Sicilian uplands and placed himself upon the road to Palermo. But
in order to open that road before him he had still a battle
to fight with General Landi, who on the same morning,
May 13, had marched from Alcamo to Calatafimi.

On the evening of that day the news of the landing at
Marsala reached official circles at Turin. An hour before
midnight on May 13 a stout gentleman in spectacles passed
down the Via Carlo Alberto to his own house, whistling to
himself in meditative glee and rubbing his hands together.
He turned in to his door and vanished, but not before a
passer-by had recognised Count Cavour.

* There is a road to-day, but in 1860 the artillery had to go miles
round to the south in order to get up the hill into Salemi at all.

CHAPTER XIV

THE BATTLE OF CALATAFIMI

'In the dark perils of war, in the high places of the field, hope shone in him like a pillar of fire, when it had gone out in all the others.'—CARLYLE's *Cromwell*, iii. 30.

THE news of the landing at Marsala passed like the wind over the uplands of Western Sicily, fanning the embers of the insurrection into sudden flame.   On the mountain ridges of Inserra that look down over Palermo, Rosolino Pilo roused his faithful remnant to fresh activity with the news that his rash promise of Garibaldi's coming was at length fulfilled.*   Far away in the interior of the island, near Roccamena, an Albanian band from Piana dei Greci, true to the old Balkan instincts, was wandering about, vainly exhorting the more timid Sicilian rustics to join them, and taking their firearms when they refused.   This forlorn hope learnt the great tidings on May 12 from a solitary horseman.   Instantly marching on Corleone, they were welcomed by the inhabitants, who had themselves gone mad over the news, and were forming *squadre* for the field.   On the 13th and 14th, at Salemi, Garibaldi himself was joined by about 1000 men, some from Alcamo, but most from Monte S. Giuliano, the village perched on Mount Eryx, out of reach of the garrison of Trapani.

The members of the *squadre* represented the hardiest type of rustic ; some wore their untanned sheep-skins, but the more well-to-do farmers' sons came mounted, and in velveteens, which with the low top-boots of the Sicilian countryman

* See p. 161 above.

made a picturesque costume. Most were armed with flint-
locks or blunderbusses. The age of the greater number
of them, according to a native writer who saw the whole
movement, was scarcely twenty, and they had therefore
been nicknamed the *picciotti*, or ' little fellows.' They
knew no drill and acknowledged no discipline, but came
on like a mob behind their ex-feudal chiefs, just so far as
they felt inclined to follow. But until the battle of Calatafimi showed their unfitness for warfare in the open field,
great things were expected of them alike by friend and
foe, and the rising of the Sicilian peasants had important
military consequences in the moral effect produced on the
Neapolitans, more particularly on their too impressionable
commanders.

Before Garibaldi sailed from Quarto, there were already
24,864 regular troops in Sicily,* of whom nearly four-fifths
guarded Palermo and its neighbourhood. Yet the aged
Governor Castelcicala, who had fought in the English army
at Waterloo, felt no security even within Palermo itself, after
he knew that Garibaldi was in the island. On receiving the
news of his landing on May 11, he had wired the same day
to Naples for more troops to be sent to Marsala by sea,
in order to co-operate with General Landi in placing the
invaders between two fires, as near as possible to the point
of their disembarkation. The plan was promptly accepted
by King Francis and his ministers, and on May 11–12 a
force under General Bonanno, three or four battalions
strong, left Neapolitan waters for Marsala, where they were
expected to land within twenty-four hours. But on May 14
they had not yet rounded Cape S. Vito, and as Garibaldi had
long before escaped into the hills of Salemi, it was thought
useless to send them further in pursuit of him. They were
landed instead at Palermo to join the immense force already
protecting the capital.

Meanwhile General Landi, himself no less belated than

* Throughout this book the numbers of the Neapolitans are taken
from Neapolitan official sources only.

Bonanno, with whom he was to have co-operated in catching the invaders near Marsala, was slowly and half-heartedly
moving away from his base at Palermo.   He was seventy
years of age, and followed his troops in a carriage.   In
six days they had marched thirty miles, as far as Alcamo,
where, on May 12, the aspect of their artillery, never seen
before in the upland towns, struck a damp into the hearts of
the patriots, who wondered whether even Garibaldi could
fight against such terrible machines.   That night they
marched to Calatafimi, a squalid town built on the slopes of
a hill, of which the conical summit was crowned by the ruins
of a Saracen castle.   In every epoch Calatafimi had been a
position of strategic importance, because it commanded the
junction of the high-roads from Trapani and Salemi, which
ran on through Alcamo to Palermo.   In 1860 they were
the only roads in that part of the island that could bear
wheeled traffic, so that if Garibaldi wished to advance
direct on the capital with his famous cannon, he must pass
that way.

Landi, when he reached Calatafimi on the morning of
the 13th, was in command of only one battalion besides
cavalry and artillery, but he was there strengthened by two
more battalions from Trapani, which had been sent thither
by sea from Palermo in order to join him.   The newcomers,
drawn from the 10th line and from the fine regiment of the
8th *Cacciatori*, under Major Sforza, raised Landi's force to
3000 regular infantry, with a full complement of cavalry and
guns.   He was aware that Garibaldi lay at Salemi, eight
miles to the south, but he was ignorant of his numbers, and
unable to obtain information owing to the hostility of the
population.   The disturbed state of the country-side daunted
him to an unnecessary degree.   Because the banditti were
out on the road behind him, and had broken the electric
telegraph and the semaphores communicating with the
capital, he was already anxious about his base and his
retreat on Palermo.   He remained inactive in Calatafimi
until the 15th, sending off nervous reports to Castelcicala,

who was scarcely less alarmed than he at the occupation of
the roads and telegraphs by the rebel bands.

On the morning of the 15th he heard that the enemy was
moving out of Salemi and advancing towards him along the
high-road by way of Vita. The choice of three rational
courses lay before him. Either he could assume the
offensive and meet them half-way ; or he could concentrate
his battalions under his own eye for the defence of Calatafimi ; or he could still retreat, inglorious but undefeated, on
the capital—and indeed he declares that he received orders
to do so that very morning from Castelcicala. But not having the sense to adopt any one of these plans, he remained in
the hill town under the shadow of the old Saracen castle,
while sending out portions of his force in different directions
' to impose morally on the enemy,' as he himself expressed
it, by ' marching about through the country-side.' With this
object, the battalion of the 8th *Cacciatori* under Major
Sforza occupied the high hill known as the Pianto dei
Romani whereon the battle monument stands to-day ; it
happened to be a good defensive position, though it had not
been selected for that reason.*

From the afternoon of the 13th till the morning of the
decisive 15th of May, Garibaldi had remained in Salemi.
There he rested his men, who were made welcome in the
monasteries and private houses ; he had gun carriages
hastily manufactured for his artillery ; he procured pikes or
muskets for those of the *squadre* who had come in unarmed ;
and he caused himself to be a second time proclaimed
Dictator of Sicily in the name of Victor Emmanuel, with
more pomp and publicity than had attended the hasty and
unnoticed proclamation by the Municipality of Marsala.
The ceremony of assuming the Dictatorship at the invitation

---

* I have kept in my narrative the romantic name of *Pianto dei Romani*
—' the wailing of the Romans '—because Garibaldi and his men were
struck with the name when they had won the battle, and believed the
legend of a Roman defeat there. But actually the name is a corrupt'
Italian version of the Sicilian *chianti di Rumani*—' the young vineyards of
the Romano family.'

of the Decurionato of Salemi was conducted in the buildings of the old municipio, and Garibaldi then showed himself at the balcony above the stone loggia, to the enthusiastic populace in the little square below. The men of Salemi completely lost their hearts to the wonderful stranger. But they were also prudently anxious to ascertain that the great King Vittorio was really supporting him, and shrewdly questioned him as to why he wore a red shirt instead of the royal uniform.

His first act after assuming the Dictatorship was to decree a conscription for all Sicily, which remained a dead letter. But the volunteer movement of *squadre* was spreading, enhanced by reports set about by Sicilians of the Thousand deliberately exaggerating the number of the invaders, and by the oratory of La Masa, and of Father Pantaleo, a friar of the neighbourhood who attached himself to the person of the Dictator at Salemi. Pantaleo was a simple and whole-hearted enthusiast, who proved utterly fearless in battle, and in spite of many subsequent opportunities to obtain wealth and position, lived and died true to his Franciscan vow of poverty. From Salemi onwards the General made him welcome to his board. ' Here,' he said, ' is our new Ugo Bassi,' and related again how his own life had been saved in '49 by the good priest Don Verità. He rebuked Gusmaroli and the more ill-conditioned members of his staff, who frowned to see a Churchman at their table, and like bad boys showed the newcomer gross incivility when their master's back was turned.

On the 14th the General, accompanied by Türr, his chief aide-de-camp, rode out and surveyed the ground in the direction of Calatafimi, whither scouting parties and spies were sent to watch the Neapolitans. Finding that Landi would not advance against Salemi, Garibaldi had to choose whether on the 15th he should himself attack the enemy, and cut open the direct road to the capital, or whether he should take the tracks leading eastward through S. Ninfa and Corleone, whence he could either move into the interior to

play a waiting game, or approach Palermo by a circuitous
route through the mountains. Sirtori had at length found
for him at the municipio a large map of Sicily, which he
studied intently on the evening of the 14th. It is probable
that he had from the first decided on the bolder course of
giving battle at once in order to win the prestige of victory,
the only magic by which he could possibly be saved. But
he always kept his own counsel on vital military issues, and
at nightfall on the 14th the inhabitants of Salemi still feared
that he would march off to the east and leave them to
Landi's vengeance. Even the General's aides-de-camp asked
themselves as they turned to sleep, ' Where are we going
to-morrow ? '

Shortly before three o'clock on May 15 Garibaldi awoke
and called to the aides-de-camp in the adjoining room.
Bandi went in to take his orders. ' Look out of the window,'
he said ; ' is it raining ? ' ' It has been,' said Bandi, ' but
now it is beautiful (*un gran bel sereno*).' ' A good omen ! '
said the General, and rose from bed.

When the young officers had made his cup of coffee, with
which he always fortified himself for the day, four of them
were dispatched on various errands, to waken Sirtori and
Türr, and bid them rouse the army and order the march.
Bandi alone remained with his chief. Garibaldi, who had
been walking up and down the room, suddenly broke into
song. The battered warrior of fifty-three, about to attack
an enemy of vastly superior numbers in a contest in which
defeat meant death, sang like a lover going to meet his
mistress, because he was about to have his heart's desire.
' When the affairs of the fatherland go well,' he explained to
Bandi, ' one must needs be happy.'

Next moment the bugle sounded the *réveillé* through the
sleeping town, with musical variations that held Garibaldi
listening spell-bound. ' I like that *réveillé* ! ' he said to
Bandi. ' It fills me with a kind of melancholy or gladness,
I don't know which. I remember I have heard it before,

the morning of the day we conquered at Como. Run and
fetch the bugler here.' The bugler, the only one in the
Thousand, was soon in his presence, and said that he had
learnt it in last year's campaign of the Alps, and that it
was indeed the *réveillé* of Como. ' Good,' said Garibaldi.
' Always sound that one. Do you understand ? Do not
forget.'

In an hour's time the little army had assembled at the
top of the town, on the broad platform in the hill-side which
forms a natural parade ground outside the gate, in full view
of the southern sea-board on which they were now to turn
their backs for good. It was a spirited scene. Besides the
armed *squadre*, the whole population of Salemi had come to
cheer them on their way. All now knew that they were
going to battle, and raising the song sung by ' the volunteers
of the Lombard Manara ' at the siege of Rome (presumably
Mameli's hymn), the Thousand began to wind down the
northern road into the bottom of the deep valley up which
they had to pass in order to reach Vita. This valley, like
many others that cleave the treeless Sicilian mountains,
is itself filled with stone pines and cypresses, fruit-trees and
leafy hedgerows, mingled with oriental aloe and cactus,
and is watered by a clear running stream beside its line of
poplars. In the bloom of the early Sicilian summer, the
vale, fresh from the last night's rain, and sung over by
the nightingale at dawn, lay ready to exhale its odours to
the rising sun. Nature seemed in tune with the hearts of
Garibaldi and his men. As the high-road began to mount
the head of the valley towards Vita, the scene changed
and became once more mountainous and treeless, though
the corn on the open hill-sides made their slopes show green
in May.

Rounding a hill the Thousand came suddenly into the
bare and characterless streets of Vita, a village perched on
the plateau or watershed dividing the streams that flow
south towards Salemi from the streams which flow north

towards Calatafimi. The column halted in Vita, and the men bought and stowed in their pockets, oranges, lemons and other food which served them well that hot afternoon. Garibaldi meanwhile rode on to explore the heights to the north-east.

Later in the morning the march was resumed. Proceeding along the road for nearly a mile beyond Vita, they reached the northern edge of the watershed, where the road dips down into another valley. At this point, leaving the artillery on the high-road, they turned off to the right up a rough foot-track that leads to the top of the north face of the Pietralunga, a high hill on the summit of which they found Garibaldi and his staff already seated. They were watching various bodies of Neapolitan troops 'marching about through the country-side' between themselves and Calatafimi, particularly the 8th *Cacciatori* under Major Sforza, who happened at that moment to be on the top of the Pianto dei Romani, the high hill opposite to the Pietralunga, from which it was divided by a short but deep valley.

Landi's troops, sent out by him that morning from Calatafimi to 'impose morally upon the enemy,' had succeeded admirably in imposing on the *squadre*. The Sicilians had withdrawn on to the hill-tops, some to the east of Pietralunga and others to the west of the high-road, and disposed themselves to watch the battle, like spectators in a Greek theatre. Only some 200 of the *squadre* followed S. Anna of Alcamo into the thick of the fight, in support of Garibaldi's right wing. The remainder, perhaps 800 all told, fired off guns in the air and shouted on the hill-tops in the middle distance. As Enrico Cairoli wrote to his mother: 'The Sicilian bands are not accustomed to our methods of fighting. They are brave behind defences, but have not the *sang-froid* to charge with the bayonet.'

Sforza and his battalion of 8th *Cacciatori* were justly counted among the picked troops of the Neapolitan army. They were no cowards, and seeing before them on the Pietralunga, instead of the Piedmontese uniforms they had feared to see, a number of men in plain clothes, not distinguishable at a distance from the *squadre*, and others in red shirts which they took to be the red uniform of convicts broken loose from the galleys, Sforza and his men took heart of grace, and fought that day without any of the foreboding of defeat felt on many subsequent occasions by their comrades engaged against Garibaldi. Sforza had no orders to engage, but only to ' march about the country-side ' ; being, however, an officer of a very different spirit from his dotard chief, who still lingered in Calatafimi, he determined on his own responsibility to sweep this riff-raff back to Salemi.

It was a little past noon, and the heat of the day was terrible. Garibaldi was still seated among some rocks of transparent talc which glitter on the summit of the Pietralunga, and near him waved the Italian banner. Close beneath him on the broad hill-side his homely Thousand were ranged in order of battle in their companies, and the skirmishing line of the Genoese Carabineers was half-way down to the valley. On the steeper hill-side of the Pianto dei Romani opposite, he saw the well-arrayed Neapolitans in their bright uniforms. Behind them, as a background to the battle, the mountains above Alcamo, Segesta and Castellamare by the northern sea reared their bare outlines on the horizon. No shot had yet been fired, and the two armies watched each other across the valley. When, at length, Sforza's trumpets sounded the advance, Garibaldi bade his bugler blow the *réveillé* of Como. The unexpected music rang through the noonday stillness like a summons to the soul of Italy.

The Neapolitans began to descend into the bottom of the valley to the banks of a small stream, the upper course of which lies through broken and rocky ground, the lower part through a pleasant grove of poplars. They fired as they struggled across the stream and began to ascend the lower slopes of the Pietralunga. The skirmishing line of the Genoese Carabineers at length opened fire with their rifles and laid several of the enemy low. Then, by a spontaneous impulse, before the moment intended by Garibaldi, the leading companies of the Thousand leapt to their feet and dashed down the smooth but rapid slopes of the Pietralunga. At the sight of the avalanche above them, the skirmishers of the 8th *Cacciatori* halted, wavered and fled back across the valley. But they rallied round their supports on the lower slopes of the Pianto dei Romani, and prepared to defend the hill, terrace by terrace and yard by yard. The Garibaldini, in their turn crossing the stream, began to charge up the heights in the face of a determined enemy. Throughout the heat of the early afternoon, for two hours or more, the battle raged, like a heath fire painfully ascending a hill under a gusty and wavering wind.

It may be well to analyse the military conditions of the storming of the Pianto dei Romani before narrating the dramatic incidents which finally decided its issue. Probably the defenders outnumbered the assailants of the hill in the proportion of five to three. With those of S. Anna's *squadre* who took part in the battle, the Garibaldini were about 1200 men. Before the end of the fight some 2000 Neapolitans were actively engaged in defending the hill, for although Landi himself remained in Calatafimi, he sent out supports to Sforza the moment the firing began, till fourteen out of his twenty companies were actually taking part in the battle. His fears of the *squadre* in the neighbourhood, and his nervousness about his line of retreat, induced him to keep the other six companies as a reserve in Calatafimi town.

Besides their superiority in numbers, the defenders had a yet more marked superiority in weapons. Every Neapolitan had an excellent rifle. The smooth-bore muskets of the Thousand were sighted for three hundred yards, they frequently missed fire altogether, and there was such a scarcity of ammunition that some had only ten rounds. Consequently, except by the Genoese Carabineers, picked marksmen armed with rifles, who kept up a telling fire in front of the battle from beginning to end, there was very little shooting done by the assailants, who were ordered by Garibaldi to reserve their fire and go in with the cold steel. Their slender stock of ammunition was not exhausted at the end of the day. The weapon was the bayonet, the sight of which coming up from below at a few yards' distance generally induced the Neapolitan riflemen to seek ground higher up the hill.

Two Neapolitan cannon were planted on the east end of the Pianto dei Romani, apparently on the hill-side below the summit, and did considerable execution. The antique artillery of the Thousand, under the able command of the Sicilian exile, Giordano Orsini, was left on the high-road at the top of the Vita plateau, to defend itself behind a hastily constructed barricade against the enemy's cavalry. Only after the latter had withdrawn could Orsini advance down the road, and, elevating his aim, fire a few shots with a high trajectory on to the top of the Pianto dei Romani, where they produced some moral effect at the last critical moment.

Both sides were well suited to their respective tasks ; the well-drilled Neapolitans to stand in close order and fire rifle volleys down the glacis of the hill-side ; and the Thousand, with the individual initiative and educated intelligence of the best kind of volunteer, to fight in open order, rushing uphill singly or in groups from one tiny bit of cover to the next.* The circumstance that rendered victory just possible for the attacking party was that, although the slope of the Pianto dei Romani was fatally steep, level and open, with nothing on the greater part of its smooth surface but corn, vines, beans and flax, the peasantry had made some terraces, at considerable distances one from another, and in lines neither definite nor continuous, cutting them out of the soil and rock, or else building them up with rough-hewn

---

* The principle of group rushes, subsequently used by the Prussian armies on a greater scale, is sometimes said to have been invented by Garibaldi, whose method it certainly was. But in fact it invents itself whenever a force of intelligent and severally reliable men has to fight under certain conditions.

stones. Each terrace, though only two or three feet high,
afforded a kind of shelter behind which the Garibaldini
could crouch and suck lemons and recover breath, while
they beckoned to comrades below to come up and form a
party for the next rush across the open. Along the terrace
walls grew stray olive and fig trees, bushes of aloe and
cactus, hedges of grey wormwood, with orange vetch and
multitudinous flowers and weeds adorning these break-
waters of the battle.

Sometimes a terrace was held successfully by the Neapolitans, and the assailants thrust down again. Once a
Garibaldian banner was captured in hand-to-hand conflict.
A Neapolitan sergeant of gigantic size, who soon afterwards
deserted and fought in the Italian ranks at Milazzo, headed
a charge downhill, killed Schiaffino of Camogli, the bearded
sea-captain who carried the banner, wounded Menotti
Garibaldi in the hand, and tearing the flag from its staff
carried it off in triumph.* If the Neapolitans had made
more frequent charges of this kind down the hill, they would
have got more benefit from the immense superiority of
their position.

A principal feature of this, as of all Garibaldi's battles,
was the degree to which his officers exposed themselves.
The General regarded courageous example as the most important of all rules in the leadership of volunteers. Bixio,
on a white horse, seemed to be everywhere at once along the
side of the steep ascent, leading on his battalion (1st to 4th
companies), which, after forming the reserve on the Pietralunga, became the left wing of the attack when the battle
was joined in earnest. One of the very few mounted officers
on the Italian side in this battle, he was able also to pay
flying visits to Garibaldi, to warn him in vain against exposing a life, the loss of which would mean instant disaster
to the hopes of Italy, and extermination for the Thousand.

* There is a dispute as to whether it was the principal banner of the
Thousand worked for Garibaldi in South America, or only a tricolour ex-
temporised for company leadership.

Garibaldi, wrapped in his *puncio*, had descended slowly from the Pietralunga on foot, carrying his sheathed sword over his shoulder. As he ascended the Pianto dei Romani he drew the sword and began to lead the foremost rushes. All that his staff could do was to attempt to form a living shield for him in front and flank wherever he walked. In the performance of this duty Elia, the sailor of Ancona, fell desperately wounded with a bullet in the mouth which would otherwise have hit the General, as Garibaldi gratefully acknowledged. At another moment it was Sirtori who saved him, when he was surrounded with the banner in his hand. 'It was the best moment of my life,' wrote the reserved and stoical Chief of Staff, after stating the fact in a letter to his brother.

The heat of the ascent was terrible, thirst raged. The enemy grew more numerous above, as fresh supports arrived and drew together in ever closer order as the concentric attack narrowed towards the top of the hill. On the other hand, the ranks of the foremost assailants grew thinner as they mounted ; already about a hundred had been hit, while many of the less heroic lingered in the valley or lower down the hill, fatigued, discouraged, and easily dropping behind out of a movement in open order on the broad mountainside. To experienced eyes the battle seemed lost. Bixio, the second bravest man in the Thousand, said to Garibaldi what others may have thought, but no one else could say to him : ' General, I fear we ought to retreat.' Garibaldi looked up as if a serpent had stung him. ' Here we make Italy or die,' he said. Phrases of so solemn an order were not often in Garibaldi's mouth, and this one was no flourish of rhetoric, but expressed the bare truth of the political and military situation. Garibaldi was a cunning old guerilla, who knew well how to retreat, dodge, and circumvent, but he perceived that on this day of all days in his life retreat would bring worse disaster on his cause and country than an honoured death upon the field. Retreat would be the certain prelude to destruction for all the

Thousand in an ignominious man-hunt, and would cut off the chance he still saw above him on the hill-top of a bare victory, the key to the rapid conquest of the whole island and of the mainland after. Once beaten, the Neapolitan troops would lose their *morale*. The *squadre* on the heights round, and with them, as it were, all Sicily and Italy, were waiting to take their cue from this skirmish. Onwards lay the only path to Palermo, to Naples, to Rome.

His spirit bore uphill the fainting battle. On the extreme right, where the ascent is less steep near the head of the valley, the 7th company under Benedetto Cairoli, aided by those *squadre* who had consented to follow S. Anna into the battle, pressed hard on the enemy's left wing. Young Enrico Cairoli, and three other students of Pavia, rushed in on the Neapolitan battery and captured one of the cannon.

At length Garibaldi found himself standing under cover of the last terrace below the summit of the Pianto. With him stood about 300 men, the largest group of those still left in the firing line, including Bixio, Türr, and the remnant of his staff, most of the surviving Carabineers, and the students of Pavia. A few yards overhead, on the top of a steep bank, the enemy's immensely superior forces were ranged in close order, firing down in regular volleys, but fortunately too high. They were so close that Garibaldi's companions could hear the Neapolitan officers ordering their men to aim lower. At one moment the charge was sounded above, and if the Neapolitans had come on with a rush, they must have swept the slender line of patriots down the hill by sheer force of gravity. But the charge was sounded in vain.

Here, under the partial cover of the last terrace, Garibaldi remained, for a quarter of an hour as it seemed to some present, resting his men before the final rush, and waiting for stragglers to come up. During this interval Bandi and many others fell beneath the volleys, and began to drag themselves down the hill again towards a hut in the valley

where the wounded collected as by instinct, with none
to care for them since the numerous doctors were fighting
in the front.

Under the bank near the hill-top the young men, many
of them the General's closest intimates, pressed round him :
' General,' they said, ' what are we to do ? ' ' *Italiani,
qui bisogna morire* ' (' Italians, here we must die '), he
answered, and went about among the groups encouraging
them for the last rush with words more stirring than any
sure promise of victory.

Meanwhile the Neapolitans above, though they could
not be induced to charge, were conducting the defence with
an angry ferocity of purpose. Some of them ran short of
ammunition, and plucking up stones and earth began to
hurl them down the bank. Garibaldi happened to be
leaning forward with his head bent towards the ground, when
he was hit on the back by a large stone. Canzio of Genoa,
his future son-in-law, who was standing next to him, used
afterwards to tell how he heard the thud of the stone,
and next moment saw Garibaldi spring to his full height,
his eyes kindling their strange lights, and heard him cry
out, ' Come on. They are throwing stones. Their ammunition is spent.' He dashed up the bank sword in hand
and his men after him against the serried ranks, who in
fact had not spent the whole of their ammunition. No
one ever pretended to remember what happened at the top
of the bank, but when the red madness of battle subsided
the victors became aware of the Neapolitans streaming in
flight across the plateau of the summit, and rushing head-
long down the other side of the hill into the valley that
divides the battle-field from Calatafimi. And there, on the
heights of the Pianto dei Romani, where the monument
stands to-day, the Italians, in an ecstasy of love and
veneration, pressed round their chief and father.

Utterly spent with thirst, heat and fatigue, the victors
lay panting on the hill-top, and as they cooled themselves
in the breeze of evening, watched the lines of fugitives

winding across the deep valley and up the hill to Calatafimi town. From one point in the ravine across which the Neapolitans fled, could be seen the lonely temple of Segesta, diminished to a toy by distance, but none the less majestic in the harmony of its perfect proportions. On the morrow many of the Thousand, tired as they were with battle, went three miles out of their way into the wilderness to admire this symbol of the wealth, art, and dignity of the men who once inhabited that poverty-stricken island.

The loss on the victorious side amounted to thirty killed and upwards of a hundred severely wounded—probably a larger loss than that of the enemy. Nearly fifty more had been slightly wounded, but most of these, including Sirtori and Menotti Garibaldi, continued at their posts. Of all the cities of Italy Genoa claimed the heaviest losses ; both Bixio and Canzio wrote that she had fifty-four wounded. The sufferers were carried first to miserable quarters in Vita, whence some were moved to Salemi, Calatafimi, and Alcamo, being taken from place to place in the small country carts, gay with mediæval carving and colour, that form a peculiar feature of Sicilian life. The wounded fared ill, for the Italian doctors, after doing all they could for a day, marched on in the ranks to take Palermo, and the Sicilians among whom the wounded were left had no great resources either of material or of skill.

Several dear comrades were lost to Garibaldi by the day of Calatafimi. Besides the good seaman Schiaffino, his friend and aide-de-camp Montanari was gone, a stern and somewhat impracticable Republican idealist of the old school, who in '49 had followed him from Rome to San Marino and thence to the sand-dunes north of Ravenna, where at Garibaldi's express command he had parted from Anita and himself. Struck at Calatafimi, Montanari died at Vita on June 6 after the amputation of his leg. The staff was also deprived for a time of the services of Bandi, Elia, and young Manin, though all three eventually recovered. Luigi Biffi, a boy of thirteen, whose

Alpine home Garibaldi had freed the year before, and who had come among the Thousand, lay dead on one of the terraces of the Pianto.

When darkness fell, the victors slept on the hard-won summit, and dreamed of home and of those who would hear of this day's work in the cities of Italy. And the stars shone down on them and on their leader, who wrapped his *puncio* round him and turned to sleep like a child.

But in Calatafimi there was terror and confusion that night. The defeated troops had fought bravely, but now they knew that it was indeed Garibaldi and his men with whom they had to deal, and that there was only too much truth in the tales told of him in every Neapolitan barrack-room for eleven years past. Their demoralisation was completed by the belief, fostered by Major Sforza, that Landi had betrayed them in that he had never shown his face on the Pianto dei Romani, and absurd stories were soon afloat of his having been bribed by the invaders. The unhappy old man was bewildered by the events of the day which he had done so little to control. That evening he penned a dispatch to Castelcicala in Palermo, of which the first words, ' Help ! Prompt help ! ' indicated at least some intention of yet making good the formidable position of Calatafimi hill and town against a foe still greatly inferior in force. The dispatch boasted that they had ' killed the great captain of the Italians,' whose name he seemed afraid to write down, and announced more truthfully that they had ' taken his flag.' The letter was waylaid on the road by the Sicilian bands and brought into the Garibaldian camp, where its odd account of a battle, which the author had not himself witnessed, caused mingled indignation and merriment.

But when night had fallen Landi abandoned all idea of further resistance, fearing as he tells us that his communications would be cut by the rising of the country-side, and alarmed by a certain shortage of food and ammunition. He

had also, as he declares, received previous orders to retreat
on Palermo, which he ought, if we judge by his own account,
to have obeyed that morning instead of allowing Sforza to
become entangled in a conflict with the enemy.   Now that
the battle was over he was unnerved by defeat, and unable
any longer to rely on the *morale* of his beaten soldiers.   For
all these reasons together he determined to retreat on the
capital.   At midnight the Neapolitans evacuated Calatafimi, and reached Alcamo at two in the morning of May 16.
Thence, after a few hours' rest, they made a forced march
on Partinico, where the inhabitants fell on them.   In
that last vendetta of the old blood-feud between Neapolitan soldiery and Sicilian people, the horrors perpetrated
on both sides left ghastly traces which a few days later
sickened the senses of Garibaldi and his Northerners,
when they marched by the charred remnants of houses
and of human bodies.   From Partinico Landi's men fled
on at evening by the mountain road through Montelepre, near which town the exhausted army was again
attacked by local *squadre*, and lost part of its baggage.   At
dawn of May 17 they dragged themselves into Palermo in
sorry plight, a living assurance to the delighted populace
that Garibaldi was indeed in the island, and no less formidable in fact than in legend.   Landi had traced back in a
little over twenty-four hours the thirty-five miles of road
that divided Calatafimi from the capital, which it had
taken him a whole week to traverse on the way out.

On May 16, from the town of Calatafimi, Garibaldi sent
a message to Rosolino Pilo, with whom his communications
were now opened up along the route of Landi's retreat.
He announced his victory, and bade Pilo kindle beacon
fires along the crests of the mountains surrounding the
Conca d'Oro, to be a sign to the inhabitants of Palermo to
lift up their eyes to the hills, where their friends were already
gathering in strength, and whence they would soon descend
to bay the enemy in his last lair.   A few days after the
battle, the authority of the Dictator was acknowledged in

9

almost all Western Sicily, save in the garrisoned capital and its Conca d'Oro, where men watching the hill-fires night by night were consumed with a silent fury of expectation.*

* In Trapani, too, there was a Neapolitan garrison, but its power did not extend as far as Monte S. Giuliano.

CHAPTER XV

IN THE MOUNTAINS ROUND PALERMO

' One had need to be a lion-fox and have luck on one's side.'—CARLYLE, *French Revolution*, III. bk. i. chap. iv.

EVEN before the battle of Calatafimi it had been determined at Court to withdraw the incompetent Castelcicala from the governorship of Sicily, and to send out in his stead a viceroy with plenary powers, distinguished by the lofty title of the King's *alter ego*, or ' other self.' Among the impressionable populations of the south, this new move might have done much to counteract the spell cast over them by Garibaldi's name, if it had been possible to find a man with sufficient prestige and ability to fill the part. There was only one such man in the kingdom. Filangieri was summoned from his retirement to a Council of State held at Naples on May 14, at which the ex-minister had the satisfaction of hearing his reactionary rivals join with their royal master in imploring him to forget the past and to go once more to save Sicily and the kingdom. But Filangieri would not go. He had advised reform and friendship with Piedmont, his advice had been rejected, and the consequences which he had prophesied had occurred. He refused to try to mend what his opponents had marred, pleaded age and ill-health, and was deaf to the King's repeated entreaties. But when Ischitella, and, it is said, Nunziante, had in turn declined to go, and the difficulty of finding an *alter ego* became pressing, Filangieri so far relented in his Achillean wrath as to advise the sending of a most incompetent Patroclus, Ferdinando Lanza.

General Lanza was a Sicilian, aged seventy-two, who had

served in his native island as Filangieri's Chief of Staff, and was best remembered as a source of innocent merriment to Palermo, where he had tumbled down with his horse on a rainy King's birthday, and soused his magnificent review uniform in some particularly ample puddles. It was an accident that might have happened to anyone, but it had seemed specially appropriate when it befell Lanza, and the announcement that he was now returning as the King's *alter ego* caused more amusement than alarm among the Sicilian rebels.

On May 16 he sailed to Palermo, in time to witness the entry next morning of Landi's beaten troops and the general panic that ensued on the news of Calatafimi. Thoroughly unnerved by a situation that was in fact serious enough, he began on May 17 to send home alarmist reports. ' The city,' he wrote, ' is in great ferment, and has a sinister appearance. . . . A rising seems imminent. All the villages round Palermo are in arms, and are only waiting for the arrival of the band of foreigners to break into the city.'

The *alter ego* wavered between two plans of campaign which had been discussed in high quarters at Naples. The first plan, which was to hold Palermo and send out strong columns to take the offensive against Garibaldi, was favoured by the King, by Nunziante, and by the majority of the Council. But Filangieri had put on paper a rival policy, namely, to leave a garrison in the Castellamare fortress, well victualled and in touch with the fleet ; evacuate the rest of the capital ; send the troops thus set free to join with the garrisons of Girgenti and Messina ; make a real occupation with these forces of the east and centre of the island ; proclaim Liberal reforms, and when time was ripe return upon Palermo as he himself had done in 1849.

Filangieri's plan appears to have been a misreading of the actual conditions of 1860 by the false analogy of 1848–49. If once the Neapolitans had left Palermo, Cavour would have seen that they never came back. The abandonment of the capital before the mere terror of Garibaldi's name would have meant a blow to their prestige in Sicily which only Filangieri himself could possibly have made good. And as he refused to execute his own plan, the proposal of it only served further to confuse and weaken the mind of his nominee Lanza, who, while actually concentrating his troops for a defence of Palermo, argued and wrote in favour of a retreat to Messina. No real confidence was placed by the King in his *alter ego*, even at the moment of his departure from Naples. His ' plenary ' powers were in practice as restricted as those of former governors of the island. Indeed, as early as May 18, General Nunziante was sent to Palermo to see that he assumed the offensive against Garibaldi, who was already drawing near the capital.

Popular Italian art usually represents the Thousand as a number of well-shaved and well-appointed young men in military gaiters, smart képis, and clean red shirts. Such, no doubt, was the impression produced at certain moments by some of the regiments of volunteers who joined Garibaldi later in the year, but the Thousand, when they marched on after a day's rest in Calatafimi town, presented an appearance more resembling that of a Boer commando towards the close of the South African war. After their scramble up the Pianto dei Romani, the plain clothes in which nine-tenths of them were dressed were falling off them in rags, their boots were dropping to pieces, many limped painfully along, and many had head or limb bandaged. Before they stormed Palermo at the end of the month, forced marches, sleepless nights, and exposure on the mountains to semi-tropical rains and sun had reduced them to veritable scarecrows.

But if their legs were weary, their hearts were light, not indeed with the assurance of victory, but with the sense that they were enviable above all Italians, that their unique campaign was poetry made real.* After Calatafimi they

---

* 'Cara Mammina, t'assicuro che questa spedizione è così poetica . . .' writes Enrico Cairoli. Such expressions are constant in letters and memoirs of the Thousand.

knew that they had at least avoided *fiasco*, and that even if they now died with Garibaldi they would be well remembered in the annals of the cause. While many, like Sirtori, had never bargained for more than a good death, some began to complain that they had been enticed by false reports as to the fighting power of the Sicilian rebels. Others shared the now confident hopes of the native population. But all alike, seeing that Garibaldi was among them and was well pleased with them after the battle, were happy in a situation characteristically summed up by Bixio, who said to his battalion, ' We shall soon be either in Palermo or in hell ' (*a Palermo od all' Inferno*).

On the sunny morning of May 17, Garibaldi and his men marched out of Calatafimi, crossed the valley of the Freddo, and ascended the high-road to the city of Alcamo, built on a ridge which overlooks the gulf of Castellamare. In the corn-fields outside the town, men and women fell on their knees as he passed. Their primitive minds could not fail to attach some idea of supernatural power to any greatly admired object, but with the help of Father Pantaleo the Dictator found a means of diverting this embarrassing idolatry from himself into its natural channels, without losing the help of popular superstition for his own and his country's cause. He consented to assume the part of crusader sanctified by religion, as the champion of the Sicilian clergy and people against the foreign tyrant. When the Thousand entered Alcamo, they were led to the principal church, where Father Pantaleo awaited them. The Dictator knelt while the friar blessed him, crucifix in hand.

Garibaldi, who was at this time of his life somewhere in process between deism and pantheism, had no belief in the supernatural, but his interpretation of nature was that of a mystic rather than of a materialist. Strongly anti-clerical, he was not by temperament anti-religious. He wished to see the world purified of priests, but he regarded Christ as the greatest of mankind, who had delivered his brothers from slavery. In North and Central Italy, where the Church

was predominantly anti-national, he would not participate
in ceremonies conducted by priests. But finding himself
suddenly transferred to an atmosphere where democracy
and patriotism were religious, and where the priest urged
the people forward on the path of political liberty, he was
at once impelled by instinct and drawn by policy to join
in the forms of popular emotion. The rest of the Thousand,
less simple than he in his equalitarian love of mankind,
did not share his feelings of fraternity with the Sicilians,
of whom for the most part they entertained a low opinion.
They were not therefore influenced as he was by the emotional atmosphere around them, and looked on with mingled
feelings at an ' outburst of mysticism ' which they recognised
as genuine on the part of their chief.

After the religious ceremony, the Dictator applied himself to political business. On the advice of Crispi, who was
now appointed Secretary of State, he instituted the office of
Governor with specified civil powers. There was ultimately
to be a Governor for each of the twenty-four districts of
the island, and for the present Baron S. Anna, who had
fought so well at Calatafimi, was nominated for his native
district of Alcamo, and Don Alberto Mistretta for the district of Mazzara, both of which were already dependent on
Garibaldi for the maintenance of public order. At the same
time he decreed the abolition for all Sicily of the *macino*,
or excise on ground corn, a concession demanded by the
peasants as the condition of their support, but destined
before long to prove embarrassing to the Dictator's finance,
since the *macino* supplied half the annual revenue.

On May 18 the Thousand made their first long day's
march since the battle. Leaving Alcamo, they followed the
high-road eastward across the uneven lowlands that decline
towards the gulf of Castellamare, cut by water-courses, and
covered with vines and corn. They hurried through the
broad, mile-long street of Partinico, to escape from the
unsavoury evidence of mutual carnage and cruelty which

marked the track of Landi's retreat through a hostile population.   Immediately outside the town they took the road to
the right, abandoned the plain and mounted to the hamlet
of Borgetto that hangs with its fruit gardens on the edge of
the first steep ascent.   There Bixio's battalion, composing
the rearguard, bivouacked amid the clamour of nightingales.
But the vanguard pushed on up the high-road, by the side of
a gorge of Alpine proportions on their left, until at nightfall
they reached the top of the pass of Renda.   There they
encamped on the water-shed dividing the streams that
irrigate the Conca d'Oro of Palermo from those that flow
westward to Partinico and the gulf of Castellamare.   The
desert spot where they lay down to sleep was called the
altipiano of Renda, a flat plain a few hundred yards long by
the side of the road, enclosed by knolls of grey rock.   Here
their headquarters were fixed during three days of almost
ceaseless rain, to which they were exposed without tents,
coats or other shelter, at a height of about 2000 feet above
the sea.*

On the morning of May 19, during a respite from the
downpour, the Thousand for the first time saw Palermo.   A
few hundred yards beyond their camping-ground at Renda,
the road, after passing between a group of grey-snouted
crags, suddenly comes to the edge of the mountains, and
there, as if startled by the sudden glory of the prospect disclosed, takes a rapid turn aside and then plunges steeply
down to Pioppo.   From this high vantage point, known as
Misero-cannone, the Thousand became aware of the theatre
of mountains, from Monte Grifone round to Monte Cuccio, on
the middle part of which they themselves stood ; while down
below, enclosed between these stately barriers and the sea,
was spread the *Conca d'Oro* itself, one vast grove of oranges,
lemons, olives, and cactus, the magnificent legacy to modern

* Henceforth use Map IV., end of book.   The *altipiano*, clearly distinguishable, is now under vines, but in 1860 was uncultivated, as I was
told by a local peasant who claimed to have lived there all his life, viz.
since 1850.

times of the Arab methods of irrigation. There, like a rich jewel set in the ' *shell of gold*,' lay Palermo on the edge of the azure sea ; and there in the harbour rode the warships of Naples and of various other nations, set to watch the issue of this wild adventure, for news of which all the world was waiting. In plain and city, that seemed asleep and dreaming in the peaceful distance, a disarmed population was chafing in frantic expectation of their arrival, and 21,000 soldiers with artillery, fortresses, and all the panoply of war, stood ready to guard the city from their assault. Who were they, a band of forlorn and hungry watchers on the mountain tops, that they should take a capital from a kingdom's army and fleet ?

To advance direct on Palermo and attack such a garrison in face would be certain destruction. Garibaldi's only chance was to make such skilful use of the screen of mountains as to be able to conceal the weakness of his force and to effect a rush into the city at some ill-guarded point. If once he and his Thousand could appear in the heart of the city, the population would rise and fight in the streets as in 1848, and so place the invaders on something a little nearer equality with the immense forces of the Neapolitan garrison.

The peaks, ridges, and long, deep valleys of the mountains, among which Garibaldi from May 19–26 gradually worked out this the supreme military problem of his life, resemble in size, shape, and general character the highest part of the English Lake District. It may give some notion of the character of the ground to imagine the hills between Helvellyn and Scafell with all their water-courses dried up, and instead of an universal and undying plenty of wet grass and moss and bracken spread between one precipice and the next, a sparse and short-lived crop of green herbs and bright-coloured flowers filling the interstices of the grey rocks after the asphodels of spring are withered, with here and there an underwood of aloe and cactus, and in valley bottoms a sudden wealth of olives and fruit-trees in some rocky Eden loud with nightingales.

The roads in this region were very few, and a small and mobile force, prepared to abandon its cannon and traverse the wildest recesses of the hills, with the aid of the inhabitants as guides, spies and transport agents, might, under a great leader, achieve some masterpiece of strategy. Calatafimi had been a soldier's battle, though the soldiers had fought with the spirit breathed into them by their general on the field itself ; but the entry into Palermo was rendered possible only by the genius of the man who was as cunning in war as he was brave in battle.

Half-way along the high-road between Renda and the capital, almost at the foot of the hills and close above the orange groves of the Conca d'Oro, lies Monreale, famous for its Norman cathedral encrusted with the most magnificent mosaics in Europe. It was so strongly occupied by an advance guard of the garrison of Palermo that to storm it would have cost the Thousand more than they could afford as the price of a mere outwork to the enemy's main position. Although Garibaldi was ready to dare anything, he was equally determined to waste nothing. If he spent his Thousand prematurely, he would be a beggar indeed. If, however, the few hundred *squadre* whom Rosolino Pilo was keeping together in the hills, could occupy precisely those heights at the foot of which Monreale lay, its garrison would then be forced to retreat. Garibaldi at Renda, and Pilo three miles north at Sagana were in close communication, and it was agreed between them that Pilo should advance from Sagana to support his outposts at the Monastery of S. Martino, a vast edifice buried in the heart of those wild valleys. Using S. Martino as his headquarters, Pilo was to occupy in force the heights to the south-east of the monastery, especially the hill of the Castellaccio, an old ruined castle visible from afar as it towers above Monreale. Garibaldi supported this movement by a reconnaissance along the high-road through

Pioppo, but the bulk of the Thousand remained on the heights near Renda until the result of Pilo's operation should be known.

The Neapolitans, however, did not wait to be attacked. A courageous Swiss officer, Colonel Von Mechel, with an energetic subordinate, the Neapolitan Major Bosco, had been sent by Lanza with 3000 men to strengthen the garrison of Monreale. On the morning of May 21 they took the offensive, pushed a column along the road against the skirmishers of the Thousand, and drove them back along the flanks of the mountains from Lenzitti through Pioppo village, back on to the heights of Misero-cannone and Renda. In this affair, in the Vallecorta, was killed Piediscalzi, the spirited leader of the Albanians of Piana dei Greci, many of whom were now fighting side by side with the Garibaldini.

Meanwhile two other columns were dispersing Pilo's bands in the mountains overhead. One column moved up the San Martino valley to occupy the monastery, while another from Monreale climbed the steep hills of Castellaccio and Giardinello, and before the *squadre* were aware that they were the attacked instead of the attackers, fired down upon them as they stood on the lower Neviera hill. Pilo, who had seated himself among some rocks to write a letter to Garibaldi asking for help, was shot dead with the pen in his hand, and his men fled over the mountains.

The brave Sicilian and Italian patriot, who thus died on the eve of the consummation of his life's work, would readily have acknowledged that, in his own and Mazzini's eyes, the real object of his mission to Sicily had already been accomplished when Garibaldi had landed at Marsala. Yet his defeat and death were at the moment a severe blow to the cause, and not only checked the advance but endangered the position of the Thousand. For the camp at Renda, high placed though it was, lay in a hollow of the mountain-tops, and now that the Neapolitans had disposed of Pilo's force, they might at any moment appear on the heights com-

manding Renda from the north-east. Garibaldi was therefore obliged, as the result of the fighting on May 21, to shift
his camp without delay.

Thus compelled to abandon the Partinico-Monreale road
by which he had first approached the capital, the General
determined to move across country, to the other great road
connecting Palermo with the interior, which runs to Corleone
through Parco and Piana dei Greci. He would there enter
upon a new sphere of operations in the mountains to the
south-east of the Conca d'Oro, which were already occupied
by *squadre* under La Masa more numerous than those that
had followed Pilo. Immediately after the battle of Calatafimi, the Dictator had wisely detached La Masa to travel
through the island and rouse the people to arms. Unlike
other Sicilians of the Thousand—such as Carini, Orsini,
and Calvino—La Masa had no marked military talent,
but he had influence as an orator and ability as an organiser,
and was well fitted to play the part of a Sicilian Danton.
With less than half a dozen comrades, he made a dangerous
cross-country journey from Calatafimi through districts
still infested by police and *compagni d'armi*, through Roccamena and the precipices and forests of Ficuzza, till he
reached the more open country of Mezzojuso and Villafrate.
In that region and along the coast from Termini to Bagheria,
he was known and trusted as a local man and a leader of
1848. His appearance among his own people dispersed
their fears and uncertainties, and he was able to dissipate
a strange rumour that Garibaldi had not really landed at
Marsala at all, but was being personated by a Pole. In
a few days he formed a camp of some 3000 *squadre* at
Misilmeri and Gibilrossa, and extended his outposts and
lit signals fires at night on the top of Monte Grifone. He
was much indebted to the patriotism of the citizens of
Termini, who, in spite of the Neapolitan garrison holding
the fort and bombarding their town, supplied his camp at
Gibilrossa with men, food and such arms and ammunition
as they could provide. Garibaldi's desire to get into touch

with La Masa's *squadre* was one of his principal objects in moving from Renda to Parco.

This difficult operation, to be effected in the face of the enemy occupying Pioppo and Monreale, was carried out with secrecy and success on the night of May 21–22. It was necessary to march round the head waters of the Oreto across the stony and desolate moor in which it rises, some miles above the groves of the Conca d'Oro. Starting along the road that leads back from Misero-cannone towards San Giuseppe Jato, the Thousand turned off it after two and a half miles, at a solitary and deserted toll-bar house (*Catena*), and began to cross the moor, at a height of some 2400 feet, by a bridle track so marshy in some places and so rocky in others as to be difficult walking even on a fine day, and almost impassable on that dark and windy night when torrents of rain seemed to carry the ground from under their feet. ' Not a soldier but fell,' wrote one who made the march. ' I fell thrice, many others ten or a dozen times.' Thus they stumbled and rolled in single file along a path of much the same general character as the passage of the Esk Hause in Cumberland, from the top of the Sty Head to the top of the Rossett Gill Pass. Close above them to the right, unseen in the darkness, were the precipices of Carpaneto and Moarda. But the local guides were faithful and competent, walking with Garibaldi in front to feel out the invisible way, and on the early morning of May 22 the Thousand, soaked, bruised and utterly exhausted, many of them without shoes on their feet, staggered down into Parco, where they were made heartily welcome to all the food and fire that the inhabitants could supply. The cannon, left near the toll-bar house during the hours of darkness, were dismounted, and next day slung on poles and carried by Sicilian mountaineers along the same path which the infantry had traversed during the night. By this difficult march Garibaldi had given the slip to Von Mechel at Monreale and gained a full two days' respite.

The small town of Parco lies at the foot of the mountains,

on the very edge of the Conca d'Oro. Straight above its roofs the Cozzo di Crasto rises to a height of about 2000 feet above the sea, and presents a natural fortress of immense strength against an enemy approaching from Palermo. On its rocky summit, attainable by means of the winding high-road that leads towards Piana and Corleone, Garibaldi fixed his camp, dug trenches, and planted his ancient artillery. He wrote to La Masa on May 22 that he ' liked the position well, and would defend it, and then take the offensive '—no doubt against the capital itself. On the evening of the same day he sent orders to La Masa, which he repeated on May 23, bidding him descend from Gibilrossa into the plain and attack the Neapolitans in flank and rear as soon as they developed their expected attack on the Cozzo di Crasto.

The plan was not ill-conceived. An action, beginning in the defence of the formidable position above Parco, aided by La Masa's flank attack on the Neapolitans, might well develop into a counter-attack which should lead the victors into Palermo at the heels of the defeated enemy. But the position which it was proposed to defend in the first instance had a weak point. The Cozzo di Crasto, high as it stood and steep as were its slopes towards Palermo, was only a spur projecting from the still higher range of Moarda and Rebottone. Early on May 24 Garibaldi became aware that part of Von Mechel's four battalions were moving from Monreale across the head waters of the Oreto, clearly intent on occupying the Rebottone mountains above and behind the Cozzo di Crasto, while the remainder of the forces occupying Monreale, joined by two fresh battalions from Palermo under General Colonna, were to make a frontal attack by way of Parco. To save himself from being at once outnumbered, surrounded and overlooked, Garibaldi ordered the Thousand to retreat on Piana dei Greci. La Masa's *squadre*, who had meanwhile begun to descend into the Conca d'Oro by way of Belmonte-Mezzagno to attack Colonna's flank, fled back into the hills in panic and anger, declaring that Garibaldi had deceived them, that he was retreating into the interior and that all was lost. La Masa with difficulty prevented a general dispersion, rallied his disheartened forces at Gibilrossa, and wrote next day to implore Garibaldi not to retreat to Corleone, but to join him at Gibilrossa for a united attack on Palermo.

Meanwhile the Thousand began to ascend the winding mountain road from Cozzo di Crasto to the pass that leads over to Piana dei Greci. To cover their retreat, the Genoese Carabineers fought a rearguard action with the Neapolitans coming up from Parco. The other part of Von Mechel's column, who had ascended the Rebottone mountains by the Portelle-Puzzilli pass and threatened to head off the retreat, were met on the rocks of Campanaro, more than 3000 feet above the sea, by a small detachment of the valiant Albanian *squadre*, supported by the main body of the Thousand, who had to turn off the road to repel the flank attack. At sight of the determined front of the Garibaldini, the Neapolitan vanguard shrank back and let them pass. Having thus cleared the way, they crossed the water-shed near the Madonna del Bosco, and descended the high-road into Piana dei Greci, on the side of the mountains facing away from the Conca d'Oro into the interior of the island.

On the evening of May 24, while the Thousand were sadly filing into the street of Piana dei Greci, and far away on Gibilrossa La Masa was doing all that oratory and gesticulation could do to prevent the dispersion of his discouraged *squadre*, the general belief was that the revolution was at an end. The Sicilians, who had sincerely wished and expected Garibaldi to attack Palermo, could hardly believe their eyes when they saw him retreat ; they began to doubt the magical powers which they had attributed to him, and took offence at the imperturbable calm of his demeanour in retreat, which they declared to be ' indifference.' At Piana many of them disbanded and made off for their homes. If now the two battalions under Colonna, and the four under Von Mechel, had pressed hard along the road into the Albanian village, it would have fared ill with the hopes of Italy. But Colonna returned to Palermo, and Von Mechel, though he had the merit so rare in the Neapolitan service of taking and keeping the offensive, was no less slow than he was sure. Consequently Garibaldi was left to his own devices at Piana dei Greci during the critical evening and night of May 24, and was able, then and there, to carry out unobserved a plan that turned the tide of war, and caught the enemy in the snare of his own success.

Piana dei Greci, ' the plain of the Greeks,' was a flat, fertile Alp, about two miles across from side to side, lying about 2000 feet above the sea-level, but almost entirely surrounded by rocky mountains rising from one to two thousand feet more. Its well-watered soil had for nearly four centuries been cultivated by the Greek-Albanian colonists, who lived in their little town on the northern edge of the basin, where the road from Palermo entered it. To the east of the plain a by-road led through a gap in the circle of mountains to the hamlet of S. Cristina Gela, and there came abruptly to an end. On the south, the high-road wound conspicuously up the mountain-side, leading to Corleone and the interior of the island. If Garibaldi left Piana by the high-road, it would mean that he finally turned his back on Palermo and abandoned all hope of success. And that way he sent his baggage, his sick and wounded, and his five cannon under the command of Orsini, with fifty artillerymen and an escort of about 150 *squadre*, many of them returning to their native Corleone. Before darkness fell on May 24, this column was clearly seen by everyone in the plain winding up the mountain-side by the southern road, and it was assumed by all that the infantry were about to follow.

And, indeed, soon after nightfall, the Thousand were mustered in the street, and following in the track of the artillery, crossed the plain by the Corleone high-road, avoiding the by-road to S. Cristina Gela. But when they were two miles from the town, near the foot of the southern mountains and on the banks of the river that waters that side of the plain, they turned off the road at dead of night, unseen by friend or foe, and passing by the water-mill of Ciaferia, were led across country to the hamlet of S. Cristina Gela. Skirting its southern side, they took to a rough drove road that led eastwards towards Marineo, across rolling hills and valleys. Late at night they bivouacked in a wood, among the lonely pastures of Chianettu.

It was a starry night, and Garibaldi gazed at the unwonted brightness of Arcturus. Half in jest, he told his aides-de-camp that Arcturus was his star, which he had chosen for himself when he was a sailor-lad, and that its splendour foreboded victory. The word was passed round the camp and gave joy to all, not merely as an omen, but as a token of the General's happy mood and the renewed prospect of an attack upon Palermo.

Next morning (May 25), descending from the higher prairie land, they followed one of the most lovely foot-paths in Sicily, across rocky ravines filled with olives and fruit-trees, and with poplars in the stream bottoms, until they reached Marineo, a large and dirty town, planted amid nature's fantastic magnificence beneath a precipice pillar resembling the Gibraltar rock.

From Marineo, where they rested for several hours, a paved road led down a broad and fertile corn valley to La Masa's headquarters at Misilmeri and Gibilrossa. The General sent word to La Masa that he would arrive at Misilmeri on the following day, but late in the afternoon, growing impatient of delay, he ordered the weary Thousand on to the road, and kept them afoot till they entered Misilmeri an hour before midnight on May 25. The inhabitants, in the wildest delight at the resurrection of their magical Garibaldi, illuminated the town in his honour. At eleven o'clock he sent the following message to La Masa in the camp of the *squadre* at Gibilrossa: 'Dear La Masa, I hope to see you at three to-morrow morning to make important arrangements' (*per combinare cose importanti*).

All knew that the combined forces would now fall upon the capital.

Not only had Garibaldi shaken off Von Mechel's pursuit, but he had deluded that officer into leading three or four thousand of the best troops in the Neapolitan army, including a battalion of German mercenaries, upon a wild-goose chase into the middle of the island. The troops defending Palermo, with whom Garibaldi was about to try conclusions, were weakened by the absence of the bravest officers and men, and were put off their guard by the positive belief that he and his Thousand had fled in rout to Corleone, and would never trouble them again.

For when Von Mechel on May 25 tardily entered Piana dei Greci, he had, of course, been told that the Garibaldini had left the town by the Corleone road. In happy ignorance that they had subsequently doubled back to Marineo, he sent back messages of victory to make Lanza, the nervous *alter ego*, feel secure in the capital, while he himself set forward once more to run Garibaldi to earth. But though determined and obstinate, he was singularly slow in pursuit, and about the time that the man whom he thought he was pursuing was really breaking into Palermo city, he himself had only reached the royal forest of Ficuzza, eight miles south of Piana. There the King's gamekeepers gave the Neapolitan officers some warning that a division had been effected in Garibaldi's forces, whereupon Major Bosco, at least according to his own and his friends' account, urged his superior either to return at once to Palermo, or else to march on Marineo by a road that turned off thither from the spot where the discussion was being held. But the Switzer was obstinate ; he did not love his able but pushing subordinate, and gave orders to continue the advance on Corleone. There the artillery officer Orsini, to whom Garibaldi had given the powers of pro-Dictator, with instructions to take every occasion for making a display, roused the populace, and on May 27 fought a spirited rearguard action on the hills behind the town. The Neapolitans lost some men, but captured two of the five cannon ; many of Orsini's followers dispersed. Having tasted blood, Von Mechel pressed on past Corleone, probably still hoping that he was on the traces of Garibaldi, or at least of the bulk of his force. Led on by the *ignis fatuus* of three obsolete cannon and a few score tired men and horses, he passed by way of Campo Fiorito as far as Giuliana and Chiusa, within fifteen miles of the south coast of Sicily. There, on May 28, a messenger reached him with the news that, since dawn on the previous day, Garibaldi and his Thousand had been fighting in the heart of Palermo. A former messenger, sent off from the capital on the morning of the 27th, whose safe arrival might have changed the fate of Italy, had been arrested by the Albanian villagers as he passed through the street of Piana dei Greci.

CHAPTER XVI

GIBILROSSA—PALERMO ON THE EVE

'Spread in the sight of the lion,
   Surely, we said, is the net
Spread but in vain, and the snare
Vain ; for the light is aware,
And the common, the chainless air,
Of his coming whom all we cry on ;
   Surely in vain is it set.

'Surely the day is on our side,
   And heaven, and the sacred sun ;
Surely the stars, and the bright
Immemorial inscrutable night ;
Yea, the darkness, because of our light,
Is no darkness, but blooms as a bower-side
   When the winter is over and done.'
        SWINBURNE. *Songs before Sunrise :*
                Halt before Rome.

DURING the few hours between midnight and dawn on the 26th, the Thousand flung themselves down to rest, some in the cafés and private houses of Misilmeri, others in the church, which Bixio insisted upon using, in spite of the lamentations of the inhabitants, who considered its occupation as an act of sacrilege which would bring bad luck on the cause. At three in the morning La Masa, in obedience to Garibaldi's summons, arrived in the town from his camp on the surrounding hills, and at dawn a council of war was held in the house where the General lodged. Probably before leaving Piana, certainly before leaving Marineo, Garibaldi had already determined to fall on Palermo, but seeing that he was about to ask his friends to stake their

lives on so desperate a cast, he thought good to lay before
them the alternative of a retreat into the interior, indicating
that his own opinion was for the bolder course.   La Masa,
rightly representing the feeling of the Sicilians, demanded
the attack on the capital for which he had been pleading
in his letters to the Dictator for six days past.   No serious
opposition was made : as Bixio said, ' There was no discussion, there could be none.'   At a quarter to six, the final
decision having been formally taken, Garibaldi sent off a
dispatch to Corrao, who had rallied the remnant of Pilo's
squadre on the mountains at the other side of the Conca
d'Oro, bidding him break into Palermo that night from the
west.   Since Garibaldi himself intended to enter it by surprise from the south-east, we may suppose that he wished
Corrao to divert attention from the side where the serious
attack was to be made.   But Carrao started nearly twenty-
four hours late, and consequently his movements in no
way helped the entry of the main force.

About seven in the morning, the Thousand marched
out of Misilmeri to the other side of the low hill whereon
stands the dismantled edifice of an Arabic-Norman castle.
There, among the olives and vines, they encamped during
the greater part of May 26, on the east side of the Piano
della Stoppa, a flat crater bottom, now drained and highly
cultivated, but then half full of water after the recent
rains.   Beyond the crater, to the north-west, rose the pass
of Gibilrossa, more than 1000 feet high, the lowest point
of the Grifone range that still divided them from the Conca
d'Oro and the capital.   They were to mount and cross those
heights at sunset, by way of the little white-walled convent
that they could see shining amid cactuses and olives on the
mountain side above them.   Once across that ridge and
down in the Conca d'Oro they must conquer or perish.
' To-morrow,' said Garibaldi to his friends, ' I shall enter
Palermo as victor, or the world will never see me again
among the living.'

That morning, as it chanced, a carriage, with three

British naval officers on the spree, drove out from Palermo by the coast road through Villabate to Misilmeri,

'where, to their surprise,' as they afterwards reported to Admiral Mundy, ' they heard the great national chief had arrived from Parco, only a few hours before, and was then at dinner in a neighbouring vineyard. The General, on hearing that three English naval officers were driving through the village, sent one of his attendants with a message requesting them to visit his headquarters. They accepted the invitation.'

Lieutenant Wilmot and his two brother-officers found Garibaldi standing amid a group of men dressed for the most part, like their chief, in grey trousers and red flannel shirts. Beside him stood his son, the finely-built and good-natured Menotti, his hand still bound up for the wound he had received at Calatafimi, and there, too, was the priest, Pantaleo, who, as the Englishmen were told, had fought in the battle, crucifix in hand. Garibaldi received his visitors with the impressively simple courtesy that charmed alike the men of all races and of all ranks. He feasted them on fresh strawberries, spoke, in good English, of his affection and respect for their country, hoped that he should soon meet the British Admiral—presumably in Palermo—and related how, on his retreat over the mountain-tops to Piana dei Greci two days before, he had witnessed ' the beautiful effect produced by the royal salutes from all the ships of war in honour of Her Majesty's birthday.' His guests drank his health and that of Italy, and did not appear at all embarrassed by the interview.

Almost simultaneously with the Englishmen, there had arrived in the camp two officers of the United States war-ship *Iroquois*, one of whom gave Garibaldi a revolver which he carried in the fight next day. The Anglo-Saxons made friends with the Thousand, and drove back to Palermo laden with letters for the post, messages that might prove to be the last to many an anxious home within sight of the circling Alps.

At the very hour in the morning when these friendly

neutrals were visiting headquarters, there arrived by the same route the Hungarian Eber, acting as correspondent for the *Times*, which was now strongly pro-Italian. Eber had made no secret among his English friends in Palermo of his intention to seek for a command under Garibaldi, and he came out to Misilmeri as the bearer of messages and information of high importance. The Central Revolutionary Committee of the capital also sent two other representatives to Gibilrossa in the course of the day. Eber gave Garibaldi and his staff an exact account of the location of the Neapolitan troops. Monreale, Parco, Porrazzi, and the Conca d'Oro in the direction of those places, he reported to be occupied by many thousands of the enemy. Near Palermo itself they were massed yet more thickly near the Vicaria prison and behind the Palace—that is, on the northern and western outskirts of the town. But the indecipherable labyrinth of ancient alleys and lanes, that constitute the heart of Palermo, was left almost unoccupied. If, therefore, Garibaldi could penetrate into these recesses, he could call out the inhabitants to barricade the narrow arteries of the city, and be safe, at any rate for a while, from the immense forces in the exterior positions of the Palace and the Vicaria.

But how was the entry to be effected ? Palermo was a loaf with a soft centre but a hard crust. Eber, however, reported that the easiest way to force an entrance into the city would be by the south-eastern gates. For, strange to say, Lanza had most neglected that side which lay towards Gibilrossa : the easily defensible line of the lower Oreto river was guarded only by a weak detachment, and Eber described in detail the barricades erected, and the points occupied by a few companies of infantry and two guns at the south-eastern gateways of Termini and S. Antonino. Guided by this accurate information, Garibaldi wisely decided to try and storm the Porta Termini.*

* Such is the information which Eber reports in the *Times* (June 8) as having reached Garibaldi at Misilmeri ; as *Times'* correspondent, sup-

Having formed his plan, the Dictator convoked the leaders of the Sicilian *squadre*, and asked their concurrence. Some few murmured that they had little or no ammunition, but the greater part cried out ' *A Palermo ! A Palermo !* ' On being asked which was the most direct and secret route to the Porta Termini, they declared, with some exaggeration as the event proved, that a practicable path led down from the top of the Gibilrossa pass into the Conca d'Oro in the direction of Ciaculli. It was, therefore, decided to go by this route, instead of by the circuitous and public road through Villabate, by which the naval officers and Eber had driven out that morning.

The enthusiasm now shown by the Sicilian chiefs, and their jealousy of being sent to the rear, induced Garibaldi to make his one mistake, destined to imperil the whole enterprise. He granted a change of plan, to the effect that La Masa's *squadre* should march in front of the North Italians. There was, however, to be a vanguard, consisting of the scouts and a body of men picked from all the companies of the Thousand, who with the local guides should lead the whole column.

In whatever order they marched, it was a strange undertaking. What with sickness, wounds, and the absence of the detachment gone to Corleone with the artillery, Garibaldi's ' Thousand ' were some 300 fewer than when he had landed at Marsala. With these 750 musketeers, or more properly bayonet-men, with rather more than 3000 peasants armed some with blunderbusses and sporting guns, some with pikes and scythes, and with the prospect of such help as he could hope to get from the disarmed citizens of the capital, if he could ever penetrate into its streets, Garibaldi was setting out to attack the garrison

posed to be a neutral, he naturally does not say in so many words, ' I brought this information.' But we know it was he who brought it. Türr said to me in conversation that it was Eber's information which decided Garibaldi to choose the Termini gate. Any other gate, added Türr, even the neighbouring Porta S. Antonino, would have been fatal. The Termini gate was the least strongly defended.

of Palermo and the Conca d'Oro, variously estimated by its own chiefs at 16,000 to 20,000 riflemen, cavalry, and artillery, not counting the four battalions that Von Mechel had led to Corleone.

In the cool of evening on May 26, the Garibaldini ascended from their camping ground, near the Piano della Stoppa, to the monastery and pass of Gibilrossa, by a track running up the mountain side between gigantic cactus hedges that gave an oriental character to the scenery. Halting for awhile on the solitary platform of grey rock, whereon the picturesque and lonely convent hangs perched amid olives, aloe, and cactus, they reached, a few hundred yards further on, the broad moor on the top of the pass, where the Garibaldi monument stands to-day. It was an enchanted hour that threw its spell on all. The ground was still fragrant with the last flowers of spring, and there lay below their feet the evening view of the plain, the city, and the sea. There were the navies of the world riding at anchor in the bay, and there, on the opposite side of the Conca d'Oro, the shoulder heights of Hamilcar's Monte Pellegrino glowing like a furnace in the rays of sunset, as though the mountain itself were alight with all the fierce draughts of sun that it had drunk through unrecorded æons of time. Close at Garibaldi's feet, between him and the city, was spread a variegated carpet of foliage, masses of grey, olive, and of yellow-green lemon, broken by streaks of the dark-green orange leaf. The Cathedral and the Palace, the heart of the enemy's position, rose clear above the city roofs. But, whilst he was still gazing upon all this beauty, the soft, green masses below lost shape and colour, the towers and cupolas of Palermo were merged in undistinguished haze, the rosy tints upon the mountain-tops grew pale, and one by one his own signal fires of war leapt out instead along the circle of the hills, beckoning him to descend into the darkened plain.

' The evening gun in the fort had been long re-echoed by the mountains, and the moon had risen clear and bright,' before the head of the column began slowly to feel its way down the rocky clefts of the gorge that fell from Gibilrossa to the plain of Palermo.

The condition of affairs in the capital and Conca d'Oro, when Garibaldi descended on the eventful midnight and dawn of May 26–27, is faithfully presented in Admiral Mundy's Journal for the two days preceding the crisis. On May 25, having observed several Neapolitan vessels take up positions with the apparent object of being ready to bombard the sea-front, the British Admiral went up town to find Lanza at the Palace. There, in the spacious chambers overlooking the city and the sea beyond, where the greatest and most beloved, but not the wisest, of English Admirals had given the Bourbon royalties very different advice from that now proffered by the excellent Mundy, the modern representative of Britain's power along the coasts of the world expostulated with the King's *alter ego* against beginning a bombardment which was not strictly part of any military operation.

'The reply of General Lanza,' continues the Admiral, 'was frank and decisive. . . . He entertained a firm hope that Palermo would not become the scene of a sanguinary civil struggle, and all his endeavours were directed to remove from its walls the calamities of war. He should oppose the foreign invasion outside the city; in fact, he had yesterday dislodged the band of Garibaldi from their strong position at El Parco, seven miles from Palermo, and had pursued them to the summit of the mountains of Piana dei Greci. If, however, in spite of his endeavours, the rebels should make the city rise, the fire of the artillery by sea and land would concur with the troops in the repression of the revolt. . . . When General Lanza had finished his address I rose to depart, thanking him for his candid statement, but, at the same time, remarking that there was a vast difference between the indiscriminate destruction of the edifices of a great city and the use of artillery against a people in revolt. He then informed me that two Piedmontese prisoners had been brought to the guardhouse in the morning, who, though dressed as private soldiers, were evidently gentlemen. I asked him to spare their lives, which he said he would do.

' During this interview Signor Maniscalco [the Police Minister] and Colonel Polizzi entered into the discussion, with a view of justifying the resolutions which had been so clearly expounded by the Royal Commissioner. Unfortunately, in the heat of argument the former asked Mr. Goodwin [the British Consul] if he did not think a population deserved to be annihilated, should they rise up in insurrection against the constituted authorities. To this unexpected and ill-timed demand Her Majesty's Consul indignantly replied that he could not have supposed such a question would have been put to him; but that, as Signor Maniscalco had chosen to do so, he had no hesitation in saying that when a people were tyrannised over they had an inherent right to take up arms, and to fight against their oppressors. . . .'

On the afternoon of May 26, while Garibaldi was between Misilmeri and Gibilrossa, Admiral Mundy and Mr. Goodwin went for a drive in the Conca d'Oro, and visited a convent, where Mundy was surprised to hear such antiquated people as the monks profess themselves ardently on the side of the revolution. Shortly afterwards, at La Grazia, the carriage was held up by some members of the *squadre*, whose appearance did not edify the Admiral, although his nationality secured him their respect. On his way back, he writes :—

' On the outskirts of the city I gained admission into a mansion once occupied by the Moorish Governors of Sicily, from the lofty turrets of which I witnessed the burning of several of the country palaces of the nobility who were supposed by the soldiery to be hostile to the Royal cause.* In whichever direction I looked over this vast and richly cultivated plain, the smoke of ruins and devastation presented itself to my view, while the constant report of musketry and the distant sound of cannon showed that armed men were in collision on the slopes of the hills.'

On his return through the streets of Palermo, the Admiral saw with indignation a procession of working men, handcuffed and led to prison by the police, because they had visited the British ships on their Saturday holiday that

* In Mr. Goodwin's Political Journal of this week, we read that the soldiers sacked the villas of the nobility, e.g., the Villa Marutta at Passo Rigano, under pretence of searching for arms.

afternoon. They had returned with nothing more compromising about their persons than tobacco and hard biscuit ; but the fact that they had visited the floating fortresses of freedom was held to be crime enough.

Having returned to his flagship, Admiral Mundy heard from Lieutenant Wilmot how he had unexpectedly found himself in Garibaldi's camp that morning. Clearly Garibaldi was not so far off as Lanza had supposed. In the evening, about the time that the Thousand were preparing to descend from the pass of Gibilrossa, a note was handed to the Admiral in his cabin, just before he turned in. It was from an English resident in the city.

' Dear Sir,' it ran, ' I hear that a rising will take place at two o'clock to-morrow morning, at which hour, or soon after, Garibaldi will be near Porta Sant' Antonino, through which you went out this afternoon, prepared to force his way into the city with the bayonet.'

The momentous secret, known to British residents and British authorities, was common property to all the active Liberals of Palermo. A Sicilian gentleman has related to me the emotions which that night disturbed the home of his father, Signor Tedaldi, in the beautiful Quattro Cantoni, at the very centre of the city. To the grief and indignation of his younger brother, it was decided that only the father and the two elder boys should fight next day. The clothes which they were to wear were laid out in readiness, consisting of velveteen shooting jackets and highland caps. They were decorated with tricolour ribbons and cockades, sacred symbols which their mother had prepared with great difficulty, gathering bits of red, green, and white out of her own hats, for no one dared ask for the forbidden colours openly in the shops. They had no weapons, for the capital had been repeatedly searched for arms, but they expected to be able to obtain them from the Garibaldini. Through the shutters they could see the police in the square below, and wondered how they would be able to get out of the house next day. They sat up late, listening to stray shots in the Conca d'Oro, such as they had heard every night for the past month, and wondering if they heralded his coming. At last, the boys were sent to bed for a few hours' sleep, while the father sat up to watch for dawn and Garibaldi.

In the great Vicaria gaol, hundreds of political prisoners had, on the morning of the 26th, been horrified by the official news of Garibaldi's flight to Corleone, but, on the same evening, a note was smuggled in among them bearing the words, ' To-morrow Garibaldi will enter Palermo.'

That a secret so generally known was so well kept reflects credit, as Garibaldi said, on the secrecy and faithfulness of the Sicilian people. It seemed, indeed, as if the authorities were almost the only people completely ignorant of the intended attack, and of the fact that Garibaldi had doubled back to the neighbourhood of Misilmeri. As late as 12.30 noon on the 26th, Lanza telegraphed to General Bonanno at Monreale, ' Garibaldi's band is retiring in rout through the district of Corleone. He is closely followed.' The same day a proclamation to the Sicilians was issued to the same effect, but the public now no longer believed in the defeat of the ' Filibusters,' and scornfully tore the announcement off the walls. Signor Della Cerda tells me that when his mother was reading this proclamation at a friend's house, Cav. Paolo Amari said to her, ' Stop reading that. To-morrow Garibaldi will be in Palermo.' Even the Neapolitan officers, though they were not in the secret, felt by no means at their ease. Many had sent their families and goods back to Naples, and Colonel Fileno Briganti, the same who was shortly afterwards, as General, murdered by his own troops in Calabria, actually consigned his furniture to the care of his Liberal friends, the Della Cerda family, sending it across in cart-loads from the *Castellamare* to their house opposite, as though a patriot's roof were a safer shelter in Palermo than the chief Neapolitan fortress of which he was himself at that time commandant.

At headquarters in the Royal Palace, the energetic Police Minister, Maniscalco, together with General Bartolo Marro, and other officers, urged Lanza to take precautions against the rebels in the direction of Gibilrossa, but the replies of the *alter ego* were evasive or contemptuous. Even when a man came post-haste from the hills, announcing that he himself had seen the red-shirts, and that they were about to attack Palermo, he remained unmoved. When informed that the city was on the eve of insurrection, he would only repeat what he had told Admiral Mundy, that if there was a rising, he would order a bombardment. Since he took no measures to strengthen the slender guard on the line of the Oreto and at the Termini and S. Antonino gates, we may presume that, in spite of all warnings, he continued under the spell of his illusions until the rude awakening on the dawn of Sunday, May 27.*

* The situation is well rendered in a cartoon issued by the liberated press a few weeks later, in which Lanza is represented as presiding over a peep-show at the windows of which his soldiers are looking, while a Palermitan behind winks at a street boy, and the boy makes ' a vulgar, odious sign ' at the *alter ego*. Lanza is saying, ' Walk up, gentlemen ! Here are the Filibusters of the Mediterranean, led by Garibaldi, flying towards Piana. Further on you can see them, routed at Piana, flying to Corleone.' A bystander says, ' Your show is a swindle. I see nothing of the sort. I see Garibaldi entering Palermo victoriously at your heels.'

CHAPTER XVII

THE TAKING OF PALERMO [*]

' Chi è costui che cavalca glorioso
In fra i lampi del ferro e del fuoco,
Bello come nel ciel procelloso
Il sereno Orïone compar ?
    Ei si noma, e à suoi cento dier loco
Le migliaia da i re congiurate :
Ei si noma, e città folgorate
Su le ardenti ruine pugnàr.'

CARDUCCI. *Sicilia e la Rivoluzione.*

' Who is this riding on in his might
    As calm amid war's flash and sheen
As oft in tempestuous night
    Orion in glory is seen ?
Cry his name, and whole armies shall fear it
    And fly from his hundreds afar :
While the cities they blasted shall hear it
    And rise on red ruins to war.'

A WELL-MADE road now winds down the mountain-side
from the Garibaldi monument on Gibilrossa Pass, into
the plain near Ciaculli. But in 1860 there was no better
means of descent than a straight, precipitous foot-track,
which during the first and steepest part of the decline
followed a dried torrent-bed along a stony gorge. Garibaldi's men climbed down this path, of which the gloomy
grandeur, revealed, rather than relieved by the moonlight,
put some of them in mind of the way by which Dante
passed from the upper to the lower circles of his Inferno.
When the level of the plain was reached about midnight,
the rugged track continued towards Ciaculli, along a stream
bed between olive-groves, of which the low walls now bear

* See Maps IV. and V., end of book.

the inscription *Discesa dei Mille*—' The descent of the Thousand.'

Among these olives, far from the enemy or any human habitation, took place the first misadventure of the night. One of the few horses in the column began playing tricks, a cry of ' cavalry ' was raised, and a panic extended to a greater or less degree along the darkened line. Some muskets were let off, whereupon all the dogs of the Conca d'Oro invoked one another with frantic howlings. Fortunately such alarms had been so common for every night of late that the noise conveyed no warning to the Neapolitan generals in the Palace. Garibaldi restored order and the march was resumed.

Once more they advanced through the silence of the groves, each man wrapped in his reflexions, or listening keenly for sounds of war from Palermo. The tinkling of a far-distant piano, played who knows why at that dead hour, came fitfully down the breeze. On the Monte Grifone to their left, and on Gibilrossa behind them, the watchfires blazed bright, fed by men whom Garibaldi had left for the purpose, lest the Neapolitans, not seeing the accustomed nightly signals, should divine that the rebels were descending into the plain.

Passing the hamlet of Ciaculli, they approached the half-ruined palace, called La Favara or the Castello di Mare Dolce, beside its well-watered garden of lemons, where once the Saracen lords of Sicily, and after them the great Emperor Frederic II., had taken their learned pleasure. Here, in the maze of paths and fruit-groves, the *squadre* lost their way and fresh confusions followed. The leaders of the various local bands were not military men ; indeed, one of them, named Rotolo, placed in command of the front division of the *squadre* that night, was a parish priest from a village in the interior, whence he had led one hundred men to the camp at Gibilrossa. Rotolo, though by no means lacking in courage, had vainly pleaded to Sirtori and Garibaldi that his inexperience should disqualify him from marching at the head of his fellow-country-men. La Masa himself, the chief of the united bands, now began to show his incapacity as shepherd of his unruly flock. Bixio, after swearing with his accustomed energy at the helpless leader, induced the Dictator to permit Carini, the Sicilian in command of one of the two battalions of the Thousand, to go and restore order among the *squadre*, which he succeeded in doing after a fashion with the help of Father Pantaléo.

From La Favara, the column appears to have advanced in two or more divisions, some passing by the road through Brancaccio, others across country to the main road at Settecannoli. All united again at the junction of the two roads, known as the *bivio della Scaffa*, where a few of the enemy's outposts were dislodged from a mill.

The first line of the Neapolitan defences lay along the banks of the lower Oreto from the cemetery above Guadagna down to the bridges near the *bivio della Scaffa*, and at these bridges a body of some strength was posted. The Ponte dell' Ammiraglio, a magnificent relic of Norman-Arabic architecture built early in the twelfth century by King Roger's great Admiral, George Antiochenus, spans what is now the dry course of the old Oreto. A few yards farther on the modern Ponte delle Teste crosses the waters of the actual river. The Neapolitans, massed on and around the Ponte dell' Ammiraglio, and in the neighbouring buildings, were ready to receive most warmly the head of the column as it approached from the *bivio della Scaffa*. For although Garibaldi had succeeded in surprising Lanza strategically, the tactical surprise had failed altogether, owing to Rotolo's *squadre*, who, as they passed through Settecannoli a few minutes before, had shouted and let off their guns in the air at the prospect of approaching battle.

When therefore the Hungarian Tüköry, leading on the two or three score picked men of the Thousand who formed the vanguard, dashed against the Ponte dell' Ammiraglio, they were received by such a volley as checked their advance.

10

A panic instantly seized the 3000 *squadre* behind them, and the Sicilian peasants bolted into the vineyards and fruit-groves on either side of the road. For a few critical minutes a wide gap was left between the small body under Tüköry who still held their ground in front of the bridge, exposed to a terrible fire, and the remainder of the Thousand in the rear of the now rapidly dissolving column.

A minute's hesitation in the rearguard might have been fatal. ' *Avanti, Cacciatori ! avanti ! Entrate nel centro !* ' cried Garibaldi. (' Forward ! Into the heart of the town ! ') Thus incited, the Genoese Carabineers and the two leading companies of Bixio's battalion came tearing along the road from the *bivio della Scaffa*, between the garden walls over which the *squadre* had so nimbly disappeared. In front of them the ghostlike bulwarks of the ancient bridge loomed through the grey twilight of dawn, spitting fire at them as they advanced. Joined with Tüköry's vanguard and a number of Sicilians who had not taken shelter with the rest, the newcomers hurled themselves on the enemy, who after a fierce struggle turned and fled for Palermo. A body of cavalry, who had come down as far as the Ponte dell' Ammiraglio, retired without charging. The Ponte delle Teste was next carried, and the line of the Oreto passed. Domenico Piva, who ten years before had helped Garibaldi to warp out the boats at Cesenatico,* was the first officer across the river, if it was not Bixio himself. Rocca della Russa of Mount Eryx and two other Sicilians lay dead or dying by the old bridge, and several of the Thousand had fallen.

From the Oreto to the Porta Termini stretches nearly a mile of suburban road, along which the Thousand hastened at full speed. For a short while the General and the mounted officers of the staff, together with a few Sicilians of the Thousand, remained behind to drive the *squadre* out of the gardens where they had taken refuge, and induce

---

* *Trevelyan's Gar. Rome,* chapter xiv.

them to cross the bridges which were still exposed to a
heavy cross fire from the direction of Guadagna.

The side of Palermo which the Thousand were approaching from the bridges, was not, like the rest of the city,
protected by its walls and bastions, for a row of houses
had been built along the outer side of the fortifications.
But as these houses were in a continuous line, an entry
en masse could be effected only through the Porta S. Antonino
or the Porta Termini. There was no longer any gate
at the Porta Termini, but the Neapolitans had erected
an unusually high barricade effectively blocking the street,
near to the place where the gate had once stood. This
obstacle, though feebly defended, was in itself physically
impassable, and therefore sufficed to bring the charge of the
Thousand to a stand, while Bixio and others flung themselves against it and began pulling it to the ground. So
long as this work continued the Neapolitan riflemen and
their two cannon posted outside the Porta S. Antonino,
in front of the church of that name, fired down the broad,
straight *stradone*,* into the left flank of the Thousand
held up in front of the Porta Termini barricade. From
the opposite direction a Neapolitan war vessel fired up
the *stradone* from the sea. Here fell Benedetto Cairoli—
yet destined to be the only one of five brothers to survive
the wars of liberation—and Canzio of Genoa, Garibaldi's
future son-in-law. Here the brave Hungarian, Tüköry,
who had led the vanguard, fell wounded to death.

At this critical moment, Garibaldi, having done his
share of rallying the *squadre*, galloped up to the Porta
Termini, still crying aloud, ' *Avanti! Avanti! Entrate
nel centro!* ' Then the high barricade yielded to the fury
of Bixio, undeterred by a bullet in his breast. Nullo of
Bergamo was the first man to enter the city, and after him
the tide of war surged over the fallen barrier. A space
was cleared to enable Garibaldi to ride his horse through

* Now the Via Lincoln.

the ruins, and all that remained of the Thousand, with their chief aloft in the midst of them, roared down the narrow street between the mediæval palaces and over-hanging balconies of Palermo.*

Meanwhile the *squadre* were following up. At the *stradone* they came to a halt, afraid to pass over to the Porta Termini across the open road, which they saw slippery with the blood of the Thousand and swept by two cross fires from S. Antonino and from the sea. Eber and several of the Thousand who had been left to bring them into the city had a hard task to accomplish. The only way was to show them how badly the Neapolitans were in fact shooting. For this purpose Francesco Carbone, a Genoese lad of seventeen, planted a chair, with a tricolour flag floating above it, in the middle of the *stradone*, and himself sat down on it amid the storm of ill-directed missiles. 'The thing took at last decidedly,' wrote Eber ; first by ones and twos, then in larger bodies the *squadre* crossed the danger zone, some even halting in the middle of the road to fire off their muskets. Finally, a barricade was erected across the *stradone* to cover the entrance for further bands from the mountains, of whom many penetrated into the capital by this way in the course of the following days. These undrilled peasants learnt to behave with ever increas-ing courage during the street fighting that followed. Eber wrote that they reminded him of the Bashi-Bazouks, because they ' can be led on after the first unpleasant sensa-tion has passed away, especially when they see that it is not all shots that kill or wound.'

Garibaldi made no halt until he reached the Fiera Vecchia, ' the ancient market,' a little, triangular space at the end of the long, straight street by which he had entered the town. Of unknown antiquity, it is the heart of the popular quarter of Palermo. In it commenced the

---

* The street they came down, in which the Porta Termini had once stood, is now called the Via Garibaldi.

revolution of January 1848, the spark that lighted the European conflagration of that year.* In the centre of it stands a fountain, adorned by a statuette of the genius of Palermo—an old man feeding a snake at his breast, which was popularly held to represent the Sicilian capital feeding its foreign conquerors, as it had done through all the ages. In 1849 the too symbolic image had been removed as seditious by the police; it was restored in June 1860, and stands there to-day.

Here, then, in the Fiera Vecchia, at about four in the morning, Garibaldi first drew rein, and began at once to organise the occupation of the city. Around him as he sat giving his orders swayed a crowd of unarmed Palermitans, so dense that there was no room to move, all in the wildest excitement, struggling to get near and kiss the hand or knee of the impassive horseman, and yelling like maniacs ' *Viva la Tàlia e Garibardi amicu!* '† In the midst'of all this, Garibaldi embraced Bixio, pointing him out to the ecstatic gratitude of the populace as the hero of the day. Bixio was at the moment near fainting with pain and loss of blood, for he had just cut out with his own Spartan hands the bullet that he had received in his breast at the Porta Termini. He had no thought of retiring yet from the fight.

From the Fiera Vecchia, the Thousand, ceasing to act as a regiment, went out in small parties in every direction through the narrow labyrinths of the great city, to rouse the inhabitants and expel the enemy. During the three days' fighting that ensued, most of the important though not all the operations of war were performed either by small parties of a dozen or more North Italians, or else by bodies of *squadre* and citizens under their leadership.

---

* The Fiera Vecchia is now called the Piazza della Rivoluzione.
† ' Long live La Tàlia ' (Italia) ' and friend Garibaldi.' Some of the more ignorant Sicilians thought ' Tàlia ' was a princess, married to Garibaldi. At least so the Thousand were led to believe, though it has since been denied by some Sicilians.

To be one of the Thousand was to be recognised as the commander by any stray group of men in any part of the city, and on any one of the countless barricades.

On their first scattering through the town from the Fiera Vecchia, the Thousand complained of empty streets and of people watching timidly from behind shutters. The citizens had no firearms, and they had not forgotten the failure of April 4. But as the certainty of Garibaldi's presence in Palermo gained ground, the populace everywhere came out in swarms, men, women, and children, to welcome and aid their deliverers. They had nothing in their hands but swords, knives, sticks, or bars of iron, but they were bursting with noise and fury, and inspired by a fitful activity and daring. Men rushed up the *campanili* and fell to beating the toscin on all the bells of the town, with hammers since the clappers had been carried off by the police. The rural *squadre*, as they poured into the streets, fired off their guns, indifferent whether at the enemy or in the air. Palermo with its 160,000 inhabitants and 4000 friendly invaders clashed and roared and shrieked and banged like the devil's kitchen, while the 20,000 foreign troops on the outskirts rained shell and heated shot into the centre, from the Palace at one end and from the Castellamare and the fleet at the other, setting whole streets on fire and killing and wounding men, women, and children.

It had been Lanza's predetermined policy that, if the city rose, he would reduce it to submission by bombardment, instead of using every effort to occupy it with his immense forces of infantry. Against this expressed intention Admiral Mundy had protested beforehand, in the interest alike of humanity and of the great quantity of British property in the town. But fortunately for Garibaldi, this cowardly and inactive programme was strictly adhered to. In the spirit of their leader, the troops stationed near the Palace began burning and sacking houses, and murdering whole families, both in the Albergheria within and in the suburbs without the gates, instead of advancing into the heart of the city and crushing the invaders before barricades had time to spring up. The desecration and robbery of churches and convents was so large a part of the activity of the Neapolitans in these days, that the devotion of the clergy and superstitious populace to the well-behaved Garibaldini became stronger than ever.* 'Thus,' wrote Captain Tommaso Cava of the Neapolitan General Staff, ' after two hours of bombardment, and several more of plunder and arson, General Lanza thought he had done enough, and became almost entirely inactive, while Garibaldi occupied all the points which he most required.

The Dictator himself, at the head of one of the small groups into which his Thousand were now divided, advanced from the Fiera Vecchia into the centre of the town in the direction of the Quattro Cantoni, the crossing place of the two streets of Spanish origin, the Toledo and the Macqueda, each a mile long, which cut Palermo into four symmetrical quarters. As the invaders drew near, the Tedaldi family, from behind the shutters of their house in the Quattro Cantoni, saw the sentinels below bolt up the Toledo for the Palace. Thus set free, the father and two elder boys descended unarmed into the streets, as so many of their fellow-citizens were doing at that hour, to seek for weapons and for allies. They soon met one of the Thousand, Paolo Scarpa, almost unconscious from prolonged exposure and want of sleep. They helped him into their house, where he

---

* Admiral Mundy, June 3, writes :—' A whole district, 1000 yards in length by 100 wide, is in ashes ; families have been burnt alive with the buildings : while the atrocities of the Royal troops have been frightful. . . . The conduct of General Garibaldi both during the hostilities and since their suspension, has been noble and generous.' In the *Morning Post*, June 26, the correspondent writes on June 6 from Palermo that in the Alberghería quarter ' a part of the town exclusively inhabited by the poorest classes, not even a single house is left standing, and one may fairly calculate the number of houses at about 200. These houses were not destroyed by the bombs or other projectiles, but by the soldiers themselves, who first entered and completely sacked them, and on leaving set fire to them, and heaven knows in each they could have found little more than the value of 2s. or 3s.'

dropped on a bed and slept where he fell.   When the servant
tried to remove his clothes, which he had not taken off since
Marsala, they fell to pieces.   Armed with his musket,
the Tedaldi went out again to the fight.   When Scarpa
awoke many hours later, he was in despair at the disappearance of his weapon, but by that time his hosts were
able to supply him with another musket, procured on a
barricade from one of the *squadre*.

Meanwhile Garibaldi, with a few followers, had occupied
the neighbouring Piazza Bologni, from which important
position Landi of Calatafimi hastily fled with his troops
towards the Royal Palace.   The Dictator took up his
quarters for a couple of hours in the courtyard of the
Villafranca Palace, on the Piazza Bologni.   It was noticed
that even at that moment he insisted on unsaddling his
horse himself, according to his custom.   As he placed the
saddle on the ground, a pistol in the holster went off and
missed him so closely that it carried off a piece of his trousers.
There was a momentary cry of ' He is assassinated.'

While the Dictator was still in the Piazza Bologni, he
became aware of Bixio, staggering for loss of blood from
his wound, but all in a rage because the citizens had not
yet come out in sufficient numbers in that part of the town.
He was crying out that they would certainly all be killed in
a couple of hours, since the city would not rise, and that
for his part he would lead any twenty men who would follow him to attack the headquarters at the Royal Palace.
Garibaldi countermanded the feverish plan, calmed his
worthy lieutenant, and finally ordered him off to have
his wounds dressed, as he should have done several hours
before.   Once in bed, Bixio was unable to leave it during the
next three days of battle, during which the absence of
the dreaded, indefatigable man was a relief alike to friend
and foe.

From the Piazza Bologni the Dictator recrossed the
Via Macqueda to the Piazza Pretorio, or municipal square
of the capital, and fixed his headquarters here during the

next three weeks. He had nominated a General Committee of leading Palermitans to govern the town, subdivided into five Committees of War, Provisions, Interior, Finance, and, last but not least, Barricades. With these, his State Secretary Crispi carried on the Dictatorial government in the Pretorio or municipal building, where Garibaldi also occasionally worked, and took his modicum of sleep. But he spent most of the days of battle sitting on the steps of the great fountain in the square below, among the statues with which it is decorated, between heaps of flowers and fruit brought to him by the people. The enemy soon discovered his whereabouts and aimed the bombardment specially at the Piazza Pretorio. Although every building on the square and in its neighbourhood suffered greater or less damage, the Municipality itself was strangely intact. Similarly, though many persons in the square were hit, Garibaldi had his usual luck. The populace cried out on a miracle. At some hazard to themselves they would stand in crowds gazing at him as he sat on the steps, as composed as one of the statues, paying no attention to the shells and abstractedly twirling round and round the string of a little whip which he held in his hand. The Palermitans whispered to each other in awe-struck tones ' *Caccia le bombe* ' (' He is keeping off the shells '), believing the whip to be a charm which he thus set in action.* In habits of thought and imagination the modern Palermitans had much in common with those ancient peoples of the Mediterranean for whose pagan souls the followers of Christ and Mohammed strove with the sword. When they saw sitting before them a stranger so beautiful, so kind, so strong to deliver and to slay, they felt as their remote ancestors felt when some god or hero was thought to have become the guest of man. And so during these days the belief became very general and profound that the Liberator was related to Santa Rosalia, the patroness of Palermo, who doubtless protected her

* Told me by Professor Pitré, the famous collector of Sicilian folk-lore and traditions. He saw and heard this himself as a boy in Palermo.

kinsman in battle. For all agreed that a hero named
Garibaldi must needs be descended from the famous *Sini-*
baldi, Santa Rosalia's father. So they looked on him and
took fresh courage.

Of many scores of street fights that raged throughout the
city, the most important and the fiercest of all was the
contest for the Toledo—the broad, straight, level street which
connected the Neapolitan headquarters at the Palace with
the centre of the town and thence with the sea. At the
marine end of the Toledo the *squadre*, under the leadership of one of the Thousand, captured the Porta Felice
under a hot fire. But that did not prevent the warships
from firing through its arch up the whole length of the town.
An immense cloth was therefore stretched across the
Quattro Cantoni, as had been done under similar circumstances in 1848, to prevent the Palace and fleet from
communicating by signals, and to hide from the ships
the fighting in the upper part of the Toledo. For it was
there that the battle was hottest, Lanza's troops making
serious if belated efforts to fight their way down the great
street from the Palace into the heart of the city, and the
rebels to work up it from the Piazza Bologni. The palace
of Prince Carini, ruined by the bombardment, and the
Jesuits' College opposite, were the sites most hotly contested during the 27th and 28th. The Neapolitans easily
maintained themselves in the Cathedral, round the east end
of which the fighting remained hot and evenly balanced.

By midday on May 27, eight hours after Garibaldi's
entry, the whole city was in the hands of the insurgents,
except the large district round the Palace, and the two
isolated positions of the *Castellamare* and the Mint at the
other end of the town. Outside the walls, in the suburbs
near to the Vicaria prison and the barracks along the
northern quays, a strong body of Neapolitans lay under
General Cataldo. During the first day's fighting they were
cut off from the Palace by the advance of the citizens, who,
having taken the Porta Macqueda in open fight, pushed out

to S. Francesco di Paola and even as far as the English Gardens.

During the afternoon of the 27th and the next morning, the large bodies of men stationed under Bonanno near Parco and Monreale were recalled to headquarters at the Royal Palace. Lanza, infatuated by the apparent safety of his position at that point, conceived the false strategical notion of concentrating there all his forces except the small garrisons of the *Castellamare* and Mint. The Palace was an ill-chosen spot for the concentration of 18,000 men, because there they were cut off from further supplies of food and ammunition, and from all communication with the shore and the fleet, except by means of semaphores signalling to each other on the roofs of the Palace and *Castellamare*.

In pursuance of this bad policy, on the afternoon of May 27, the *alter ego* sent a fatal order to Cataldo in the Northern suburb, bidding him join the main body at the Palace.

Meanwhile the remnant of Pilo's *squadre*, rallied by his companion Corrao on the hills to the north-west, were working down to Palermo by way of Uditore and Lolli. During the night of May 27–28 they fell on the Neapolitans under Cataldo, who had not yet carried out the order to return to headquarters. After some fighting Corrao, wounded by a shell led his men into the city by the Porta Macqueda, and at dawn on the 28th Cataldo brought his troops round from the Vicaria to the Royal Palace.

The second day of the fighting in Palermo (May 28) began with the eruption of the prisoners from the gaol-fortress of the Vicaria. The gaolers, a detestable set of men, had wisely taken themselves off even before the departure of Cataldo's infantry. Early in the morning, as soon as the last sentinels disappeared from the ramparts, the many hundreds of political prisoners in the Vicaria burst their cells, and the foremost of the crowd began to

attack with crowbars and naked hands the inside of the
great iron door that denied them exit. Minute after
minute its strength resisted their frenzied efforts, and
the terrible cry was raised ' The soldiers are returning ! '
But the alarm was false, and finally the door was opened
from the outside by a man to whom the departing gaoler
had confided the keys. He had hastened first to let out
the common criminals, among whom he had some friends.
An eager mob of the best and worst men in Sicily, some
2000 all told, rushed into the town by the Porta Macqueda,
and flew to the barricades.

The original barricades, which on the first day had
been improvised of carriages and household furniture,
were gradually being replaced by carefully-built erections
of the flagstones with which the streets of Palermo are
paved. Many, even, were loop-holed for musketry, or faced
along the top with sandbags. The Committee of Barricades
saw to their scientific disposal, at intervals of a hundred
yards, down the length of every street, until the whole
town was protected from the centre outwards by a network
of successive lines of defence. The populace, women as
well as men, was ready with scalding water and heavy
objects to hurl from the balconies on to the troops below.
The noise of bells and the clamour of the multitude was
appalling, and there was in fact ever physical and moral
discouragement to the advance of the enemy's infantry
down the streets. On the other hand, the fits of lethargy
that seized the Sicilians from time to time were the despair
of all the Northerners except Garibaldi ;* the small quantity
and bad quality of the firearms, of which there were few
in the city beyond what the peasants and the Thousand
brought with them from the hills, and still more the

---

* ' Not so energetically seconded by the Palermitans as one could
have expected from their enthusiasm. There is a semi-oriental *laissez-
faire* about them which only produces fits of activity. . . . Even the
ringing of bells, the most demoralising sound to an army in a populous
town, can, in spite of all injunctions, be only kept up in fits and starts.'
End of letter, May 27 eve., in *Times*, June 8.

shortage of ammunition, which the *squadre*, with their childish love of noise and smoke, wasted in the most heart-rending manner, were circumstances which left the final success of the patriots still dependent on their amazing good luck and on the continuance of Lanza's imbecile conduct of affairs.

Early on the morning of May 28, the *alter ego* opened communications with the British Admiral by means of semaphore messages to the *Castellamare*, conveyed on board H.M.S. *Hannibal* at eight o'clock by Captain Cosso-vich, now in command of the Neapolitan vessels in the harbour. Lanza's first request was to obtain the use of the British flag to enable officers from the Palace to pass along the Toledo and hold a conference with the commanders of the fleet and *Castellamare* on board H.M.S. *Hannibal*. The use of the British flag in the streets of the town was refused, but Admiral Mundy, with the consent of Captain Cossovich, sent Lieutenant Wilmot,—the same who had shared Garibaldi's strawberries at Misilmeri,—to find the Dictator in the heart of the besieged city and ask him to allow the Neapolitan officers to pass down the Toledo. Garibaldi consented, but Lanza for the present refused to accept the concession as coming from the filibuster, since the use of the British flag in the town was not to be obtained. While these first abortive negotiations were pending, Captain Cossovich, who hated the service assigned to him of de-stroying a splendid city, had willingly, at Admiral Mundy's request, suspended the naval bombardment for several hours, though the *Castellamare* and the artillery at the Palace continued to fire.

May 29, the third and last day of continuous street fighting, saw the severest conflict of all. In the morning the Sicilians and the Garibaldini made a determined advance against the Cathedral, which the men of Bergamo succeeded at last in taking. From its high, western *cam-panile* they were able to pour such a rain of bullets down

on to the Archbishop's palace that this also became untenable
by the enemy. The buildings commanding the great
square in front of the Royal Palace thus fell into the
hands of the insurgents, and Lanza's headquarters were
closely threatened. Driven to bay, the hosts of the Neapolitans rallied after midday, and from the Porta Nuova
swept their assailants back again through the Archbishop's
palace, and through the Cathedral. As Garibaldi sat on
the steps of the Pretorio fountain early in the afternoon,
with a map of Palermo spread on his knees, his old companion
in arms, Piva, who had been the first man across the river
two days before, rushed up with the news that the Neapolitans were advancing from the Cathedral and bade fair
to penetrate to the heart of the town. ' I must go myself,'
said Garibaldi, and taking Türr and some fifty men who
happened to be at hand, mostly Sicilians, he walked to
the scene of action. At first the Neapolitans stood their
ground, and one of the *squadre*, shot through the head, fell
dead into Garibaldi's arms. But when he ordered his
bugler to sound the charge, and the whole party dashed
forward, the enemy fled back into the Cathedral. The
east end of that magnificent edifice became once more,
as in the morning, the boundary of the Neapolitan position.

In these fierce fights of May 29, for the possession of
the upper Toledo, the members of several Sicilian aristocratic families behaved with distinction. The brothers
Pasquale and Salvatore di Benedetto fell dead together
at a corner of a street ; a third brother, Raffaele, had
been wounded two days before, and was destined in after
years to give his life for Italy under the walls of Rome.
The Di Benedetti were the Cairoli brothers of Sicily.

The revolution had scored one important success that
day. In the morning a small handful of men, chiefly of the
Thousand, North Italians under the leadership of Sirtori
and of the two Sicilians Ciaccio and Campo, captured
the gate and bastion of Montalto and the neighbouring

buildings, including the S. Giovanni degli Eremiti. The latter, with its cloistral ruins and little garden, well known to travellers as one of the most beautiful relics of Arabic-Norman architecture, was retaken in the afternoon by the Neapolitans issuing from the Palace. But the Montalto bastion and gate remained to the insurgents as the one solid gain to either side of that day's fighting.

On the night of May 29-30, two fresh battalions of so-called 'Bavarian' troops, German recruits of a rather indifferent quality under Colonel Buonopane, who had landed near the *Castellamare* off two steamers recently arrived from Naples, marched right round behind the scene of conflict by way of the English gardens, and coming in at the rear of the Royal Palace, reported themselves in the isolated and overcrowded headquarters, where the scarcity of supplies was already beginning to be felt.

Throughout May 29 Lanza had persisted in his refusal to communicate with Garibaldi. But he had once more feebly attempted to beg the use of the British flag to cover the passage of his own officers through the town, a negotiation of which the only results were to irritate the British Admiral, and to give to the humane Captain Cossovich an excuse for suspending the naval bombardment on the 29th as on the former day. But during the night of May 29-30 the *alter ego* began to reconsider his position. The failure of the serious effort made in the afternoon to penetrate from the Cathedral into the heart of the town, the threatened shortage of food, and the state of the eight hundred wounded, cut off from all necessaries, most of them suffering under his own eyes in the Palace, conduced to shake his infirm resolution. On the morning of May 30 he awoke prepared to treat with his enemy in a manner unnecessarily humiliating to the Royal cause, and penned the following letter, of which the address alone marked his changed attitude towards the ' filibuster.'

'GENERAL LANZA TO HIS EXCELLENCY GENERAL GARIBALDI.

'May 30, 1860.

'Since the English Admiral has let me know that he would receive with pleasure on board his vessel two of my Generals to open a conference with you, at which the Admiral would be mediator, provided you would grant them a passage through your lines, I therefore beg you to let me know if you will consent thereto, and if so (supposing hostilities to be suspended on both sides) I beg you to let me know the hour when the said conference shall begin. It would likewise be advantageous that you should give an escort to the above-mentioned Generals from the Royal Palace to the Sanità, where they would embark to go on board.

'Waiting your reply,
'FERDINANDO LANZA.'

If a man on his way to execution were asked by the prison authorities whether he would be so good as to change places with the hangman, he would feel much what Garibaldi felt in his heart, when with calm and serious countenance he finished reading this letter in the presence of the two Neapolitan officers who brought it to the Pretorio. The fact was that he had practically no ammunition left. He secretly sent one of his men to steal across the harbour in a boat at night, and beg ammunition from the Piedmontese vessel commanded by the Marquis d'Aste, who refused to commit any such breach of neutrality. Garibaldi and many of his circle remembered this against Cavour, whose black purposes they saw in the ' correct ' attitude of a patriotic but much perplexed naval captain.

So Garibaldi arranged with Lanza's messengers that firing should forthwith be stopped on both sides and more particularly that an armistice should commence at stroke of noon, after which hour the parties to the conference would as soon as possible proceed on board the British flagship.

Before thus sending off, about nine o'clock, his petition to His Excellency General Garibaldi, the *alter ego* had received a piece of intelligence that would have made any commander of sense and spirit postpone all thought of negotiations. At dawn, the look-out on the Palace roof had sent word that he saw Von Mechel's four battalions, at last returned from Corleone and from the pursuit of the phantom Garibaldi. They were on the edge of the town, between the Ponte dell' Ammiraglio and the Porta Termini. Lanza for several hours neglected this significant news, and when it was forced upon his attention, instead of ordering a general attack in co-operation with the newly-returned column, he sent his letter to Garibaldi none the less, and even enclosed in it an order to Von Mechel, bidding him observe the armistice that was about to be concluded.

' If Von Mechel had returned a day earlier, we should have been lost.' So said General Türr, the year before he died, to the writer. Von Mechel and Major Bosco were the two fire-eaters of the army, and their regiments were the fighting regiments, especially the 3rd Light Infantry, a battalion of Germans of much finer quality than those recently landed under Buonopane. There can be no doubt that, if they had returned on the 29th, the officers would have overruled Lanza's timid counsels, and the men would have borne themselves well in battle. The reason why Von Mechel did not return on the first or second day after Garibaldi's entry, was partly that the messenger sent after him on the morning of the 27th had been stopped by the villagers of Piana dei Greci, and partly that the brave Switzer, whose motto was 'slow but sure,' had no idea of forced marches. On the latter part of the journey back, instead of taking the direct route across the Conca d'Oro from Parco to the Palace, he had passed along the foot of Monte Grifone by way of S. Maria di Gesù, crossed the Ponte dell' Ammiraglio, and spent the night of May 29–30 near the Botanical Gardens. His bivouac there, just outside the Porta Termini, had been seen before sunset on the 29th by the watchmen on the *Castellamare* roof, who did not however semaphore the news to the Palace.

Late on the morning of the fateful May 30, many

precious hours after dawn, Von Mechel began to move
into the city, outside the walls of which he had been content
to camp all night without making his arrival known at
headquarters. It was not until a few minutes after the
stroke of noon, when the armistice had just come formally
into operation, that the stillness was broken by volleys
from the Porta Termini and the Fiera Vecchia, which
announced simultaneously to the Dictator at the Pretorio,
to the British Admiral on his flagship, and to the *alter ego*
at the Palace, that Von Mechel was forcing his way into
the town by the very route that Garibaldi had followed
three days before. Great was the surprise, confusion
and rout of the slender guard of Sicilians under La Masa,
thus taken in rear, in time of truce, and almost without
ammunition. The newcomers occupied the Fiera Vecchia,
and would have pressed on at once to the Pretorio, but for
the activity of Sirtori. The gaunt, ill-dressed, meditative
ex-priest, poised inexpertly on an immense horse, his
trousers perpetually rising up to his knees, was during
these days in Palermo compared by his comrades in arms
to the figure of Don Quixote. But he was no mere tilter
at windmills, and in this moment of rout and dismay the
Chief of Staff rallied enough men to keep Von Mechel's
Bavarians within the compass of the Fiera Vecchia, until
the peacemakers had time to come on the scene. He did it
at the cost of a severe wound, the third which he had received
since he entered Palermo. Carini, the finest soldier among
the Sicilians in the Thousand, was also badly hit while
endeavouring to induce both sides to observe the truce.

One of the next to arrive on the scene was a chance-
comer, Lieutenant Wilmot. Having been sent on shore
again to make final arrangements for the conference on
his Admiral's flagship that afternoon, he was going round
by what he thought to be the safest route to the Pretorio,
by way of the Fiera Vecchia. He suddenly found himself
between a cross fire of *squadre* and Bavarians. Waving
his handkerchief, he walked straight up to the Royalist

troops, and, pointing to the hands of his watch which indicated that it was already past noon, he remonstrated against the breach of a truce in the observation of which the honour of the British Admiral was involved. The foreign officer and his men were, however, ' very much excited,' and seemed to be on the point of advancing, taking the indignant Englishman with them as a sort of prisoner, when the two Neapolitan officers who had carried Lanza's letters to Garibaldi, arrived on the scene from the Pretorio and saved the situation—and perhaps Italy. They made it clear to the unwilling mind of Von Mechel, and to his yet more eager and enraged lieutenant, Major Bosco, that an armistice had indeed come into force at noon, and that Lanza had given special orders that the newcomers should observe it. Garibaldi appeared almost immediately afterwards, furious at the breach of the truce, and had an angry altercation with the Royalist officers, who consented to halt, but refused to retire from the ground which they had occupied.

Meanwhile in the Palace the *alter ego* and his Staff were eagerly disputing whether they should advance in force down the Toledo, and order Von Mechel to meet them at the heart of the city. Victory was in their grasp, unless honour obliged them to observe the truce until the Garibaldini had time to hem Von Mechel into the Fiera Vecchia with a network of barricades. Good faith carried the day in Lanza's mind, aided perhaps by the natural inertness of the old General's disposition. Much to the disgust of several of his Staff, he effectively stopped Von Mechel's advance, and gave orders for Generals Letizia and Chretien to proceed forthwith on board H.M.S. *Hannibal* to the promised conference.

When Lanza's two delegates drove down to the quay-side at the Sanità, Garibaldi was there before them, signalling with his handkerchief across the inner harbour to the riflemen in the *Castellamare,* who were characteristically trying to shoot him in time of truce, and equally characteristically failing in the attempt. Generals Letizia and Chretien, who had hoped to deal with the British Admiral alone, were disgusted at finding themselves literally and metaphorically ' in the same boat ' with the filibuster ; they did not know which way to look when Garibaldi stepped in after them, and the British officer cried, ' out boat-hooks ' and ' shove off,' before they had time to protest. They were none the better pleased when, on their coming aboard H.M.S. *Hannibal*, the guard of marines saluted Garibaldi, again dressed for the occasion in his uniform of Piedmontese General, with the same honours as were accorded to themselves as representatives of the king of Naples.

In the Admiral's cabin, where the conference began about 2.15 in the afternoon of May 30, Letizia's ill-humour burst out. He objected in no courteous way to the presence of the French, American, and Piedmontese commanding officers (the Austrian Commodore had not wished to come), and still more to the presence of Garibaldi. He argued with doubtful logic that Lanza's idea in proposing the conference had been that the Neapolitan officers and Admiral Mundy should draw up terms for an armistice, which the rebel chief could then either accept or refuse. Garibaldi and the Piedmontese captain, the Marquis d'Aste, held their peace, while the French and American commanders expressed their indignant astonishment at Letizia's language, and Mundy made it clear that for his part he was not acting as mediator, but was merely offering his cabin as a neutral meeting-ground for the convenience of the two parties, who must confer together and on equal terms, if there was to be any conference at all.

Letizia gave way and proceeded to read the terms proposed by Lanza for the armistice. Garibaldi made no objection to the proposals for free passage of the Royalist wounded to the ships, and of provisions to the Palace. But when Letizia had read the fifth clause—

' That the municipality should address a humble petition
to His Majesty the King, laying before him the real wishes of
the town '—

he thundered out ' No ! The time for humble petitions
has gone by,' and then, giving rein to his pent indignation,
inveighed against the recent treacherous attack on the
city in time of truce, and the refusal of Von Mechel to
withdraw from the positions so occupied. The conference
would have broken up, had not Letizia been, in fact, prepared to grant everything, in spite of his offensive and
bullying manner, which was not shared by his amiable
colleague Chretien. After some bluster, seeing that
Garibaldi appeared quite indifferent as to the failure
of the negotiations, he withdrew the clause about the
humble petition, and an armistice was signed, to last until
noon next day.

Thus Garibaldi, by playing out to the end a game of
dignified and courageous bluff, had secured twenty hours
at least in which to provide himself with ammunition.*
Before he left the British flagship, he took aside Captain
Palmer, the United States commanding officer, and asked
him to assist the cause of freedom with a supply of powder.
Probably the American was no more compliant than
the Piedmontese captain, and, in any case, he could have
spared but little from a slender store. As Garibaldi
returned to land, between four and five o'clock, the idea
of a retreat to the mountains crossed his mind, though no
one would have guessed it from his imperturbable manner.
But the populace, whose zeal, though fitful and unreliable,
was proportionately terrible in moments of exaltation, after
being much depressed while the conference was still sitting,
showed such a warlike spirit on the critical evening of
May 30, as to put confidence into Garibaldi and fear into
his opponents. The last shadow of doubt was removed
from the Dictator's inmost soul, after he had addressed

* Canzio, the year before he died, said to the writer, ' We had scarcely
any ammunition left. But for the armistice we should have been destroyed.'

the Palermitans from the balcony of the Pretorio. When he told them how the Neapolitan General had asked that Palermo should send a humble petition to King Francis, and how he had refused it in their name, the roar of joy and rage that went up from the fountain-square was so appalling that Major Bosco, who happened to be present on business of the armistice, grew pale and trembled, being even more affected than the Garibaldini by the spectacle of popular rage which he knew to be directed against himself and his comrades.

From that moment, about five in the afternoon of May 30, until noon next day, when the armistice was to come to an end, the whole population worked with a will at the manufacture of ammunition and arms, and at the erection of barricades to surround and isolate Von Mechel in the Fiera Vecchia. Under cover of darkness, a Greek vessel which had entered the port with a cargo of powder, sold a certain quantity to Garibaldi, together with an old cannon. That night the city was brilliantly illuminated. Discouragement proportionately set in among the Royalists. Desertions, especially by non-commissioned officers, began to be frequent. During the armistice Neapolitan soldiers were sometimes inveigled into conversation, taken into the town and treated to wine, with the result that they lost their rifles or came over to the ranks of Italy.

At nine o'clock on the evening of May 30 a council of war was held at the Palace, at which it was decided to attack next day at noon, the moment the truce had expired. Exact orders were sent to Von Mechel and given to the other heads of columns, detailing the routes by which they were to penetrate through Palermo and meet in the centre. But after the council of war had broken up, Colonel Buonopane, who had been in the heart of the town treating with Garibaldi about the transport of wounded, gave Lanza so alarming an account of the perfection of the barricades and the spirit of the populace, that the *alter ego* changed his mind once more. The Dictator was asked to prolong the armistice for three days, and when he consented, at eleven o'clock on the morning of the 31st, the elaborate preparations for the attack were all countermanded. Under the new armistice, the isolated position of the Mint, with the very large sums of money which it contained, was handed over to Garibaldi.

It is perhaps from this moment of the signing of the second armistice, that the chances may be said to have turned in favour of the revolution. For every hour that the truce lasted made it more difficult to recommence hostilities. General Letizia and Colonel Buonopane were sent to consult the Court and Ministry at Naples, where Buonopane's account of the military strength of the revolted city frightened the King and his advisers, as it had frightened Lanza. There were also political and moral considerations. Great odium would attach to the young King, if he personally gave orders that the bombardment of his subjects should be renewed, after his generals had suspended hostilities for four days. It might so far alienate England and France as to compromise his chances of preserving the throne of Sicily, or the throne of Naples, if Sicily were already lost. It was felt that if the generals had wanted to renew the fight, they should have taken the responsibility on their own shoulders, and the application to the authorities at home seemed to imply that those on the spot knew that the game was lost.

Capitulation was the most obvious way out of the immediate difficulties in which they had involved themselves, and the want of moral strength and purpose in the men of the Bourbon *régime* allowed them to grasp at it for want of any alternative policy. And so, by the consent of the Royal Government, after another temporary prolongation of the armistice, a final capitulation was signed on June 6. The Neapolitans were forthwith to abandon the Palace and all other positions in the city except the *Castellamare*. They were to march out with the honours of war, and to take up temporary quarters in the northern suburb and on the great plain behind it that stretches to the foot of Monte Pellegrino. Thence they were as rapidly as possible to be shipped for Naples. When they were all gone the *Castellamare* was, last of all, to be handed over to Garibaldi, together with the six State prisoners of noble Palermitan family which it still contained.

If the Neapolitan generals had known the thoughts that were passing in the mind of Nino Bixio during the first days of June, they might never have signed this humiliating treaty. ' The second of the Thousand ' was afoot again since May 30, and from what he saw of the discipline of the forces defending the town he lived in constant terror of another attack. The Sicilians could not be relied on to perform regular and irksome military duty. The *squadre* were many of them going home to their villages. The conscription decreed by the Dictator was proving a flat impossibility. Many of the island warriors were in the habit of carrying off for personal use the muskets of the Thousand and the rifles captured from the enemy. On the morning of June 7, the day fixed for 20,000 Neapolitans to march defeated out of the city, there were only 390 muskets among the remnant of the Thousand. Those who survived of that gallant body, now all dressed in red shirts to give them distinction and authority, were the one reliable element in the situation, and they had consequently to do continuous duty at the outposts, partly in order to preserve the truce, as the maddened Palermitans were liable to insult and shoot at the men who had murdered so many of their women and children. Garibaldi put his trust in the rage felt against the soldiery who had inflicted such horrors on the town, and believed that if the Neapolitans attacked again the incensed populace would fight with a furious desire for vengeance. But the slender and irregular character of the military defences were such that even the General, according to Bixio's observation, was ' sometimes confident, but sometimes anxious.'

In these days, when there was little sanction for law
except the personal ascendency of Garibaldi, the safety of
life and property was extraordinary in a city into which
the criminal population had recently been emptied from
the Vicaria.   Some of Maniscalco's spies were hunted down
and slaughtered, although Garibaldi managed to save
most even of these.   No one else had anything to fear, and
the British Consul praised both Government and people,
writing home that public order was far better than in the
first days of liberty in 1848.

The terms of the capitulation were executed without a
hitch.   On June 7 more than 20,000 regular troops in two
long columns under Lanza and Von Mechel respectively
evacuated the Palace and Cathedral, and the Fiera Vecchia ;
passing round the outside of the town they marched to their
new camping-ground under Monte Pellegrino.   Von Mechel's
column passed from the Porta Termini by way of the sea,
where, in front of the barricade at the Porta Felice, sat
Menotti Garibaldi on a black charger, with a dozen red-
shirted comrades, while before them filed along the esplanade
an army in battle array.   It was as though Goliath in his
armour were surrendering to David with his sling.   The
British Admiral and his captains who witnessed the scene
from their ships were filled with a sense of mingled exultation
and disgust.   A similar scene was enacted at the Porta
Macqueda, where Lanza and his column filed off before
Türr and another group of red-shirts.

Of the loss of the victors in the three days' fighting
from May 27 to May 30 there is no reliable estimate, but,
counting the victims of the bombardment, it must have
run into many hundreds.   The Neapolitans had lost about
a thousand—800 wounded and over 200 killed.

Twelve days passed before the whole army of twenty to
twenty-four thousand soldiers could be embarked for Naples
in the limited number of transports available.   After a week,
9000 still remained.   As the Neapolitans grew weaker,
Garibaldi's strength increased, till even Bixio began to sleep

at nights, instead of constantly patrolling among the sentinels. Soon after the enemy's evacuation of the Palace, a consignment of arms and ammunition had arrived from Genoa by way of Marsala ; and on June 18, the day before the last batch of Neapolitans sailed, Medici with the ' second expedition ' of 2500 well-armed men landed in the Gulf of Castellamare, twenty-five miles west of Palermo.* During the latter and most dangerous part of their voyage, between Sardinia and Sicily, a Piedmontese war vessel scouted in front of them—so far had Cavour already dared to advance in the benevolence of his neutrality towards Garibaldi.†

On the night of June 18-19, when the Dictator himself had gone to meet the newcomers, Palermo was roused from its slumbers by the sound of heavy firing out at sea. Had the Neapolitans broken faith at the last moment ? Were they returning in force ? Were they waylaying Garibaldi, who was expected to come back by boat along the coast ? The whole population rushed into the streets at midnight and flew to arms. In the morning it was discovered that the disturbing sounds had come from the British sailors, practising gunnery by night—the eccentric, indefatigable men, with no thought for the nerves of a city recently bombarded.

On the morning of June 19 the Dictator returned by land to the capital. It was the day appointed for the sailing of the last of the Neapolitan army, in twenty-four ships collected ready for them at the quays beyond the northern suburb. All Palermo went down to see their

* This Castellamare and its gulf have nothing to do with the fortress called *Castellamare*, in Palermo.

† The history and organisation of these later expeditions I leave for another volume. As early as May 31, Cavour had sent the following orders in cipher to the Marquis d'Aste in Palermo harbour: 'Follow up the overtures of the Neapolitan Commandant Vacca. Assure him in the name of the Government that the Neapolitan officers who embrace the National cause will preserve their rank and have a brilliant career assured them. A pronunciamento by the Neapolitan fleet would make the complete triumph of our cause certain.'

hated foes take themselves off for ever. At the moment of their departure, the *Castellamare*, left till now in the enemy's hand, would run up the tricolour flag, and the hostages imprisoned there would be released. Since these were none other than Baron Riso and the five young nobles arrested on April 7, the most popular citizens in Palermo since that hour, it would clearly be necessary to carry them in triumph up the Toledo.

Everyone, therefore, had gone down to the harbour; an unusual silence reigned in the upper part of the city, and Garibaldi for awhile was left in peace in the new lodging which he had chosen for himself in the Royal Palace. This was one of the humblest rooms which he could find there, the so-called Observatory over the Porta Nuova, at the extreme north wing, and detached from the State apartments in the main building. On one side, his windows looked down the mile-long Toledo to the sea; on the other, up the road to Monreale across the Conca d'Oro. It was his first day in these new quarters, and he stood gazing at the city and plain which he had freed from servitude and won for Italy. Above Monreale and Parco rose the grim and splendid mountains, where he and his Thousand had dodged with death; while from the sea, up the length of the Toledo gay with flags and flowers, was heard ever nearer and nearer the joyful roar of the people, as they came bringing the released prisoners to present them to the Liberator. When the young men, with their parents and families, at length came into his presence in the little room over the gateway, tears stood in his eyes, and it was some minutes before he could find voice to answer their words of gratitude.

EPILOGUE

THE story of Garibaldi and the Thousand down to the taking of Palermo has an historical and artistic unity. In a later volume, entitled *Garibaldi and the Making of Italy*, I have told the history of the following six months. The occupation of eastern Sicily, the battle of Milazzo, the crossing of the straits, the march through Calabria and the Basilicata, the entry into Naples, the battle of the Volturno, the meeting with Victor Emmanuel, and the return to the farm at Caprera, constitute the rich remainder of the Garibaldian epic of 1860. If it is no less extraordinary than the capture of Palermo, it is of a different character. The larger numbers and better equipment of the volunteers, never indeed equal to those of tne enemy, differentiate the story from the wild adventure of the Thousand. The entry of Victor Emmanuel and Cavour into the arena of the war, the release of Papal Umbria and the Marches by the Piedmontese regular troops, the diplomatic history of Europe at the decisive crisis of the Italian question are large matters, though they all have their origin on the heights of Calatafimi and the barricades of Palermo.

MAP IV.

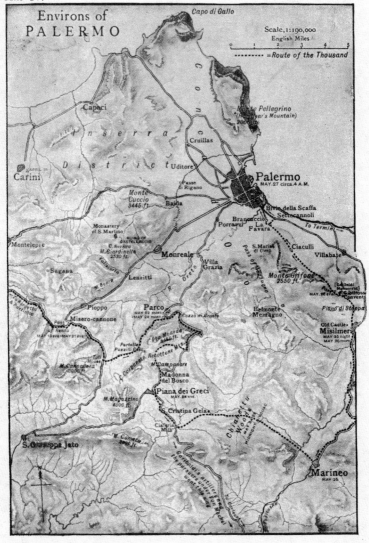

Environs of
PALERMO

Capo di Gallo

Scale, 1:190,000
English Miles

= Route of the Thousand

Conca d'Oro

Monte Pellegrino
(Robilyra's Mountain)
2056 ft.

Capaci

Cruillas

Uditore

Palermo
MAY 27 circa 4 A.M.

Carini
X APRIL 30

Monte
Cuccio
3445 ft.

Passo
di Rigano

Baida

Bivio della Scaffa
Settecannoli

Brancaccio
Porrazzi
La Favara

To Termini

Monastery
of S.Martino

Montelepre

RUINS OF
CASTELLACCIO
C.Nevara
M.Giardinetta
2530 ft.

S.Maria di Gesù

Ciaculli

Villabate

Monreale

Villa
Grazia

Monte Grifone
2550 ft.

[Gibilmanna]
Santa Rosa
Convent

Sagana

Lenzitti

Belmonte
Mezagno

Piano di Stoppa

Pioppo

Parco
MAY 22 morn
MAY 24 morn

Cozzo di Crasto

Old Castle
Misilmeri
MAY 20 night
MAY 26 morn

Misero-cannone

Portella
Puzzilli

M.Cannulera
2000 ft.

Corleone Rebottoni

Et.Moarde
2000 ft.

M.Campanura

Madonna
del Bosco

S.O.seppa Jato

M.Magazzino
4000 ft.

Piana dei Greci
MAY 24 eve

S. Cristina Gela

Chiarelli Woods

M.Cometa
4000 ft.

Ciaierisi
Mills

Marineo
MAY 26

MAP III.

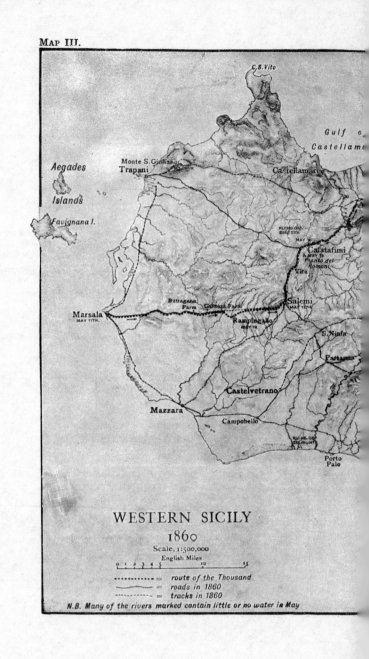

WESTERN SICILY

1860

Scale, 1:500,000

English Miles

0 1 2 3 4 5   10   15

route of the Thousand

roads in 1860

tracks in 1860

N.B. Many of the rivers marked contain little or no water in May

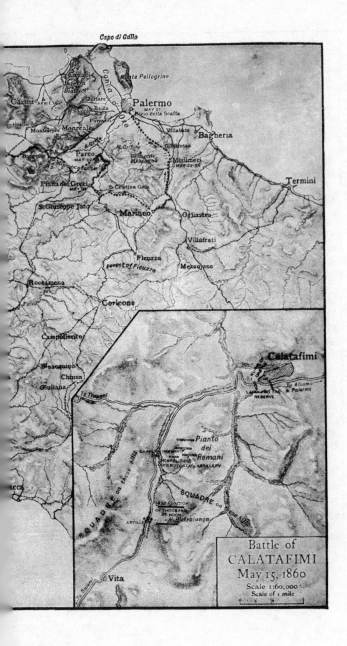

Capo di Gallo

Monte Pellegrino

Capaci
Isola
Distretto

Cannita
APRIL 17

Cinisi

Pioppo

Sardinello

Montelepre

Monreale

Baida
Duccio
Baida
Porrazzi

Palermo
MAY 27
Divio della Scaffa

Villabate

Bagheria

Bagnotto

Piana dei Greci
MAY 1st

Parco
MAY 22

Boccannone

M. Grifone
Belmonte
Mezagno

Misilmeri
MAY 20-26

Gibilrossa

Termini

S. Giuseppe Iato

S. Cristina Gela

Marineo

Ogliastro

Villafrati

Roccamena

Fienzza
Forest of Fienzza

Mezzojuso

Corleone

Campofioritoe

Bisacquino

Chiusa

Giuliana

To Trapani

Calatafimi

LANDING THE
RESERVE

To Alcamo
& Palermo

Pianto
dei
Romani

SQUADRE on these hills

CAVALRY MOVEMENTS
NEAPOLITANS
UNDER SFORZA'S ARTILLERY

SQUADRE on these hills

FIRST POSITION
OF THOUSAND
AT NOON

ARTILLERY

M. Pietralunga

Vita

**Battle of
CALATAFIMI
May 15, 1860**

Scale 1:60,000
Scale of 1 mile

0   ¼   ½

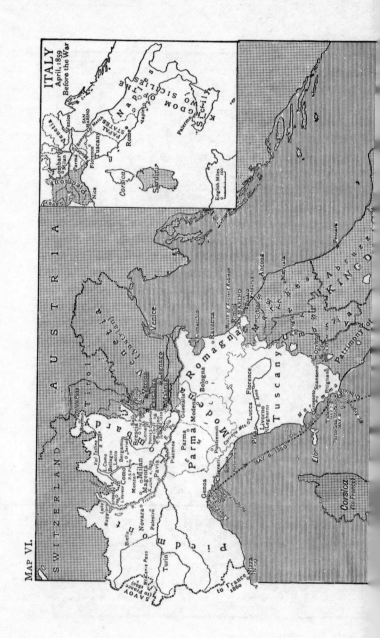

MAP VI.

ITALY
April, 1859
Before the War

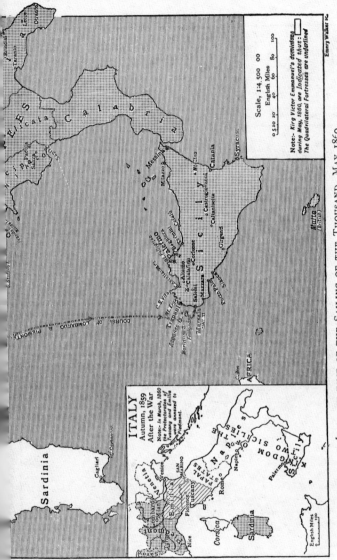

[ITALY AT TIME OF THE SAILING OF THE THOUSAND, MAY 1860.]

Emery Walker sc.

MAP V.

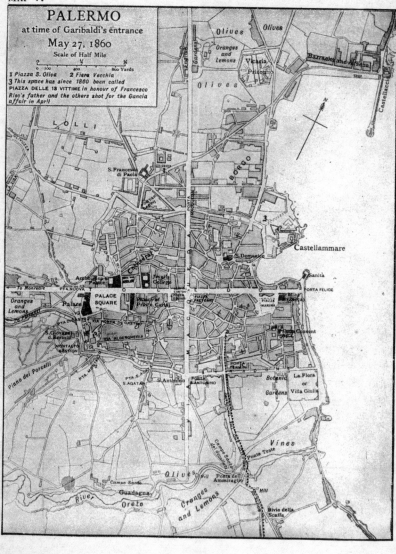

PALERMO
at time of Garibaldi's entrance
May 27, 1860
Scale of Half Mile

1 *Piazza S. Oliva*   2 *Fiera Vecchia*
3 *This space has since 1860 been called*
PIAZZA DELLE 13 VITTIME *in honour of Francesco
Riso's father and the others shot for the Gancia
affair in April*